Common Core Literacy for Math, Science, and Technical Subjects

Strategies to Deepen Content Knowledge (Grades 6–12)

KATHERINE S. MCKNIGHT

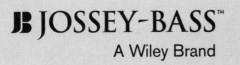
JOSSEY-BASS™
A Wiley Brand

SDE Staff Development for EDUCATORS™

Published by Jossey-Bass
A Wiley Brand
One Montgomery Street, Suite 1200, San Francisco, CA 94104-4594—www.josseybass.com

Jossey-Bass books and products are available through most bookstores. To contact Jossey-Bass directly call our Customer Care Department within the U.S. at 800-956-7739, outside the U.S. at 317-572-3986, or fax 317-572-4002.

Wiley publishes in a variety of print and electronic formats and by print-on-demand. Some material included with standard print versions of this book may not be included in e-books or in print-on-demand. If this book refers to media such as a CD or DVD that is not included in the version you purchased, you may download this material at http://booksupport.wiley.com. For more information about Wiley products, visit www.wiley.com.

Library of Congress Cataloging-in-Publication Data
Library of Congress Cataloging-in-Publication Data has been applied for and is on file with the Library of Congress.
ISBN 978-1-118-71020-3 (pbk); ISBN 978-1-118-71021-0 (ebk); ISBN 978-1-118-71034-0 (ebk)

Printed in the United States of America
FIRST EDITION

PB Printing   10 9 8 7 6 5 4 3 2 1

CONTENTS

Common Core Literacy for Math, Science, and Technical Subjects

ABOUT THE AUTHOR

Katherine S. McKnight, PhD, began her career as a high school English teacher in the Chicago public school system. She currently serves as a distinguished professor of research at National Louis University and travels worldwide as a professional development consultant. She lives in Chicago with her family. To learn more, go to www.katherinemcknight.com.

ABOUT STAFF DEVELOPMENT FOR EDUCATORS

Providing educators with sustained professional development that is research-based, rigorous, and innovative, as well as practical, motivating, and fun, Staff Development for Educators' (SDE) mission is to create meaningful improvement in student attainment, teacher fulfillment, and school success.

Dedicated to helping build classrooms where all students can succeed, SDE's foundational work in the area of Differentiated Instruction and early advocacy of Singapore Math Strategies have helped it gain recognition as one of the nation's leading providers of professional development in education. SDE's Crystal Springs Books imprint exemplifies these same attributes to deliver important and timely resources right to the educator's desk.

For Jim, Ellie, and Colin, who bring joy to my life

PREFACE

It was more than twenty-five years ago that I first became interested in adolescent literacy. As a college senior, I finally made the decision to become a high school English and social studies teacher. In my first position as a high school educator, I taught my subjects passionately, but I knew that I lacked the knowledge to support struggling readers in my content area. It's often assumed that English teachers know how to teach reading and remediate students who struggle; yet this is one of the greatest educational myths. My teacher education program did not require any courses on teaching reading, and I did not know how to help my students. Furthermore, I was constantly given the message and expectation that "all teachers are teachers of reading and writing." As a high school educator I knew how to teach my content areas—English and social studies—but I was truly at a loss for strategies to support all kinds of readers.

During my years in the classroom, I earned my master's degree and eventually my PhD in reading and literacy. Both degrees broadened my professional knowledge of reading and literacy methods and of strategies that could support all kinds of learners. I learned how to use reading and writing strategies as pedagogies to develop my students' literacy skills while also developing their content knowledge.

Fast forward to twenty-five years later: I am relieved to witness the renewed interest in developing the literacy skills of our middle and high school students. I envision the Common Core State Standards as a vehicle to reemphasize the development of literacy skills and content knowledge. This book is a response to this reality.

Many teachers contributed to this book. In particular, I want to thank Bradley Berlage, Holly Young, and Androush Danielians for their mathematics content expertise. I also want to thank the following teachers from George Washington Community School, Indianapolis, Indiana; their professional input and copious student samples were invaluable to the development of this book:

Michael Anderson
Deboarah Aquino
Andrew Gatza
Rhonda Jennings
Brooke McCray
April Partee
George Simms

My teacher friends, Deanna Gallagher and Warren Thomas Rocco, read multiple versions of this text.

I am also grateful to my professional friends at Jossey-Bass: Dimi Berkner and Tracy Gallagher. My Jossey-Bass editor Margie McAneny's professional knowledge is a gift. Margie and I have worked on eight publications together. In addition to having a tremendous skill set in publishing, she is a dear friend who makes me laugh and supports me when I am plagued by those author demons.

Elaine Carlson, my unflappable assistant for her word-smithing skills and sense of humor. She keeps me organized. The designs and graphics originated from the talented Kris Lantzy—who also happens to be one of the funniest people I know.

Without the support of my husband, Jim, and my children, Ellie and Colin, these books would not have been written. Finally, I want to thank the other teachers in my family, including my sister, Mary Scruggs (1964–2011), a writing teacher at the famous Second City in Chicago, who inspired a generation of writers to find their voice and conquer their own writing demons, and my mom, Patricia Siewert (1934–2008), a Chicago public school teacher for more than thirty-five years. I can still hear her whisper to me her mantra: "Teaching is an act of love and social justice."

Common Core Literacy for Math, Science, and Technical Subjects

CHAPTER ONE

Why Does Content Literacy Matter?

I have a confession to make. When the Common Core State Standards were first introduced in 2010, I was skeptical. Actually, I was more than skeptical—I wanted to find every reason I could to hate the new standards.

I was coming from the point of view that the state standards developed ten years previously, during the No Child Left Behind (NCLB) movement, were reductive and that the corresponding overemphasis (and overspending) on standardized testing was horribly misguided. In the classrooms that I worked in as a literacy consultant all over the United States, I saw the same pattern during the NCLB decade: more focus on test prep and less focus on research-based teaching methods. As a career-long educator I found this terribly disheartening, and I shared my frustration with my teacher colleagues and students alike.

So when the Common Core State Standards (CCSS) were first introduced, I was poised to attack and rip the CCSS to shreds; I felt certain that they were going to be yet another nail in the coffin of research-based, effective teaching methods. I had only made it to page 4 when I had a Jerry McGuire moment. I realized that the Common Core standards were nothing like the No Child Left Behind nonsense. Here's the part that "had me at hello":

A focus on results rather than means. By emphasizing required achievements, the Standards leave room for teachers, curriculum developers, and states to determine how those goals should be reached and what additional topics should be addressed. Thus, the Standards do not mandate such things as a particular writing process or the full range of metacognitive strategies that students may need to monitor and direct their thinking and learning. Teachers are thus free to provide students with whatever tools and knowledge their professional judgment and experience identify as most helpful for meeting the goals set out in the Standards.

(CCSS 2010, p. 4)

Hallelujah! Educators were finally being acknowledged and credited for their professional knowledge. Reading this paragraph, I felt refreshed and excited that we could finally get back to what I knew, in my head and heart, great teaching and learning should look like in a middle school or high school classroom.

As I continued to read the standards, I grew increasingly "geeked out" about what this new framework could do for our students. If you've felt similarly skeptical about the Common Core State Standards, let me give you a quick overview of some CCSS basics and explain why the new standards are a great thing for our schools.

THE STRUCTURE OF THE COMMON CORE STATE STANDARDS

For sixth through twelfth grade (at the time of press for this book) the following CCSS documents are available:

▶ *Common Core State Standards for English Language Arts* and Literacy in History/Social Studies, Science, and Technical Subjects
▶ *Common Core State Standards for Mathematics*

In this book, we are going to focus on the first document, *Common Core State Standards for English Language Arts in Science and Technical Subjects* (which include mathematics). Before we begin, I need to clarify a couple of things as they are articulated in the CCSS documents for interdisciplinary literacy. (If you need a full copy of the standards, the documents can be downloaded at www.corestandards.org.)

1. There are *four* strands in the English language arts (ELA) standards:
   Reading

Writing

Speaking and listening

Language (including grammar and vocabulary)

2. For the literacy in science and technical subjects (and, by implication, in the mathematical standards), there are *two* strands: reading and writing. Although the speaking, listening, and language strands are not included in this set of standards, strategies for these literacies are included in this book, since both are necessary for students to learn new content and to express what they know and understand about that content.

THE NEED FOR CONTENT LITERACY

As many middle school and high school teachers already know, our teenagers are struggling with their reading skills, and there are very specific reasons why. You've no doubt heard many explanations in staff development workshops. The National Assessment of Educational Progress (NAEP) data shows that a majority of American eighth-grade students aren't proficient readers. This means that most students aren't able to comprehend grade-level texts when they enter high school. The 2006 ACT, Inc., report, *Reading between the Lines*, is cited by the CCSS authors as evidence that about half of high school students who took the ACT in the 2004–2005 academic year lacked the reading and literacy skills necessary for success in an introductory, credit-bearing college course (CCSS 2010, appendix A, p. 23). In fact, it is estimated that more than 40 percent of students entering college must take remedial courses in reading and writing before they are able to enroll in college credit courses.

To address this stark reality, the Common Core State Standards authors drew from research in the field of adolescent literacy as they identified the skills in reading, writing, speaking and listening, and language that would prepare students in the twenty-first century for college and career readiness. In the introduction to the standards the authors identify what it means for students to be college and career ready.

As students advance to the grades and master the standards in reading, writing, speaking, listening, and language, they are able to exhibit with increasing fullness and regularity these capacities of the literate individual.

   They demonstrate independence

   They build strong content knowledge.

They respond to the varying demand of audience, task, purpose, and discipline.
They comprehend as well as critique.
They value evidence.
They use technology and digital media strategically and capably.
They come to understand other perspectives and cultures.

(CCSS 2010, p. 7)

As you read through this list, I'm sure you'll agree that these literacy skills are integral to the development of content knowledge and competency.

At the sixth through twelfth grade levels, the literacy standards for English language arts are divided into two sets. There are standards that focus on **English language arts classrooms**, and there are **interdisciplinary literacy standards**. The latter were created to address the literacy needs of adolescent students in subject areas other than English. This doesn't mean that content area teachers are English teachers! It **does** mean that the interdisciplinary literacy standards are designed *"to complement the specific content demands of the disciplines, not replace them"* (CCSS 2010, p. 60).

WHAT DOES THIS FRAMEWORK MEAN FOR CONTENT AREA TEACHERS?

The ELA standards and the literacy standards for science and technical subjects share the same anchor standards in reading and writing. The ELA standards also embody anchor standards in speaking, listening, and language. This book contains strategies for speaking, listening, and language, since these are necessary for college and career readiness, although not included in the literacy in science and technical subjects standards.

Common Core State Standards

Looking at the standards from a more macro-level view, one can see that particular emphasis is placed on reading and writing in content area classes. Students are expected to develop their literacy skills as they learn content, with a particular emphasis on reading informational texts and argumentation in writing.

The emphasis on content literacy as articulated in the CCSS is not a new idea for middle school and high school teachers. The difference is that the CCSS emphasize that all content area teachers are responsible for developing student literacy skills; this effort is not the responsibility solely of English language arts teachers. Learning and integrating literacy strategies and skills in the teaching of content are pedagogies for effective instruction. **This is the focus of this book: to provide specific strategies that content area teachers can use to boost students' literacy and deepen their understanding of content area material**.

A Close Reading

When students read to develop content knowledge, they're often working with complex texts. In order to develop knowledge in a specific content area, students need to be able to **analyze and synthesize** literary and informational texts.

> *Reading is critical to building knowledge in history/social studies as well as in science and technical subjects. College and career ready reading in these fields requires an appreciation of the norms and conventions of each discipline, such as the kinds of evidence used in history and science; an understanding of domain specific words and phrases; an attention to precise details; and the capacity to evaluate intricate arguments, synthesize complex information, and follow detailed description of events and concepts. In history/social studies, for example, students need to be able to analyze, evaluate, and differentiate primary and secondary sources. When reading scientific and technical texts, students need to be able to gain knowledge from challenging texts that often make extensive use of elaborate diagrams and data to convey information and illustrate concepts. Students must be able to read complex informational texts in these fields with independence and confidence because the vast majority of reading in college and workforce training programs will be sophisticated nonfiction. It is important to note that these reading standards are meant to complement the specific content demands of the disciplines, not replace them.*
>
> (CCSS 2010, p. 60)

Although these goals are embedded within the literacy standards there are clear implications to the development of content knowledge. Specifically, students need to know how to read **content-specific text** like charts and graphs in science, math, and technical subjects. Teaching and developing specific literacy skills facilitate content learning, including science and mathematics.

Up for Debate

Another important feature of the literacy standards is the emphasis on argumentation. For college and career readiness, students need to be able to demonstrate what they know and understand through written text. Specifically, students should be able to make a claim, provide evidence, and make counterarguments. The introduction to the interdisciplinary writing standards articulates these expectations:

> *For students, writing is a key means of asserting and defending claims, showing what they know about a subject, and conveying what they have experienced, imagined, thought, and felt. To be college and career ready writers, students must take task, purpose, and audience into careful consideration, choosing words, information, structures, and formats deliberately. They need to be able to use technology strategically when creating, refining, and collaborating on writing. They have to become adept at gathering information, evaluating sources, and citing material accurately, reporting findings from their research and analysis of sources in a clear and cogent manner. They must have the flexibility, concentration, and fluency to produce high-quality first-draft text under a tight deadline and the capacity to revisit and make improvements to a piece of writing over multiple drafts when circumstances encourage or require it. To meet these goals, students must devote significant time and effort to writing, producing numerous pieces over short and long time frames throughout the year.*
>
> (CCSS 2010, p. 63)

The CCSS authors identify argumentation and writing as essential skills for developing content knowledge and being able to express what a student knows and understands in any given content-based discipline.

The interdisciplinary literacy standards are consistent with the K–12 ELA anchor standards; close reading, technology integration, and text complexity are all referenced. The strategies in this book specifically address these areas to support the development of students' literacy skills while also developing content knowledge. Although there are many similarities between these sets of standards, there are a few differences to note. For example, writing anchor standard 3, which emphasizes narrative writing ("*Write narratives to develop real or imagined experiences or events using effective technique, well-chosen details and well-structured event sequences*"), is not included in the interdisciplinary writing standards. It is expected that narrative writing is more suited for the English content curriculum, although the CCSS authors note that students do need to develop their narrative voice in writing argumentation.

> *Students' narrative skills continue to grow in these grades. The Standards require that students be able to incorporate narrative elements effectively into arguments*

and informative/explanatory texts. In history/social studies, students must be able to incorporate narrative accounts into their analyses of individuals or events of historical import. In science and technical subjects, students must be able to write precise enough descriptions of the step-by-step procedures they use in their investigations or technical work so that others can replicate them and (possibly) reach the same results.

(CCSS 2010, p. 65)

In addition to narrative writing, reading literature is included in the English content area standards but not in the interdisciplinary standards. This is logical, since literature is the primary content text for English courses.

Reading the Framework

As mentioned previously, the CCSS include anchor standards, which are consistent skills statements for grades K–12. These are macro-level expectations that students are to meet at the conclusion of twelfth grade. Under each anchor statement, there are grade-level articulations. These grade-level articulations are year-end goals and must be broken down into smaller lesson-level and unit-level goals (see figure 1.1).

THE BIGGEST CHANGES WITH THE COMMON CORE

The architects of the Common Core State Standards examined the recommendations of the National Reading Panel, data from the National Assessment for Educational Progress, and research-based methodology for literacy skill development. In the chapters that follow we'll examine each of the strands, the associated standards, and activities and strategies that you can immediately use in your classroom. Right now, we're going to look at the big picture and the overall major shifts that are embedded in the CCSS.

As we look at the CCSS reading strand, we'll notice that there is a much greater emphasis placed on high-level comprehension skills. Whether you've been teaching for quite some time or are new to the profession, you've surely already noticed that middle school and high school students lack the more sophisticated and developed reading skills that can support their understanding of related texts in our content areas, specifically science and mathematics. If students are to become college and career ready, they must be able to tackle increasingly complex texts. Highly developed reading comprehension skills are part of the "secret sauce" for college and career readiness.

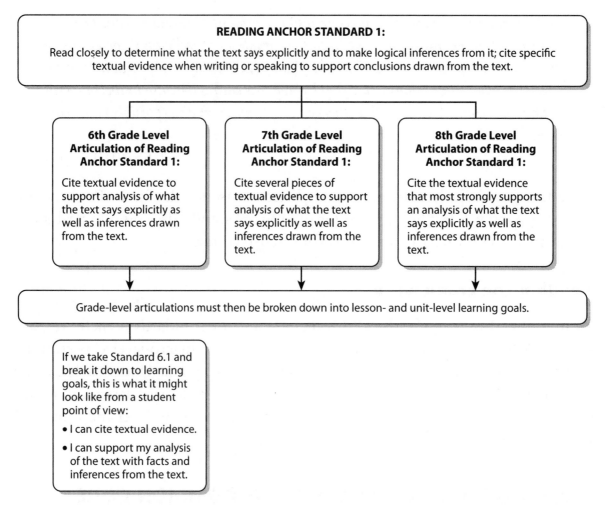

READING ANCHOR STANDARD 1:

Read closely to determine what the text says explicitly and to make logical inferences from it; cite specific textual evidence when writing or speaking to support conclusions drawn from the text.

6th Grade Level Articulation of Reading Anchor Standard 1:

Cite textual evidence to support analysis of what the text says explicitly as well as inferences drawn from the text.

7th Grade Level Articulation of Reading Anchor Standard 1:

Cite several pieces of textual evidence to support analysis of what the text says explicitly as well as inferences drawn from the text.

8th Grade Level Articulation of Reading Anchor Standard 1:

Cite the textual evidence that most strongly supports an analysis of what the text says explicitly as well as inferences drawn from the text.

Grade-level articulations must then be broken down into lesson- and unit-level learning goals.

If we take Standard 6.1 and break it down to learning goals, this is what it might look like from a student point of view:

- I can cite textual evidence.
- I can support my analysis of the text with facts and inferences from the text.

Figure 1.1   Anchor Standards and Grade-Level Articulations of Those Standards

Text Complexity

Although I'll go into greater detail about text complexity in chapter 2, we'll look at it briefly here. Text complexity is discussed in great detail in the CCSS document and articulated through reading anchor standard 10 for ELA and through the interdisciplinary literacy standard in history/social studies. In reading anchor standard 10, readers are expected to "*read and comprehend complex literary and informational texts independently and proficiently.*" What this means for middle school and high school teachers is that we must provide our students with a wide variety of texts that can develop students' reading skills, specifically in comprehension. We will discuss that in greater detail in chapter 2, and I'll provide some specific strategies for science and mathematics content.

Close Reading and Textual Analysis

Before you picked up this book, you'd probably already heard about close reading in discussions about the new standards. Close reading, or analytical reading of text, is valued as a means to develop high-level comprehension and interpretive skills. In chapter 2 I'll give you many strategies for developing close reading skills in your students, specifically science and mathematics word problems.

Argumentation in Writing

My seventeen-year-old daughter's English teacher, Mr. Gunning, began the first day of the senior English class with the following statement: "Everything is an argument." College- and career-ready students can make a claim about a text and then support it with evidence. That evidence is not always text-based. For the English class, the evidence probably would be text-based, but in social studies we would probably use text, visual documentation, graphs, charts, or lab data as evidence to support a claim. In mathematics, we would use numerical data to support a claim. There are many careers in which this kind of argumentation is relevant. For example, scientists make claims and must use data to support them. There are also many examples where numerical data, such as statistics, are used to support a claim. When adolescent students are able to establish a claim and support it with rich evidence, they are college and career ready. Appendix C in the CCSS document provides writing exemplars for your reference.

Greater Emphasis on Research

The CCSS writing standards also emphasize research. In order to be college and career ready, students should be able to analyze and synthesize a wide variety of resources, including technology or media-based resources, and present a cogent argument.

Speaking and Listening

Although the literacy standards for science and technical subjects do not include the speaking and listening strand, it is in my view a core part of the balanced literacy program and needs to be addressed, so this strand is included in the discussion in this book. Like the writing standards, the speaking and listening standards emphasize a student's ability to present an argument through speaking. Science and mathematics teachers are certainly familiar with this expectation and skill. The speaking and listening standards also emphasize a student's ability to engage in active listening in small and large group discussion. I don't know why the speaking and listening strand was not included in the interdisciplinary standards, but all content teachers—not just those in ELA—develop these skills in their students.

Language

Like the speaking and listening standards, the language standards are included only for the ELA and not for the interdisciplinary standards. I believe the CCSS language expectations also deserve attention in content areas. The ELA language standards focus on grammar and vocabulary; science and mathematics teachers are surely already addressing grammar in student written work and in speaking. If students are going to improve their overall literacy skills so that they are better able to learn content in our particular disciplines, then all of us must address grammatical issues when appropriate and needed. In addition, vocabulary is also a focus of the language standards. All content areas are vocabulary rich. Chapter 5 will provide a number of strategies for helping students develop vocabulary content knowledge.

SOME FINAL THOUGHTS

My purpose in writing this book is to provide content area teachers with ideas and resources for students to develop their literacy skills while learning content. This should be an easy process—as students learn new content, they should become more literate in that content area simultaneously and seamlessly—but, of course, it's not always that straightforward. Therefore my aim in the pages that follow is to make this process easier for you, the content area teacher. And please remember that Common Core implementation is a journey. Good teachers tinker, and this book provides tools, strategies, and ideas that will support your classroom tinkering!

CHAPTER TWO

Deepening Reading Comprehension Skills and Content Knowledge

When I became a high school English teacher twenty-five years ago, I knew my content, and I was a passionate educator. I entered the classroom excited to share my love of literature with my students. But not long after I began teaching, I realized that many of my kids were in no position to appreciate the texts we were reading, because these students lacked basic comprehension skills. These students could decode texts effectively (they understood letters and corresponding sounds), but they often found it challenging to go beyond a simple recall of information. Learning ways to teach students **reading comprehension strategies** was a glaring deficiency in my teacher preparation. It wasn't until I earned my PhD in reading that I developed a comprehensive "toolbox" to meet this need.

Twenty-five years later, I still witness this glaring need in the dozens of schools that I visit each year as a literacy consultant. Teachers often ask, "How do I support my students to understand what they're reading?" Cris Tovani's *I Read It, but I Don't Get It: Comprehension Strategies for Adolescent Readers* (2000) and Kylene Beers's *When Kids Can't Read, What Teachers Can Do: A Guide for Teachers, 6–12* (2003) both offer student/teacher case studies and strategies to support reading comprehension in adolescent readers. This chapter will help you address the demands of the CCSS reading standards by focusing on text complexity, close reading, and strategies that we can use in science, mathematics, and technical subjects to develop content knowledge and reading skills.

Before we delve into sample strategies for developing content knowledge and reading comprehension, let's take a look at the reality of adolescent literacy in schools. My consulting work takes me all across the United States, working with teachers and students to raise adolescent literacy. Everywhere I go, including international destinations, I hear similar stories from middle school and high school teachers in all content areas. I hear that students are reading below grade level and that they can decode text but don't understand the text that they are reading. Science teachers tell me that their students can't read the materials that the teachers assign. Mathematics teachers inform me that their students do not possess close reading skills needed to solve word problems. Often schools and districts rely on a "one size fits all" approach to the development of content knowledge and literacy skills. Given the diversity of kids in our schools, this approach is simply not effective.

If content area teachers and those teaching science, mathematics, and technical subjects want students to become proficient in reading *and* comprehension of content, we need to integrate comprehension strategies. This is how we're going to develop content knowledge.

Using the Common Core State Standards as a framework, let's consider the following as we work to develop our knowledge of pedagogies that foster the acquisition of content knowledge and literacy skills for college and career readiness.

> ▶ **The more students read, the more skilled they become at reading**. The authors of the Common Core State Standards emphasize the fact that our students don't read enough in school. Therefore, reading must be assigned in *all* content areas.
>
> ▶ **Giving students some choice in their reading material fosters student motivation**. When there are choices for reading material, teachers can differentiate and meet the needs of different-level readers in the content area classroom.
>
> ▶ **Using strategies that promote active reading will help build students' content knowledge and reading comprehension skills**.

This chapter will demonstrate many of these reading strategies and how they connect to the content areas of science and mathematics.

▶ **Remember, the textbook or a novel in English class is not the curriculum**. Exploring complex ideas and questions provides a context for student inquiry and content knowledge.

A LOOK AT THE INTERDISCIPLINARY STANDARDS

As we discussed in chapter 1, CCSS has two sections of standards: English language arts (ELA) and social studies. The standards that English language arts teachers should follow are divided into four strands:

▶ Reading

▶ Writing

▶ Speaking and listening

▶ Language

Remember that although you are a science or mathematics teacher, the standards that are specific to your content area always link and connect to the major anchor standards. So although things may be worded a bit differently in the ELA standards for science and technical subjects, the literacy skills that are being developed in each of the content areas are quite similar.

The filled-out activities provide examples from the Common Core Standards for Literacy in History/Social Studies, Science, and Technical Subjects. They are connected to the following reading anchor standards:

Key Ideas and Details

1. *Read closely to determine what the text says explicitly and to make logical inferences from it; cite specific textual evidence when writing or speaking to support conclusions drawn from the text.*

2. *Determine central ideas or themes of a text and analyze their development; summarize the key supporting details and ideas.*

3. *Analyze how and why individuals, events, or ideas develop and interact over the course of a text.*

Craft and Structure

4. *Interpret words and phrases as they are used in a text, including determining technical, connotative, and figurative meanings, and analyze how specific word choices shape meaning or tone.*

5. *Analyze the structure of texts, including how specific sentences, paragraphs, and larger portions of the text (e.g., a section, chapter, scene, or stanza) relate to each other and the whole.*

6. *Assess how point of view or purpose shapes the content and style of a text.*

Integration of Knowledge and Ideas

7. *Integrate and evaluate content presented in diverse media and formats, including visually and quantitatively, as well as in words.*

8. *Delineate and evaluate the argument and specific claims in a text, including the validity of the reasoning as well as the relevance and sufficiency of the evidence.*

9. *Analyze how two or more texts address similar themes or topics in order to build knowledge or to compare the approaches the authors take.*

Range of Reading and Level of Text Complexity

10. *Read and comprehend complex literary and informational texts independently and proficiently.*

The CCSS authors present the ELA standards for literacy in the content areas by reminding users of the documents about the ten anchor standards of reading. These anchor standards are then developed into grade-level articulations. Unlike the History/Social Studies, Science, and Technical Subjects literacy standards, the English content standards for reading are categorized according to the type of text being read: literary text or informational text. One of the major areas of confusion regarding this division involves the chart included in the standards that outlines the distribution of literary and informational text (see table 2.1). In my experience, the eighth-grade and twelfth-grade distributions are often misinterpreted.

The distributions for literary and informational text are across **all content areas**. If we look at the distribution for twelfth grade, where literature is 30 percent and informational texts is 70 percent, we need to ask the following question: Where is literature taught in the curriculum? Literature is primarily taught in the English content area course. The 30 percent designation of literary text represents

Table 2.1 Distribution of Literary and Informational Passages by Grade in the 2009 NAEP Reading Framework

Grade	Literary	Informational
4	50%	50%
8	45%	55%
12	30%	70%

Source: National Governors Association Center for Best Practices, Council of Chief State School Officers, *Common Core State Standards*. Published by National Governors Association Center for Best Practices, Council of Chief State School Officers, Washington, DC, copyright 2010.

the portion of English course content within an entire twelfth-grade curriculum. In short, English teachers still teach literature.

The Common Core State Standards go on to outline the specific literacy skills that should be developed in the content area. There are a few things to note regarding the reading standards for ELA in science, mathematics, and technical subjects:

▶ The ELA standards for the English content area divide reading into two areas (literature and informational text), but the reading standards for science and technical subjects do not. The focus is primarily on informational text in the science and mathematics content areas.

▶ Standard 1 relates to anchor standard 1, in that students develop the ability to cite specific textual evidence to support a claim.

▶ Standard 6 relates to the focus on point of view and perspective. In the science and mathematics content areas, reading standard 6 prompts students to evaluate different points of view on the same topic or issue.

It is also important to note that the CCSS do not specifically recommend a particular text or textbook for students to use in the study of their content areas. Instead, it is suggested that students use a wide variety of texts to develop content knowledge.

The overall goal of the reading standards is for students to develop college and career readiness:

> *Reading is critical to building knowledge. . . . Students must be able to read complex informational texts in these fields with independence and confidence because the vast majority of reading in college and workforce training programs will be sophisticated nonfiction. It is important to note that these reading standards are meant to complement the specific content demands of the disciplines, not replace them.*

(CCSS 2010, p. 60)

The CCSS for reading emphasize comprehension, and of course this is the area that concerns us the most about adolescent readers. The new standards articulate the expectation that students read books, documents, technology-based text, and other text sources as students develop their comprehension skills and content knowledge. It is critical that our adolescent students in the twenty-first century develop more advanced reading comprehension skills in order to be college and career ready.

BUILDING READING SKILLS IN A CONTENT AREA: BEFORE, DURING, AND AFTER READING

In the Common Core State Standards, close reading and sophisticated textual analysis are central to developing high-level comprehension and interpretive skills. The strategies that will be featured in this section are divided into three categories: **before reading**, **during reading**, and **after reading**. When these strategies are integrated with content study, greater reading proficiency is possible. Here's an overview of each category.

> ▶ Before-reading strategies are ones that are designed to draw out prior knowledge, or schema. Before-reading strategies provide structures in which students can work with the text for better comprehension.
>
> ▶ During-reading strategies prompt students to become more active and engaged readers. When students are not active and engaged in their reading, comprehension breaks down. During-reading strategies prompt students to make connections, monitor their own understanding, and maintain focus on the text.
>
> ▶ After-reading strategies prompt students to think reflectively about text. We know the importance of metacognition: thinking about our thinking allows for deeper comprehension. After-reading activities are important because these strategies prompt students to extend the meaning of a text, question what is not understood in a text, make personal connections about the text, and develop final conclusions about the text.

There are many interdisciplinary or content area reading strategies, and throughout this chapter I will provide additional suggestions and link the CCSS in reading to the different strategies. You will also notice that many of the strategies are not exclusively for before reading, during reading, or after reading. Most interdisciplinary reading strategies are combinations. Each featured sample strategy includes a blank template as a student sample for both science and mathematics content areas.

Before-Reading Strategies

Building background knowledge and tapping into what students know is the primary focus of before-reading strategies. Each of the following strategies accomplishes this goal.

Use Them for Yourself!

Many of the templates included in this book can be downloaded for free from the publisher's website. For details on how to access these web downloads, see appendix A of this book.

Anticipation Guide

The anticipation guide is a strategy that activates a student's prior knowledge and promotes interest in a new topic. Prior to reading, the student will respond to teacher-created statements that prompt students' prior understanding and perception about concepts in the text that the students are about to read.

How Does This Connect to CCSS?

Anticipation guides build the foundation for reading anchor standard 1, "*Cite textual evidence to support the analysis of what the text says as well as inferences drawn from the text.*" Anticipation guides are designed to draw out what students already know. Students are prepared to examine text more explicitly since major ideas and concepts were already introduced as part of the before-reading strategy. A template with examples follows in figure 2.1.

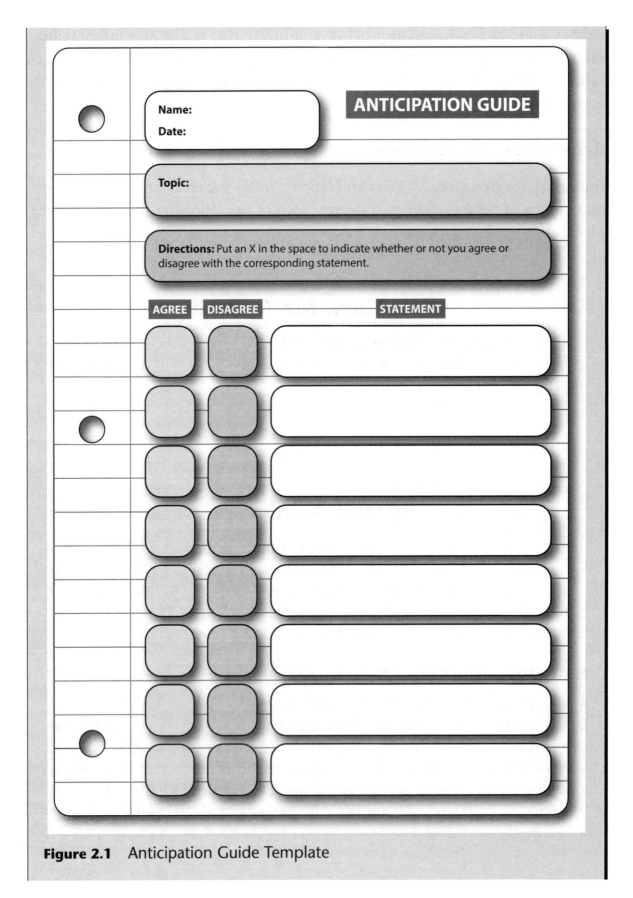

Name:

Date:

ANTICIPATION GUIDE

Topic:

Directions: Put an X in the space to indicate whether or not you agree or disagree with the corresponding statement.

AGREE	DISAGREE	STATEMENT

Figure 2.1 Anticipation Guide Template

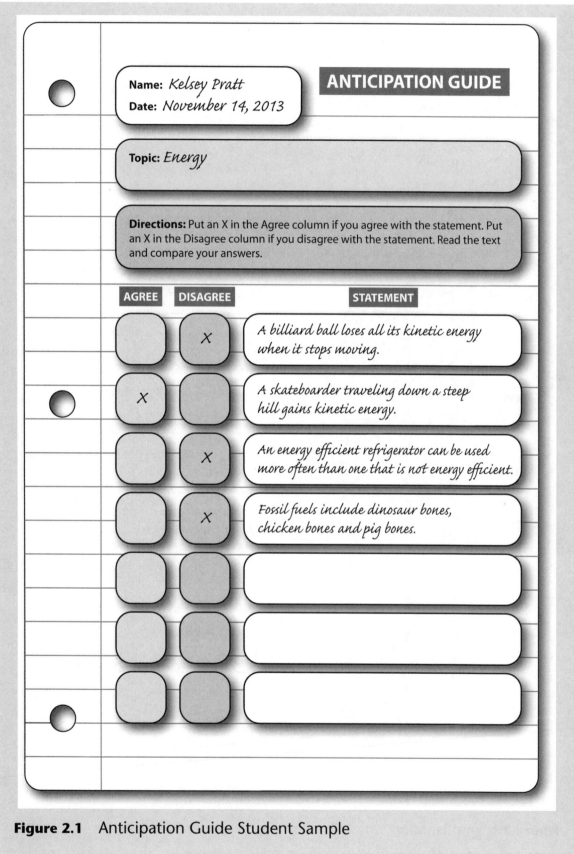

Figure 2.1 Anticipation Guide Student Sample

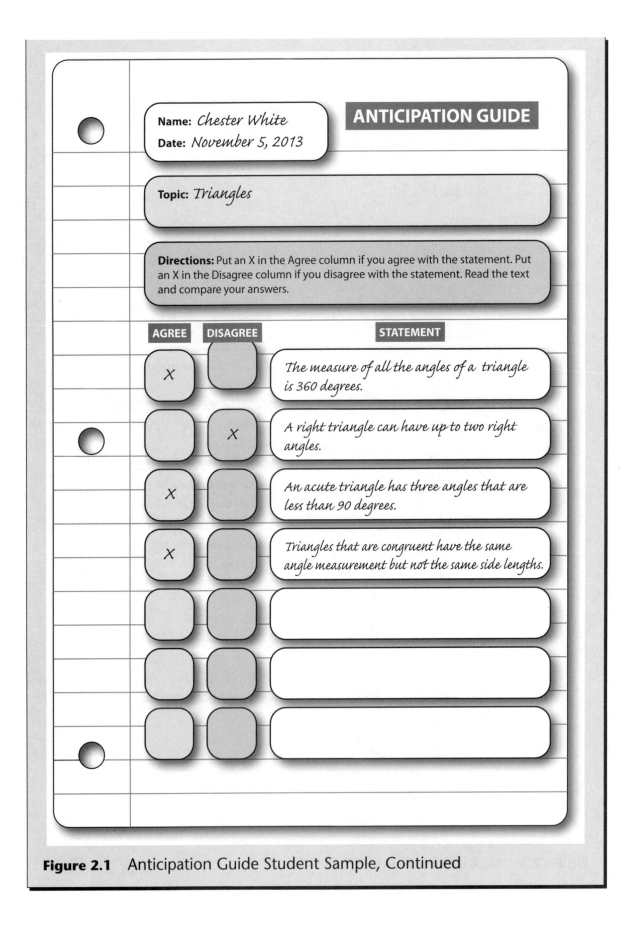

Name: *Chester White*

Date: *November 5, 2013*

ANTICIPATION GUIDE

Topic: *Triangles*

Directions: Put an X in the Agree column if you agree with the statement. Put an X in the Disagree column if you disagree with the statement. Read the text and compare your answers.

AGREE	DISAGREE	STATEMENT
X		*The measure of all the angles of a triangle is 360 degrees.*
	X	*A right triangle can have up to two right angles.*
X		*An acute triangle has three angles that are less than 90 degrees.*
X		*Triangles that are congruent have the same angle measurement but not the same side lengths.*

Figure 2.1   Anticipation Guide Student Sample, Continued

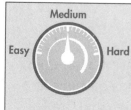

Listen-Read-Discuss

Developed by Manzo and Casale (1985), Listen-Read-Discuss builds student prior knowledge through a lecture that is paired with a graphic organizer. After the lecture, students compare what they learned during the lecture with what they learn from the text. Listen-Read-Discuss is a powerful tool for engaging struggling readers in classroom discussion, since they have some introduction to the presented content.

Here's how the strategy works.

Step 1: Listen

The teacher presents a content-based lecture on the reading. For example, if the students are about to read specific science content or a word problem, the teacher can conduct a think-aloud. Our students need to witness how we read and think about science, technology, and mathematics content. As the students listen to the teacher's lecture, they should document what they are learning in a graphic organizer.

Step 2: Read

The students will read the selected text (that the teacher read during the think-aloud). Inform the students that their reading of the text may provide another interpretation of the content.

Step 3: Discuss

Through large group discussion, prompt the students to consider the differences between what they read and what they learned from the teacher's think-aloud.

How Does This Connect to CCSS?

Learn-Read-Discuss connects to reading standard 1, which focuses on a student's ability to identify a claim or idea and then support it with textual evidence (remember, for science and mathematics, this includes numerical "text"). In this strategy, the students listen to a teacher think-aloud and record key ideas and information using a graphic organizer. As the students read, they are comparing what they read to what they learned through lecture. Throughout this entire activity, the students are constantly analyzing information and either confirming it or challenging what they know.

GIST

GIST is one of my favorite reading comprehension strategies. Students often enjoy this activity because it has gaming and problem-solving elements. Like many strategies that are featured in this section of the chapter, not all of the activities fit neatly into just one of the before-reading, during-reading, or after-reading stages. GIST is a before-reading and an after-reading activity.

Here's how it works.

Step 1

Students preview the text. Draw their attention to the headings, subheadings, and graphic elements like graphs, charts, and pictures.

Step 2

You and the students compile a list of words, phrases, and key vocabulary from the text.

Step 3

Students read the text. Since the students have already previewed the text and identified key language and vocabulary, they should have a guide to understand the text.

Step 4

Students summarize the passage, using the words and phrases that they identified, into a twenty-word statement. This is where the "gaming" element emerges. The students must create a statement that is **exactly** twenty words.

How Does This Connect to CCSS?

GIST develops the skills that are identified in reading standard 2, which requires students to identify the key ideas and concepts in a text and provide supporting evidence. This reading strategy also develops the skills that are featured in reading standard 4, which states that students are expected to closely read and analyze words and vocabulary. Students should understand the denotative and connotative meanings of words and vocabulary in a text. A template with examples follows in figure 2.2.

GIST

Name:

Date:

Title of Reading Selection:

Directions: Preview the reading selection. Write down the key words and phrases. Then write a twenty-word summary sentence using as many of the key words as you can.

Key words and phrases:

Twenty-word summary sentence

________ ________ ________ ________

________ ________ ________ ________

________ ________ ________ ________

________ ________ ________ ________

________ ________ ________ ________

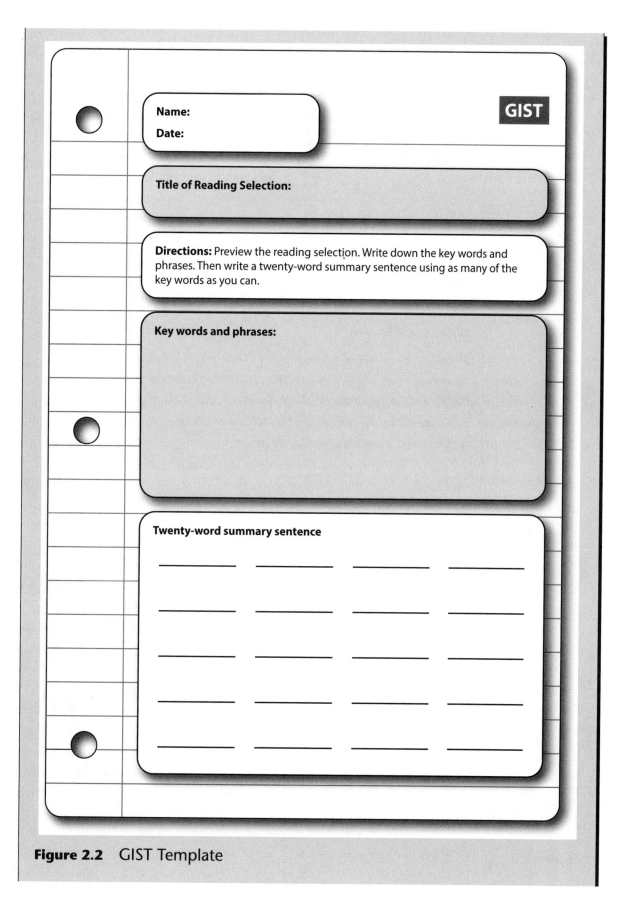

Figure 2.2 GIST Template

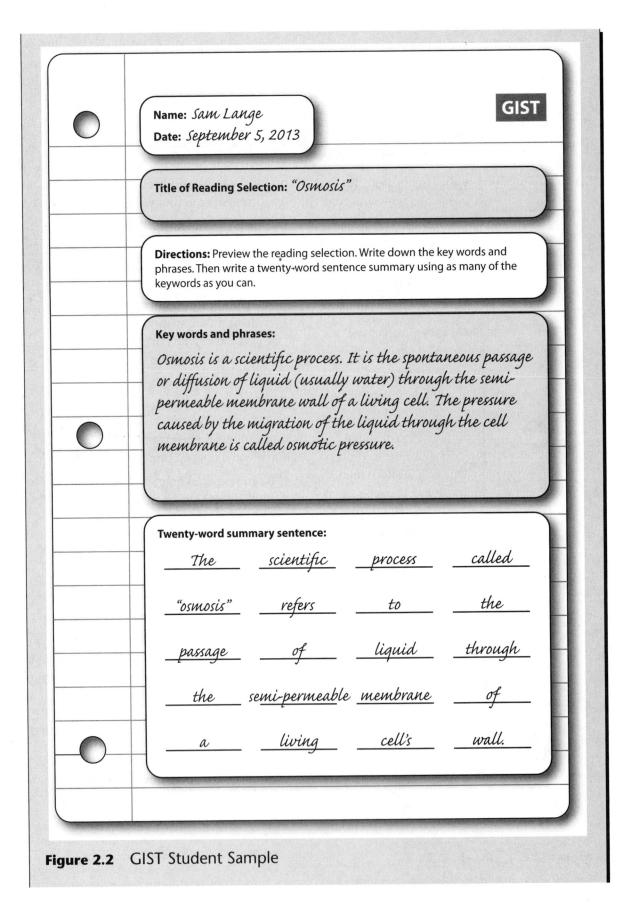

GIST

Name: *Sam Lange*
Date: *September 5, 2013*

Title of Reading Selection: *"Osmosis"*

Directions: Preview the reading selection. Write down the key words and phrases. Then write a twenty-word sentence summary using as many of the keywords as you can.

Key words and phrases:

Osmosis is a scientific process. It is the spontaneous passage or diffusion of liquid (usually water) through the semi-permeable membrane wall of a living cell. The pressure caused by the migration of the liquid through the cell membrane is called osmotic pressure.

Twenty-word summary sentence:

The   scientific   process   called

"osmosis"   refers   to   the

passage   of   liquid   through

the   semi-permeable   membrane   of

a   living   cell's   wall.

Figure 2.2 GIST Student Sample

Name: Jennifer Skinner
Date: March 17, 2013

GIST

Title of Reading Selection: Pi

Directions: Preview the reading selection. Write down the key words and phrases. Then write a twenty-word sentence summary using as many of the keywords as you can.

Key words and phrases:

Pi is the ratio of the circumference of a circle to its diameter. It is an irrational number, and the value of it is 3.14159265359, etc. etc. Mathematicians have used computers to calculate to more than 200 billion pi decimal places. Pi is used in calculations including length, area and volume.

Twenty-word summary sentence:

Pi	is	the	ratio
of	a	circle's	circumference
to	its	diameter	and
it	has	more	than
200	billion	decimal	places.

Figure 2.2   GIST Student Sample, Continued

During-Reading Strategies

During-reading strategies develop students into more active and independent readers. I know from working with teachers of adolescents all over the country that many students are able to decode but unable to comprehend text while they're reading it. Consequently we need to provide strategies that can develop content knowledge and reading skills that prompt students to make connections, monitor their understanding, and actively interact with the text. Each of the following strategies develops these goals.

Cornell Notes

Cornell Notes are probably one of the most often-used reading strategies, and it isn't difficult to understand why. Cornell Notes require students to dig more deeply into text as they connect text details to the main ideas and concepts. Developed by an education professor at Cornell University, this note-taking and active-reading strategy promotes students to analyze and think critically about the text. In the left-hand column, students identify the big ideas and concepts from the text. In the right-hand column, students write details and information that are connected to the big ideas and concepts in the left-hand column. The area at the bottom of the template is where a student can write a summative statement about the text. See figure 2.3.

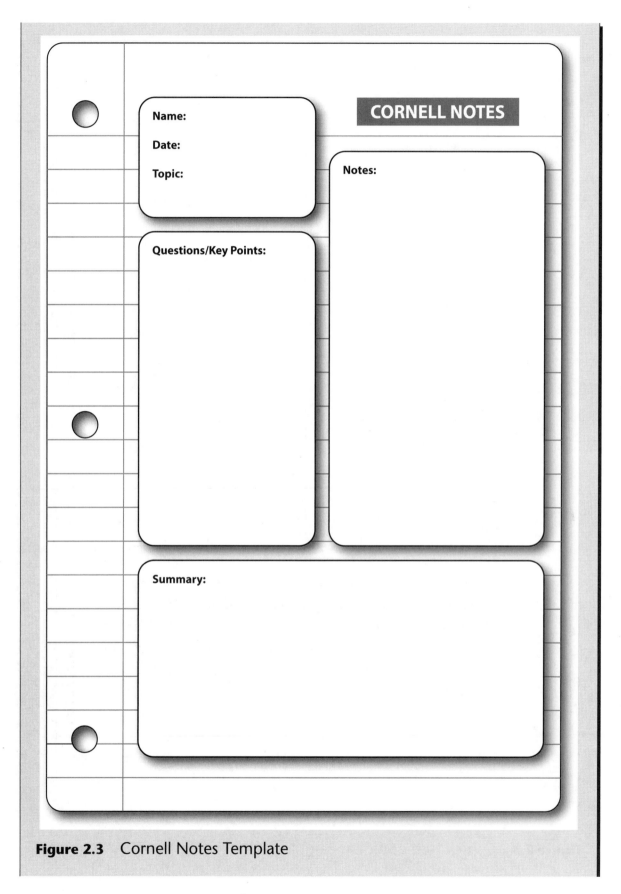

CORNELL NOTES

Name:

Date:

Topic:

Notes:

Questions/Key Points:

Summary:

Figure 2.3 Cornell Notes Template

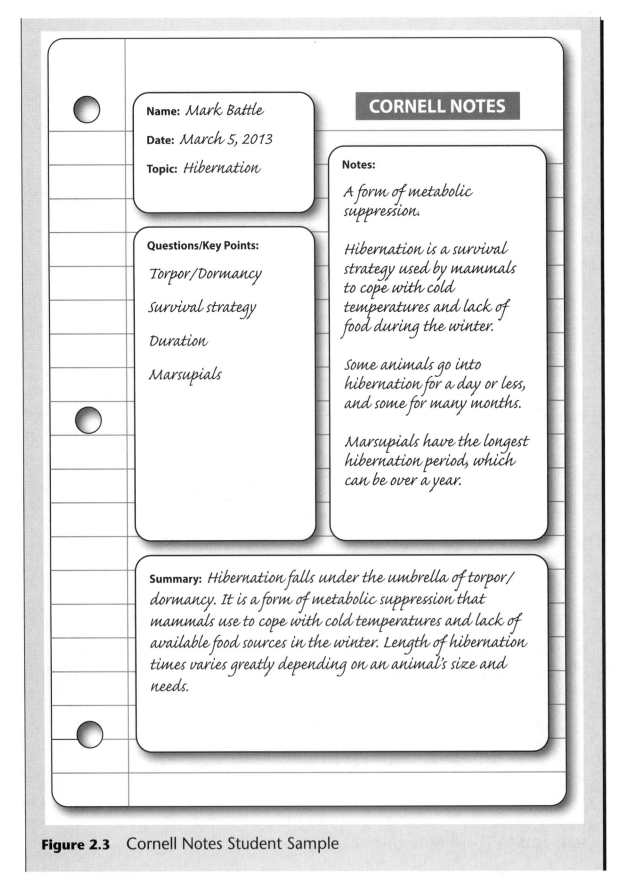

CORNELL NOTES

Name: Mark Battle

Date: March 5, 2013

Topic: Hibernation

Questions/Key Points:

Torpor/Dormancy

Survival strategy

Duration

Marsupials

Notes:

A form of metabolic suppression.

Hibernation is a survival strategy used by mammals to cope with cold temperatures and lack of food during the winter.

Some animals go into hibernation for a day or less, and some for many months.

Marsupials have the longest hibernation period, which can be over a year.

Summary: Hibernation falls under the umbrella of torpor/dormancy. It is a form of metabolic suppression that mammals use to cope with cold temperatures and lack of available food sources in the winter. Length of hibernation times varies greatly depending on an animal's size and needs.

Figure 2.3   Cornell Notes Student Sample

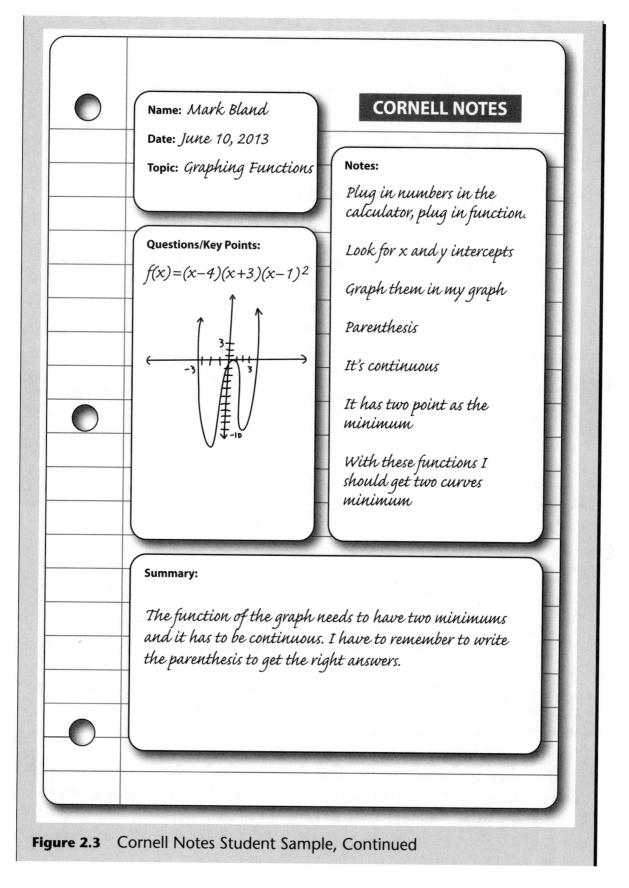

Name: Mark Bland

Date: June 10, 2013

Topic: Graphing Functions

CORNELL NOTES

Questions/Key Points:

$f(x) = (x-4)(x+3)(x-1)^2$

Notes:

Plug in numbers in the calculator, plug in function.

Look for x and y intercepts

Graph them in my graph

Parenthesis

It's continuous

It has two point as the minimum

With these functions I should get two curves minimum

Summary:

The function of the graph needs to have two minimums and it has to be continuous. I have to remember to write the parenthesis to get the right answers.

Figure 2.3 Cornell Notes Student Sample, Continued

An Additional Tip for Classroom Implementation

Many students I encounter often struggle with the summary section of the Cornell Notes strategy. The student samples (figure 2.3) demonstrate how you can scaffold the strategy for the students. In these examples, students are given a specific detail to reexamine since it will help them to summarize the text.

How Does This Connect to CCSS?

Cornell Notes connects to the CCSS reading standards on several levels.

▶ As we already discussed, reading standard 1 establishes the expectation for students to *"determine what the text says explicitly and make logical inferences from it."* Students must engage in this kind of close reading in order to identify the main ideas and concepts and connect those to specific details and evidence for the text.

▶ Cornell Notes also develops the skills that are identified in reading standard 2: *"determine central ideas or themes of a text and analyze their development; summarize the key supporting details and ideas."* When students record information in each column, they are also tracing the development of ideas and concepts that are further developed and presented in the summary statement.

Questioning the Author

This challenging interdisciplinary literacy strategy requires students to connect with the text, use prior knowledge, make inferences and develop an understanding of the author's purpose, or point of view. When students ask questions and dig more deeply into a text from a different point of view or perspective, they develop a more complex and deeper comprehension of the text. See the template that follows in figure 2.4.

This strategy is an example of how close reading is critical to sophisticated comprehension. We'll discuss more about close reading and how it is emphasized in the CCSS reading standards later in this chapter.

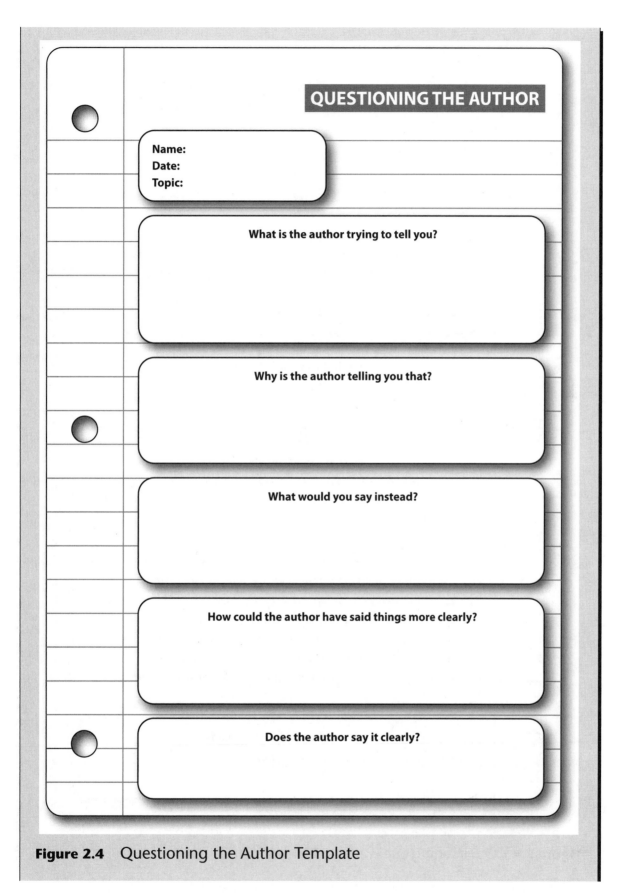

Figure 2.4 Questioning the Author Template

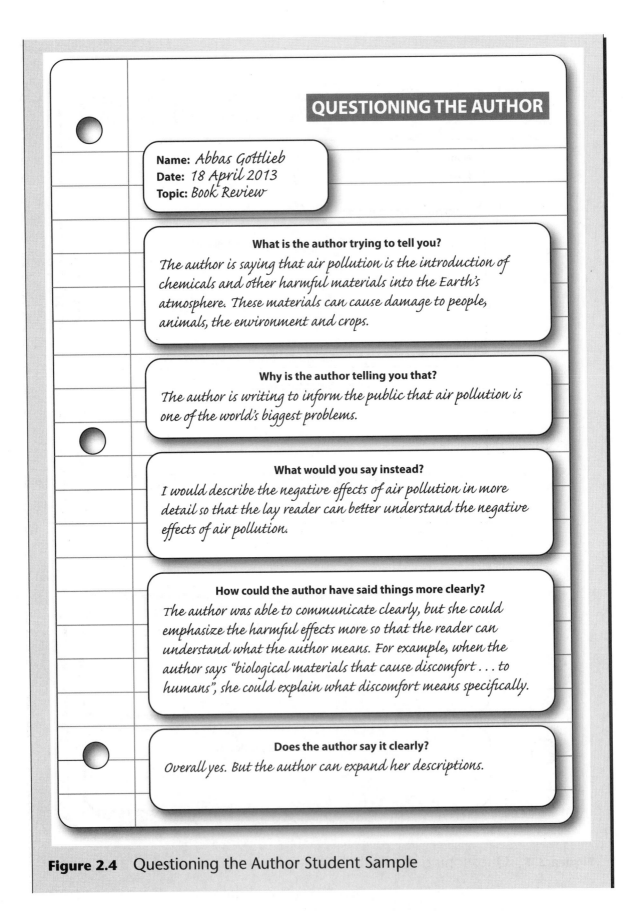

QUESTIONING THE AUTHOR

Name: Abbas Gottlieb
Date: 18 April 2013
Topic: Book Review

What is the author trying to tell you?

The author is saying that air pollution is the introduction of chemicals and other harmful materials into the Earth's atmosphere. These materials can cause damage to people, animals, the environment and crops.

Why is the author telling you that?

The author is writing to inform the public that air pollution is one of the world's biggest problems.

What would you say instead?

I would describe the negative effects of air pollution in more detail so that the lay reader can better understand the negative effects of air pollution.

How could the author have said things more clearly?

The author was able to communicate clearly, but she could emphasize the harmful effects more so that the reader can understand what the author means. For example, when the author says "biological materials that cause discomfort . . . to humans", she could explain what discomfort means specifically.

Does the author say it clearly?

Overall yes. But the author can expand her descriptions.

Figure 2.4 Questioning the Author Student Sample

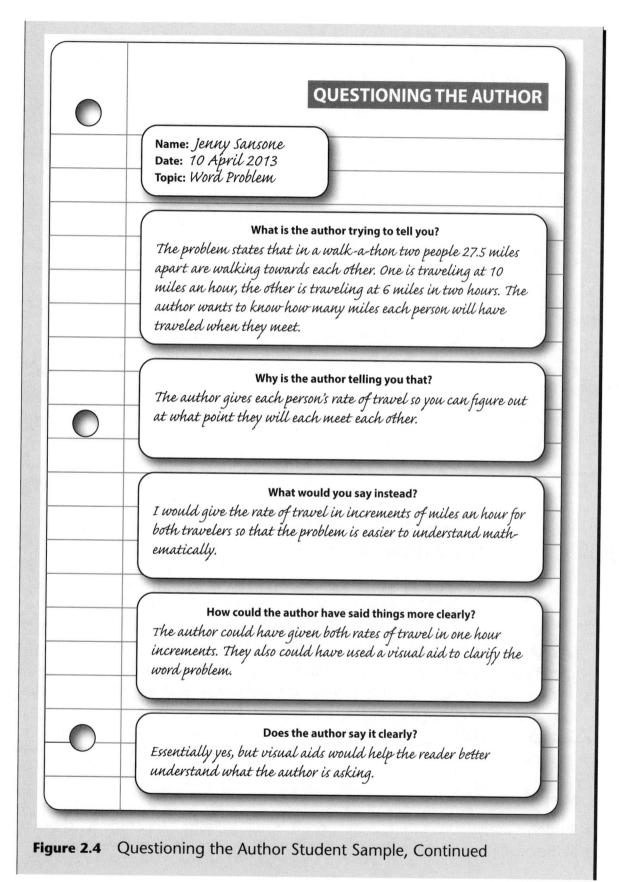

QUESTIONING THE AUTHOR

Name: *Jenny Sansone*
Date: *10 April 2013*
Topic: *Word Problem*

What is the author trying to tell you?
The problem states that in a walk-a-thon two people 27.5 miles apart are walking towards each other. One is traveling at 10 miles an hour, the other is traveling at 6 miles in two hours. The author wants to know how many miles each person will have traveled when they meet.

Why is the author telling you that?
The author gives each person's rate of travel so you can figure out at what point they will each meet each other.

What would you say instead?
I would give the rate of travel in increments of miles an hour for both travelers so that the problem is easier to understand mathematically.

How could the author have said things more clearly?
The author could have given both rates of travel in one hour increments. They also could have used a visual aid to clarify the word problem.

Does the author say it clearly?
Essentially yes, but visual aids would help the reader better understand what the author is asking.

Figure 2.4 Questioning the Author Student Sample, Continued

How Does This Connect to CCSS?

Questioning the Author develops several reading skills as identified in the CCSS reading standards. For example:

▶ Like Cornell Notes, students develop the skills that are articulated in reading standards 1 and 2. Students learn how to read closely and develop inferences and logical understanding of the text (reading standard 1). Through the development of questions for the author, students also identify central ideas and themes and connected details (reading standard 2).

▶ Depending on the text, students would also most likely develop the skills articulated in reading standard 3, which prompts students to analyze why the author chooses to develop individuals, events, and ideas.

▶ Many reading skills identified in the Common Core standards are addressed by the Questioning the Author strategy, but most notably reading standard 6 is aligned with this strategy. Reading standard 6 focuses on how point of view and purpose can shape the content and style of a text (CCSS 2010, p. 35). In this strategy, students need to consider a point of view that is different from their own as they develop questions for the author.

SQ4R: Survey, Question, Read, Recite, Review, Reflect

Easy — Medium — Hard

You may also be familiar with SQR and SQ3R. I selected SQ4R as an example since it is the most complex in this strategy group. This strategy develops several reading skills, such as predicting, using prior knowledge, monitoring comprehension, and making inferences. This is a particularly helpful strategy for the development of close reading skills. As you look at the steps for the strategy, you will also note that this is not exclusively a during-reading strategy. There are steps in this strategy that could occur before reading as well as after reading.

Here's how the strategy works.

Step 1: Survey

Students should survey the chapter prior to reading. Prompt the students to look at the heading and subheadings and to skim the introduction and conclusion.

Step 2: Question

Once students have identified the headings in the text, instruct them to change the statement headings into questions.

Step 3: Read

At this point, students read the text and answer the questions that they created in step 2.

Step 4: Recite

Once students have read the text, instruct them to close the text and orally summarize what they read. Think-Pair-Share, a common speaking and listening strategy, is an effective method for students to share their text summaries. Students will pair with a classmate and then discuss what they know and understand about the text.

Step 5: Review

Review the answers to the questions and the vocabulary word definitions.

Step 6: Reflect

This step occurs after reading. Students should write what this new information means to them and how it contributes to their understanding of the text and the content knowledge.

How Does This Connect to CCSS?

Like the other during-reading strategies that we have examined so far, SQ4R develops students' skills in identifying key concepts and details that support the main ideas and themes of the text. Depending on the type of text or subject, students will have also probably addressed perspective and point of view as they responded to the questions and reflected on the information and what it means. Another reading skill is also developed in SQ4R. In steps 1 and 2, in which students survey the text and develop questions, students develop the skills articulated in reading standard 5. In this standard, students analyze the text structure as they survey the text and headings. Students also begin to develop an understanding of how the text structure will impact the meaning or tone of the text. See the template that follows in figure 2.5.

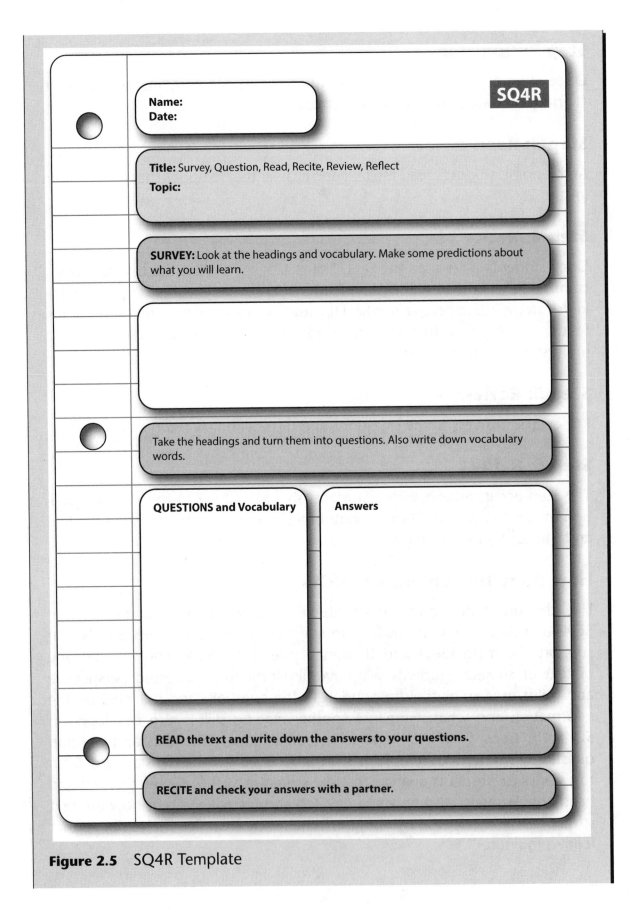

Name:
Date:

Title: Survey, Question, Read, Recite, Review, Reflect

Topic:

SURVEY: Look at the headings and vocabulary. Make some predictions about what you will learn.

Take the headings and turn them into questions. Also write down vocabulary words.

QUESTIONS and Vocabulary	Answers

READ the text and write down the answers to your questions.

RECITE and check your answers with a partner.

Figure 2.5 SQ4R Template

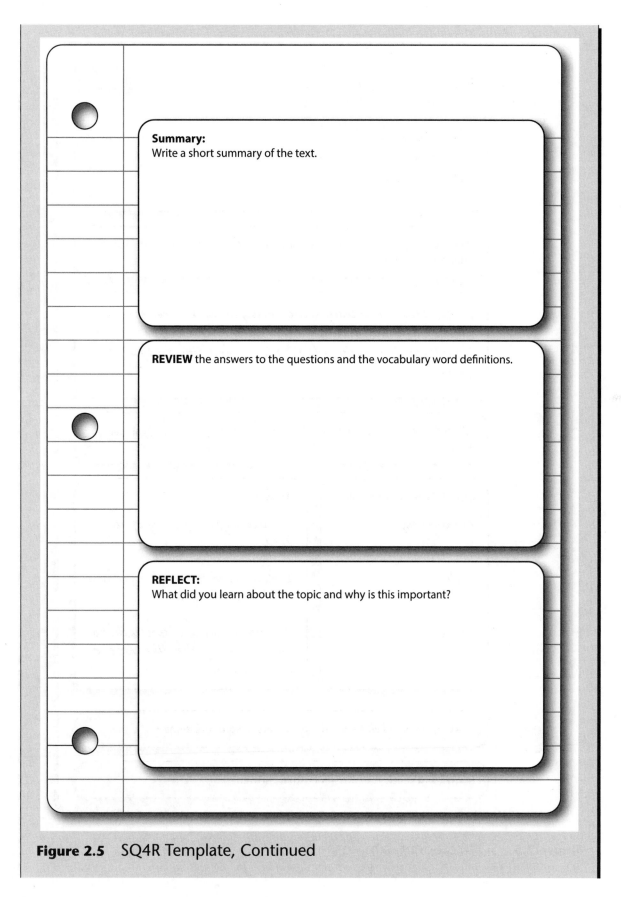

Summary:
Write a short summary of the text.

REVIEW the answers to the questions and the vocabulary word definitions.

REFLECT:
What did you learn about the topic and why is this important?

Figure 2.5 SQ4R Template, Continued

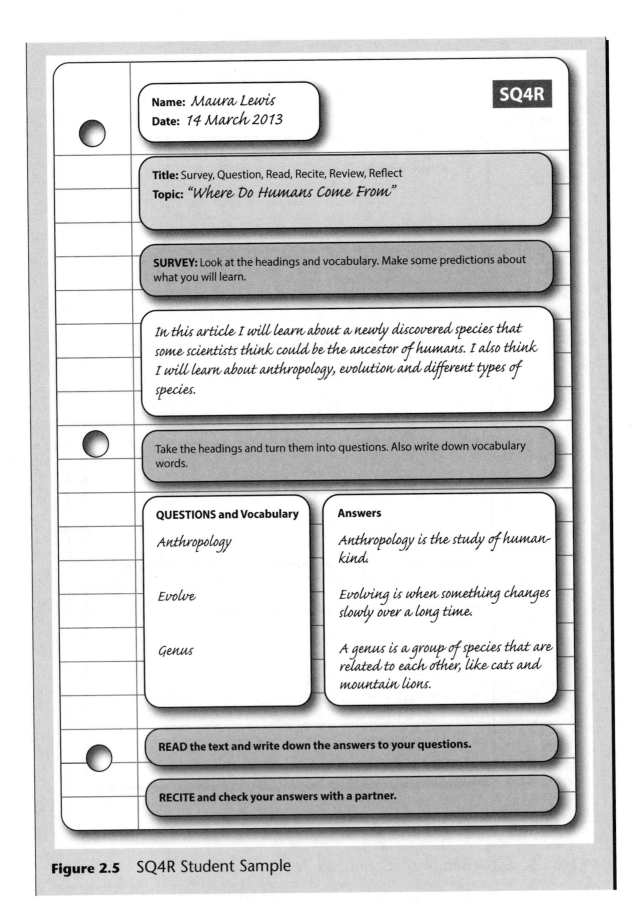

Name: Maura Lewis
Date: 14 March 2013

SQ4R

Title: Survey, Question, Read, Recite, Review, Reflect
Topic: "Where Do Humans Come From"

SURVEY: Look at the headings and vocabulary. Make some predictions about what you will learn.

In this article I will learn about a newly discovered species that some scientists think could be the ancestor of humans. I also think I will learn about anthropology, evolution and different types of species.

Take the headings and turn them into questions. Also write down vocabulary words.

QUESTIONS and Vocabulary	Answers
Anthropology	Anthropology is the study of human-kind.
Evolve	Evolving is when something changes slowly over a long time.
Genus	A genus is a group of species that are related to each other, like cats and mountain lions.

READ the text and write down the answers to your questions.

RECITE and check your answers with a partner.

Figure 2.5   SQ4R Student Sample

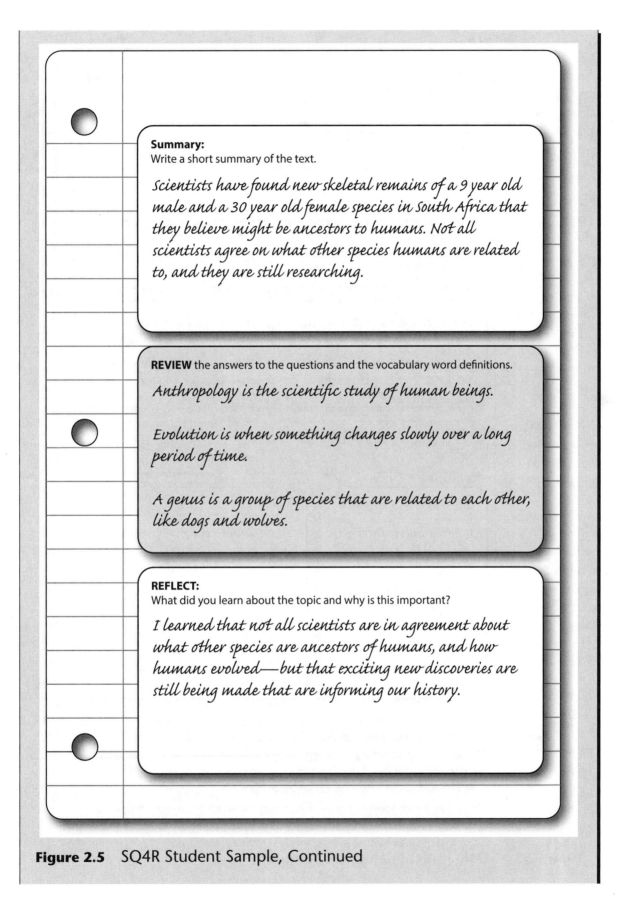

Summary:
Write a short summary of the text.

Scientists have found new skeletal remains of a 9 year old male and a 30 year old female species in South Africa that they believe might be ancestors to humans. Not all scientists agree on what other species humans are related to, and they are still researching.

REVIEW the answers to the questions and the vocabulary word definitions.

Anthropology is the scientific study of human beings.

Evolution is when something changes slowly over a long period of time.

A genus is a group of species that are related to each other, like dogs and wolves.

REFLECT:
What did you learn about the topic and why is this important?

I learned that not all scientists are in agreement about what other species are ancestors of humans, and how humans evolved—but that exciting new discoveries are still being made that are informing our history.

Figure 2.5 SQ4R Student Sample, Continued

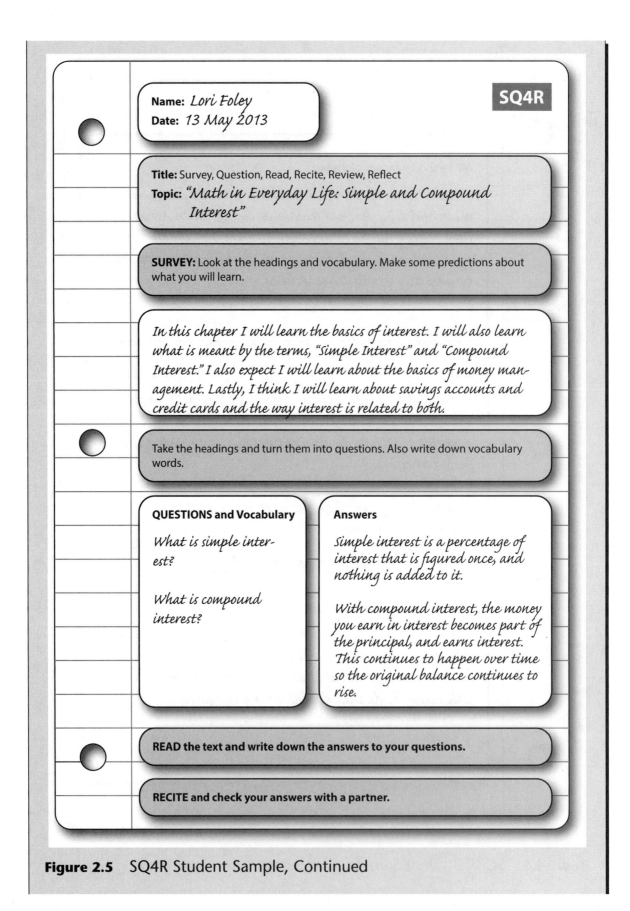

Name: *Lori Foley*
Date: *13 May 2013*

SQ4R

Title: Survey, Question, Read, Recite, Review, Reflect
Topic: *"Math in Everyday Life: Simple and Compound Interest"*

SURVEY: Look at the headings and vocabulary. Make some predictions about what you will learn.

In this chapter I will learn the basics of interest. I will also learn what is meant by the terms, "Simple Interest" and "Compound Interest." I also expect I will learn about the basics of money management. Lastly, I think I will learn about savings accounts and credit cards and the way interest is related to both.

Take the headings and turn them into questions. Also write down vocabulary words.

QUESTIONS and Vocabulary

What is simple interest?

What is compound interest?

Answers

Simple interest is a percentage of interest that is figured once, and nothing is added to it.

With compound interest, the money you earn in interest becomes part of the principal, and earns interest. This continues to happen over time so the original balance continues to rise.

READ the text and write down the answers to your questions.

RECITE and check your answers with a partner.

Figure 2.5 SQ4R Student Sample, Continued

Summary:
Write a short summary of the text.

Interest is expressed as a rate. Savings accounts accumulate interest, for example, an account with a 2% rate would earn $2 for $100 in the account.

Simple interest is added to the balance only once, whereas compound interest accumulates over time because the interest added on one day is added to the overall balance and continues to collect interest.

REVIEW the answers to the questions and the vocabulary word definitions.

Simple interest is a percentage of interest that is figured once and is not added to the overall balance. Compound interest is interest that is added to the balance and becomes part of what is used to calculate additional interest so that the balance continues to rise.

REFLECT:
What did you learn about the topic and why is this important?

Compound interest is the type of interest that makes it difficult to pay back balances on a credit card. On these types of accounts, the interest is in the bank's favor, whereas in a savings account, the interest is in your favor. It is smarter to keep no balance on a credit card, and keep as much as possible in a savings account.

Figure 2.5 SQ4R Student Sample, Continued

After-Reading Strategies

Encouraging students to self-reflect on what they've read is the main goal of after-reading strategies. Students who draw parallels to personal experience or previously encountered information, situations, and characters are more likely to experience deeper comprehension and greater retention. After-reading strategies are an important metacognitive strategy that leads to greater reflection and comprehension.

Question-Answer Relationship

The Question-Answer Relationship, or QAR, is one of the most challenging comprehension strategies to teach. It is also an outstanding strategy for developing close reading skills. In this strategy, students develop questions after they have read the assigned text. There are four types of questions.

- ▶ **Right There**: The answer is in the text and is easy to find.
- ▶ **Think and Search**: The answer is in the text, but students may have to look at several different sentences and make inferences from what they've read.
- ▶ **Author and You**: The answer is not in the text. However, readers may have some background knowledge that will help them to answer the question.
- ▶ **On My Own**: The answer is not in the text. This kind of question requires a high level of comprehension because students must analyze and then synthesize the information that they've read in order to represent the information in a unique and personal way.

How Does This Connect to CCSS?

The QAR develops numerous skills identified in the CCSS. Students are prompted to read closely as they develop their questions, which requires them to determine what the text says both explicitly (Right There questions) and implicitly (Think and Search questions) (see figure 2.6). These skills are in reading standard 1. In order to respond to the questions a student has developed in a QAR, the student needs to determine and track themes, ideas, events, and individuals, for example, from the text; this effort is aligned to reading standards 2 and 3. Students would also apply skills outlined in reading standards 4, 5, and 6 in order to develop and respond to the questions. These standards identify skills like close analysis of wording, text structures, and point of view. The skills in reading standard 8 are also developed in a QAR because students need to examine claims made in the text and analyze how evidence and reasoning are used in support. It is no wonder that QAR is one of the most challenging content reading strategies for students, since it embodies many reading skills. Although it's a challenging strategy, you will witness a tremendous growth in comprehension skills as students master the QAR strategy.

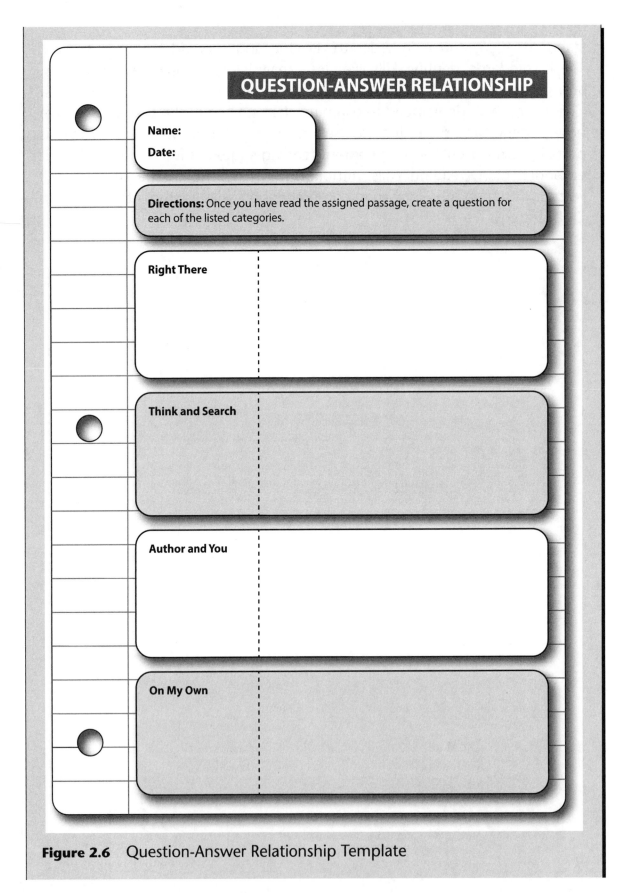

Figure 2.6 Question-Answer Relationship Template

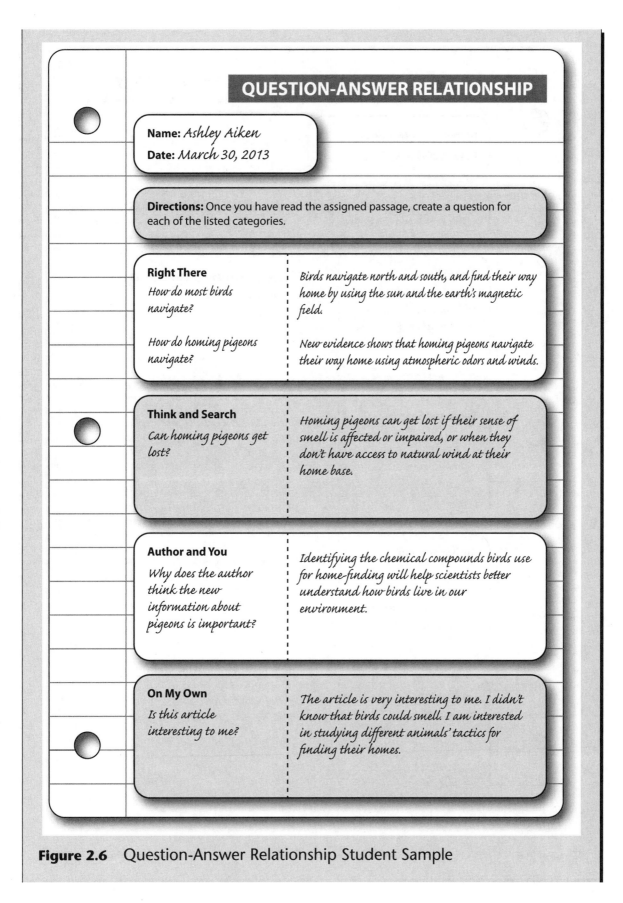

QUESTION-ANSWER RELATIONSHIP

Name: Ashley Aiken

Date: March 30, 2013

Directions: Once you have read the assigned passage, create a question for each of the listed categories.

Right There

How do most birds navigate?

How do homing pigeons navigate?

Birds navigate north and south, and find their way home by using the sun and the earth's magnetic field.

New evidence shows that homing pigeons navigate their way home using atmospheric odors and winds.

Think and Search

Can homing pigeons get lost?

Homing pigeons can get lost if their sense of smell is affected or impaired, or when they don't have access to natural wind at their home base.

Author and You

Why does the author think the new information about pigeons is important?

Identifying the chemical compounds birds use for home-finding will help scientists better understand how birds live in our environment.

On My Own

Is this article interesting to me?

The article is very interesting to me. I didn't know that birds could smell. I am interested in studying different animals' tactics for finding their homes.

Figure 2.6 Question-Answer Relationship Student Sample

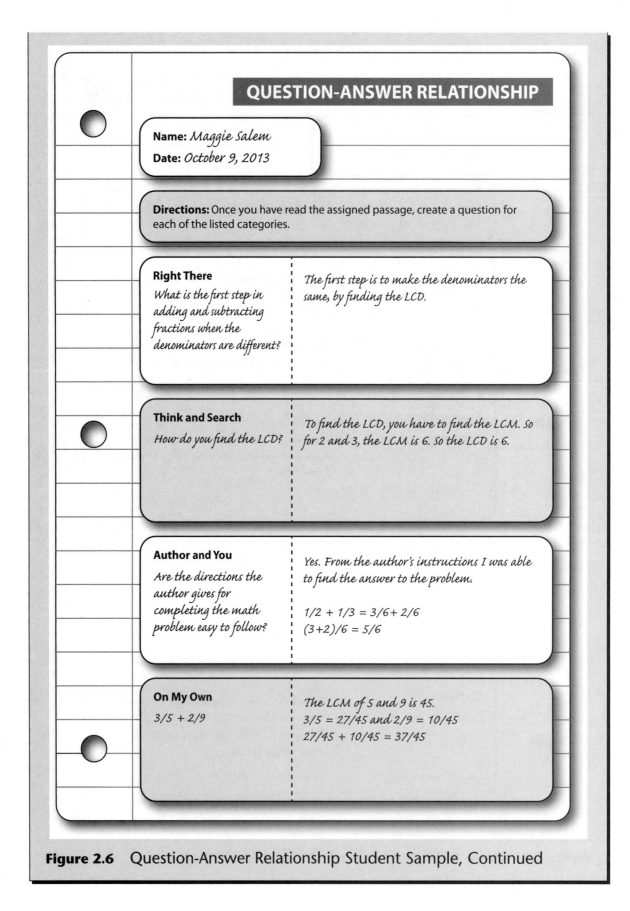

QUESTION-ANSWER RELATIONSHIP

Name: *Maggie Salem*

Date: *October 9, 2013*

Directions: Once you have read the assigned passage, create a question for each of the listed categories.

Right There

What is the first step in adding and subtracting fractions when the denominators are different?

The first step is to make the denominators the same, by finding the LCD.

Think and Search

How do you find the LCD?

To find the LCD, you have to find the LCM. So for 2 and 3, the LCM is 6. So the LCD is 6.

Author and You

Are the directions the author gives for completing the math problem easy to follow?

Yes. From the author's instructions I was able to find the answer to the problem.

1/2 + 1/3 = 3/6 + 2/6
(3+2)/6 = 5/6

On My Own

3/5 + 2/9

The LCM of 5 and 9 is 45.
3/5 = 27/45 and 2/9 = 10/45
27/45 + 10/45 = 37/45

Figure 2.6   Question-Answer Relationship Student Sample, Continued

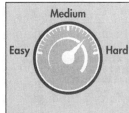

Sequence Trails

The Sequence Trails strategy offers a structure for students to identify key events from a literary text or informational text (see figure 2.7). Once the students have identified the key events in the text, they should arrange them in chronological order and create a visual representation of each event. I also prompt the students to answer the following question about the events that they selected: "Why do you think this event is important?" This is a metacognitive kind of question and prompts students to analyze, synthesize, and then explain or represent each event. This is a high level of comprehension.

How Does This Connect to CCSS?

In this strategy, students are developing several reading strategies that are aligned with reading standards 1, 2, and 3. These strategies include

- ▶ Connecting key ideas, information, and events
- ▶ Making predictions about the text and the events that are represented in the text
- ▶ Visualizing text while paying close attention to details and important text-based information
- ▶ Making inferences

As with the other interdisciplinary reading strategies from this chapter, students develop multiple reading skills as well as content knowledge.

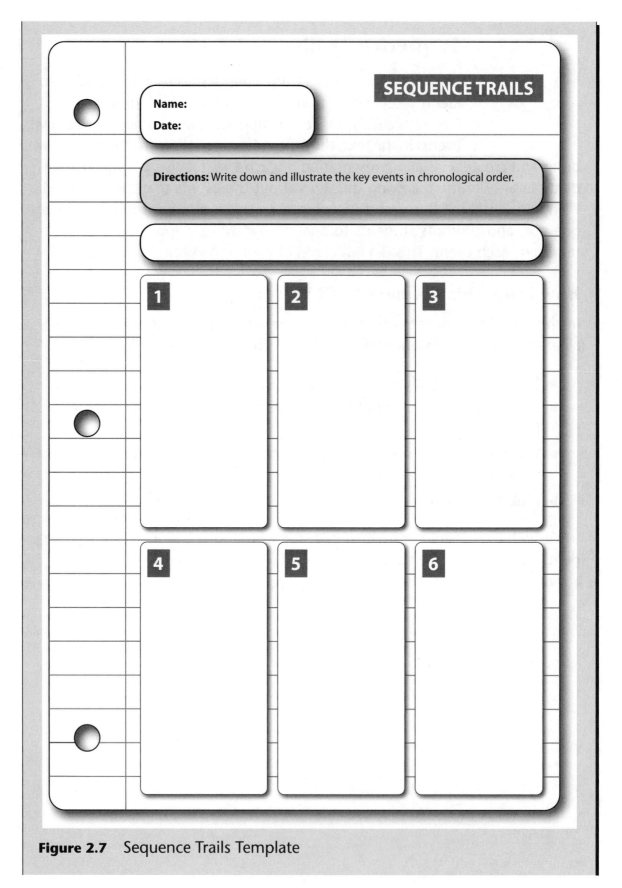

Name:

Date:

SEQUENCE TRAILS

Directions: Write down and illustrate the key events in chronological order.

| 1 | 2 | 3 |

| 4 | 5 | 6 |

Figure 2.7 Sequence Trails Template

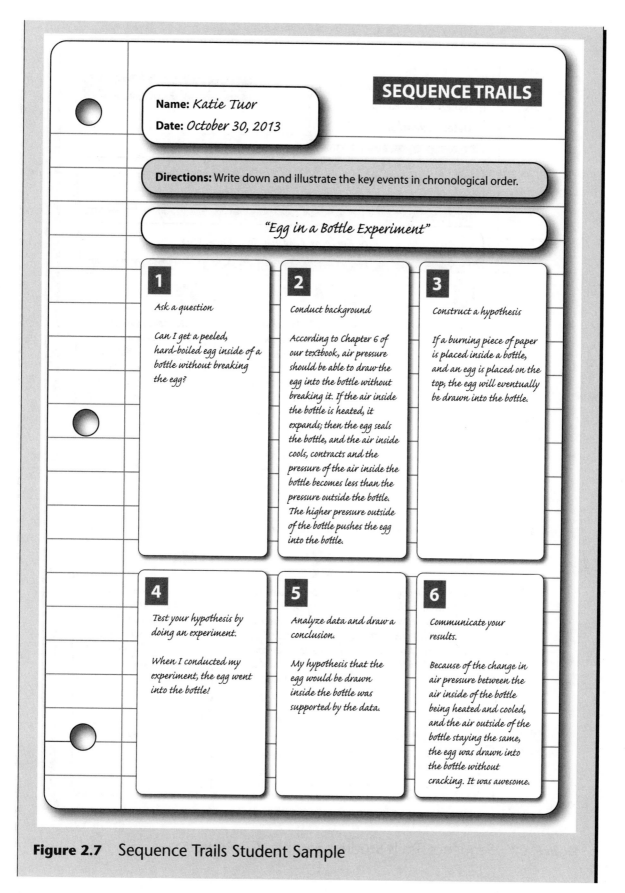

SEQUENCE TRAILS

Name: *Katie Tuor*
Date: *October 30, 2013*

Directions: Write down and illustrate the key events in chronological order.

"Egg in a Bottle Experiment"

1

Ask a question

Can I get a peeled, hard-boiled egg inside of a bottle without breaking the egg?

2

Conduct background

According to Chapter 6 of our textbook, air pressure should be able to draw the egg into the bottle without breaking it. If the air inside the bottle is heated, it expands; then the egg seals the bottle, and the air inside cools, contracts and the pressure of the air inside the bottle becomes less than the pressure outside the bottle. The higher pressure outside of the bottle pushes the egg into the bottle.

3

Construct a hypothesis

If a burning piece of paper is placed inside a bottle, and an egg is placed on the top, the egg will eventually be drawn into the bottle.

4

Test your hypothesis by doing an experiment.

When I conducted my experiment, the egg went into the bottle!

5

Analyze data and draw a conclusion.

My hypothesis that the egg would be drawn inside the bottle was supported by the data.

6

Communicate your results.

Because of the change in air pressure between the air inside of the bottle being heated and cooled, and the air outside of the bottle staying the same, the egg was drawn into the bottle without cracking. It was awesome.

Figure 2.7 Sequence Trails Student Sample

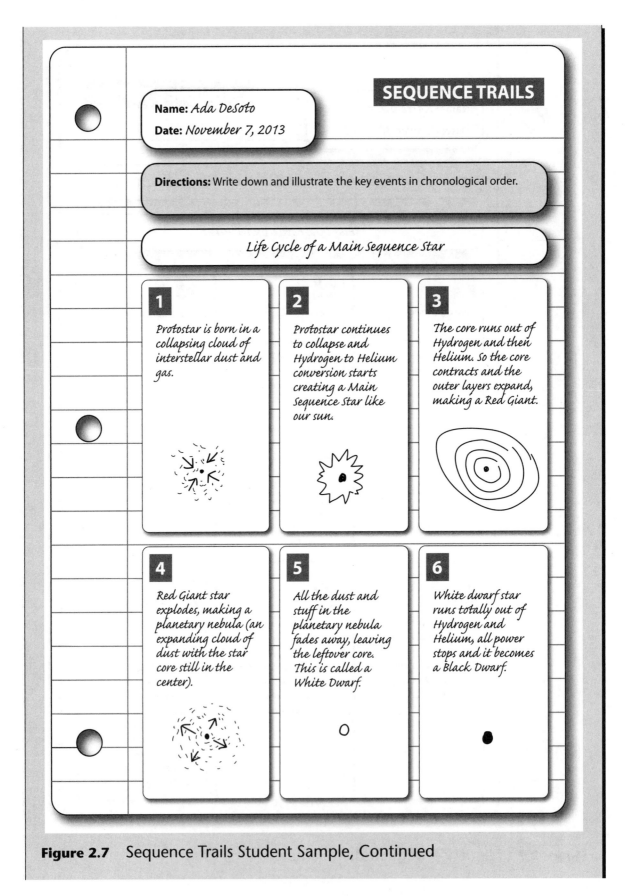

Name: *Ada DeSoto*
Date: *November 7, 2013*

SEQUENCE TRAILS

Directions: Write down and illustrate the key events in chronological order.

Life Cycle of a Main Sequence Star

1
Protostar is born in a collapsing cloud of interstellar dust and gas.

2
Protostar continues to collapse and Hydrogen to Helium conversion starts creating a Main Sequence Star like our sun.

3
The core runs out of Hydrogen and then Helium. So the core contracts and the outer layers expand, making a Red Giant.

4
Red Giant star explodes, making a planetary nebula (an expanding cloud of dust with the star core still in the center).

5
All the dust and stuff in the planetary nebula fades away, leaving the leftover core. This is called a White Dwarf.

6
White dwarf star runs totally out of Hydrogen and Helium, all power stops and it becomes a Black Dwarf.

Figure 2.7 Sequence Trails Student Sample, Continued

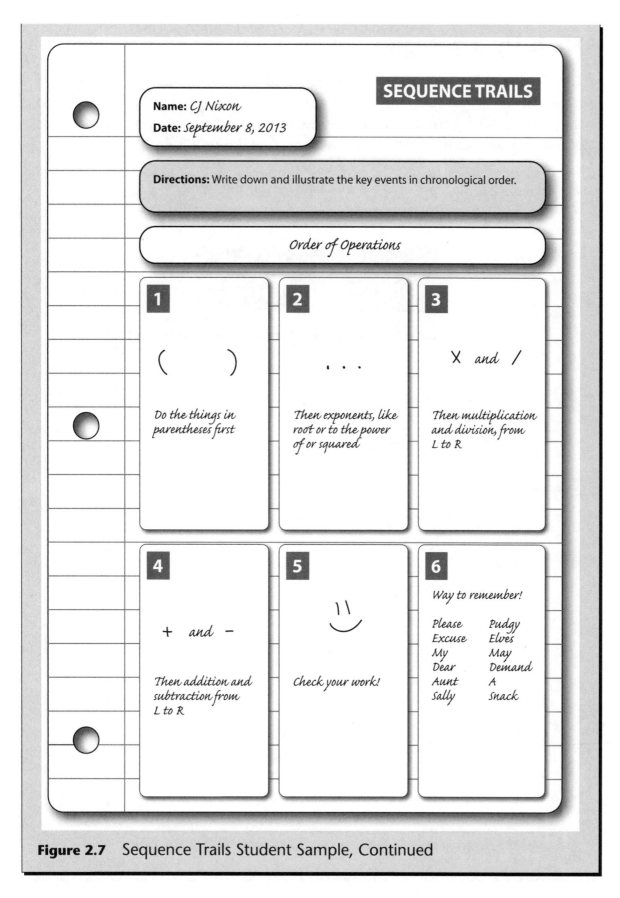

Figure 2.7   Sequence Trails Student Sample, Continued

Fix It Up Strategies

The Fix It Up Strategy chart is a guide that you can give your students to remind them what they should do when the reading becomes difficult and they get "stuck." You can use this guide and develop the students' awareness of these strategies as a think-aloud activity. See figure 2.8.

FIX IT UP STRATEGIES CHART

Are you stuck? Try doing these tricks before you give up!

Get a sense of the text before reading.

Guess what will happen.

Decide why you are reading.

Create a mental picture.

Think of what you already know about the topic.

Develop logical guesses based on the text and your own experiences.

Figure 2.8   Fix It Up Strategies Chart

Close Reading and Textual Complexity

I am fairly certain that before you picked up this book, you've probably already heard quite a bit about close reading and textual complexity. I also believe that you are already using many close reading strategies with your students. The next section of this chapter explains the meaning for us content area teachers of close reading and textual complexity as foundational features of CCSS. Remember, our first focus is developing our students' content knowledge, while also developing literacy skills. For now, we are going to continue our focus on reading.

What Exactly Is Close Reading?

Another important feature of the CCSS reading standards is that close, analytical reading of text is valued and considered as a means to develop high-level comprehension and interpretive skills. Struggling readers have great difficulty analyzing texts, and active readers always need more practice in order to develop more advanced skills. A CCSS myth that I often hear about close reading is that content teachers should not allow for reader response or personal responses anymore. This is not accurate. Even though close reading of text is emphasized in CCSS, it doesn't mean that we ignore a student's background knowledge when it comes to thinking about the meaning of a text. The importance or impact of a student's background knowledge, or schema, on a reader's comprehension of a specific text is well documented by reading theorists. **Our personal background and experiences significantly impact our comprehension**. Although CCSS does not mention reader response specifically, I would argue that close reading and textual analysis, along with a student's schema, work together to develop higher-level comprehension. Yet I also want to offer this caveat. All readers, especially struggling ones, need to develop analytic reading skills. When reader response is overemphasized, struggling readers stop at personal response and usually do not incorporate close reading and analytical skills.

Students need to learn how to work with and within a text as part of close reading. Figure 2.9, on the following pages, outlines the steps for close reading in the classroom.

SCAN THE PASSAGE

What do you think this passage is going to be about?

List things that you already know about this topic:

List at least one thing you want to know about this topic:

How many graphics (pictures, charts, graphs, and so on) are in this passage?

Figure 2.9   Close Reading Template

FIRST READ THROUGH

Read the passage from beginning to end.

Are there any confusing words, sentences, or passages? Mark them with a highlighter or sticky note.

Examine all graphics, and read their captions.

Do any graphics visually represent information that is also included in the text? If so, which ones?

Draw a line or use a sticky note to indicate when graphics relate to a specific part of the text.

Are there any graphics that provide additional information that is not also included in the text? Which one(s)?

Figure 2.9   Close Reading Template, Continued

LOOKING FOR CLUES

This is when you look for clues to help you figure out the confusing parts.

Look up any unfamiliar words or symbols, and write brief definitions here:

If the confusing sentences or passages relate to a graphic, examine that graphic and search for clues that will help you figure out the meaning. List clues here:

Read the paragraph that appears right before the confusing passages. Are there any clues that might help you figure out the meaning? List them here:

Read the paragraph that appears right after the confusing passages. Are there any clues that might help you figure out the meaning? List them here:

Using all the clues, can you say or write the confusing passages using your own words? Write your "best guess" versions here:

Figure 2.9 Close Reading Template, Continued

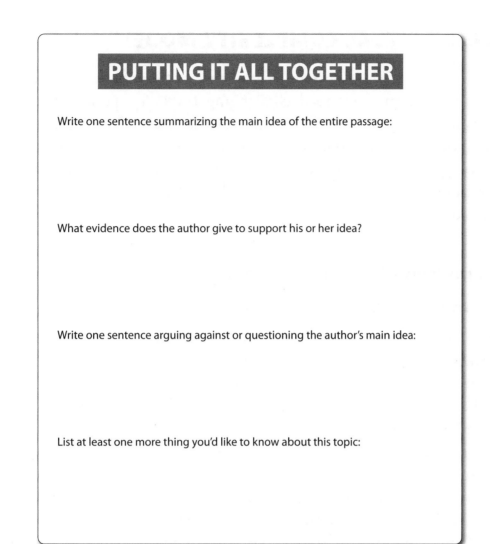

PUTTING IT ALL TOGETHER

Write one sentence summarizing the main idea of the entire passage:

What evidence does the author give to support his or her idea?

Write one sentence arguing against or questioning the author's main idea:

List at least one more thing you'd like to know about this topic:

Figure 2.9   Close Reading Template, Continued

THE CCSS TEXTUAL COMPLEXITY MODEL

Another discovery of the CCSS architects is that students—even students who regularly read—often don't read challenging texts. A separate task force for CCSS was assembled specifically to address the issue of text complexity. The resulting model illustrates the three equal components used to measure textual complexity: qualitative measures, quantitative measures, and reader and text considerations (CCSS 2010, p. 57). Figure 2.10 represents the three-part model that CCSS developed.

Text Complexity Three-Part Model

Quantitative Measures

Usually calculated by computer software, quantitative measures look at word length, frequency, sentence length, and text cohesion. CCSS depends on the Lexile Framework. Remember that text complexity is a three-part model, and no part of the model is emphasized or valued more than another. I am providing this reminder because many schools and districts are overemphasizing quantitative measures like Lexile. The following examples illustrate why text complexity is a three-part model. You would probably think that *Stuart Little* by E. B. White has a lower Lexile level than *The Hunger Games* by Suzanne Collins. In reality, it's the opposite. *The Hunger Games* has a lower Lexile score. However, there are complicated themes and ideas in *The Hunger Games*, which we will discuss in further

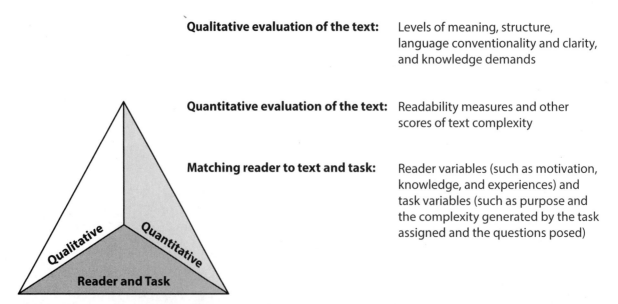

Qualitative evaluation of the text: Levels of meaning, structure, language conventionality and clarity, and knowledge demands

Quantitative evaluation of the text: Readability measures and other scores of text complexity

Matching reader to text and task: Reader variables (such as motivation, knowledge, and experiences) and task variables (such as purpose and the complexity generated by the task assigned and the questions posed)

Figure 2.10 Measuring Text Complexity: Three Factors

detail as we examine qualitative measures. Highly technical content focused texts like those in science, technology, and mathematics often have the highest Lexile scores.

Qualitative Measures

In their discussion of quantitative measures, the CCSS note that these tools and frameworks are not always reliable when considered in isolation. For example, *The Hunger Games* has a readability range of third to fourth grade, according to the Lexile Framework. However, most English teachers know that *The Hunger Games* is not an appropriate text for younger readers, when language, themes, and prior knowledge demands are considered. As we consider the qualitative measures and reader and text considerations of *The Hunger Games*, we know that this novel is more appropriate for middle school readers. According to CCSS, qualitative measures include levels of meaning, structure, language conventionality and clarity, and knowledge demands. Most often, qualitative measures are determined by teachers and curriculum specialists, who consider students' levels of background knowledge and generally use a common rubric to determine the qualitative measures for a text.

The CCSS advice is this: *"until widely available quantitative tools can better account for factors recognized as making such texts challenging, including multiple levels of meaning and mature themes, preferences should likely be given to qualitative measures of text complexity when evaluating narrative fiction for students grades 6 and above"* (2010, p. 8).

Reader and Task Considerations

Familiarity with the language, context, and setting, along with the reader's motivation, are identified in the CCSS as considerations that have direct impact on text complexity. Reader and task considerations include student or reader motivation, the role of prior knowledge, and the contextual nature of text.

Reader and task considerations can include the following.

READING SKILLS

▶ Does the reader have the inferencing skills to make connections that may not be explicit in this text?

▶ Does the reader have the visualization skills to picture what is being described in the text?

▶ Does the reader have the active questioning stance to explore the ideas in the text?

- Does the reader have comprehension strategies to actively read this text?
- Does this text support the development of inferencing skills, visualization skills, active questioning, and comprehension strategies in the reader?

MOTIVATION AND ENGAGEMENT

- Is the reader interested in the specific context of this text?
- Is the student motivated to actively engage with this text?

Additional Resources for Determining Text Complexity

- The Teachers College Reading and Writing Project has a resource-rich website.
- Lexile is explained in the following video and resources.
  - Overview video: http://www.lexile.com/about-lexile/lexile-video/
  - "What Does the Lexile Measure Mean?": http://lexile.com/m/uploads/
  - downloadablepdfs/WhatDoestheLexileMeasureMean.pdf
  - "Lexile Measures and the Common Core State Standards": http://www.lexile.com/using-lexile/lexile-measures-and-the-ccssi/

OTHER TIPS FOR DEVELOPING ADOLESCENT READING SKILLS

Middle school and high school students are often not motivated to read. I will not deny that this is a tremendous challenge for teachers and students. I do have some advice about what can actually work in the classroom:

▶ **Give students a voice in selecting increasingly challenging texts**. When we offer students a variety of texts to read and they are allowed to choose from that selection, they are often more motivated to complete the assigned reading. For example, as a science teacher, if I wanted my students to read about ecosystems, I would offer students several different texts, so they could make a choice from a variety of reading materials at different textual complexity levels. As a mathematics teacher, I might give students different word problems to match their reading ability level.

▶ **Group students into text study groups like literature circles or pairs**. Students learn from each other. As they read text together, encourage them to support each other.

▶ **Do read-alouds to demonstrate how a skilled reader thinks about and works toward text comprehension**.

▶ **Supplement the text with videos and audio versions**. All of your students, but especially the struggling readers, will benefit from the extra support as they work to comprehend more challenging texts and ideas.

▶ **If a student is motivated and keenly interested in the subject of a specific book, encourage him or her to try it**. This can be effective even if it may be challenging at first.

▶ **Use the support strategies suggested in this chapter—and learn more**. These will lead the student to develop the close reading skills to work with and within a challenging text.

SOME FINAL THOUGHTS

Students who show the most substantial growth and achievement are assigned more reading. As teachers, we need to reflect on how much reading is included in current curriculum and set goals to increase reading. Be sure to include a wide variety of texts in these assignments—and in each classroom. An easily accessible classroom library, loaded with interesting books of different levels, will promote positive attitudes about reading and reinforce the idea that reading matters.

Remember the established correlation between student achievement and extensive reading. But remember, too, that reading material needs to be appropriately challenging if students are going to meet the rigorous expectations of the Common Core State Standards.

CHAPTER THREE

Effective Content Area Writing Strategies

About two years ago, I started a long-term project with a seventh- to twelfth-grade school in the Midwest. The school had a diverse population, and over 90 percent of the students received free or reduced lunch. There was magic in this school. As I visited classrooms, I soon discovered that the teachers and students were engaged in consistent practice for the development of literacy skills and content knowledge. Some of the strongest teachers in literacy taught mathematics and science. The science teachers, in particular, share the pedagogical belief and practice that if all students can explain and talk about science, then they understand the content.

Brooke McCray, a seventh-grade science teacher at the same school, regularly implemented writing activities in her content subject. She often remarked that content writing instruction was critical to the development of science content knowledge: "If the kids can *show* me their thinking and understanding about content through writing, I'll know if they're getting it." Her room was filled with displayed student work where competent writing and science content were showcased.

Their principal, instructional leader, and former science teacher, Deb Lesser, emphasized the importance of content expertise, effective communication in writing, and academic English. The school had a coherent literacy plan that was practiced in all content areas, and during Lesser's leadership, there were strong gains in student achievement.

This is what we strive for with middle school and high school students. They need to develop the skills to express what they know and understand through written form.

When I entered the teaching profession in the late 1980s, a paradigm shift in writing instruction was percolating. Writing became more focused on process, rather than overemphasizing product. Consequently, teachers, particularly in English language arts, focused on teaching students the process of writing that includes the following steps: pre-writing, drafting, revising, editing, and publishing. Students also develop their writing skills when they write often, revise and rethink their writing, belong to a community of writers, and recognize the importance of expressing what they know and understand in written text.

English teachers focus on all of these areas. Content area teachers, however, provide students with critical opportunities to write often through a community of writers and thinkers.

In addition, writing is a vehicle for students to learn and develop their thinking about content and new information. When we write, we develop our thinking—"writing to learn," as it was called by foundational theorist James Britton (1970). His work is reflected in the CCSS in the standards that articulate the expectations for explanatory or informational writing.

In the past ten years, under No Child Left Behind, writing was not assessed in many states and school districts, resulting in insufficient instruction. Greater emphasis was placed on reading assessment. This kind of misguided direction is illogical to me. There are strong research-based connections among reading, writing, and the acquisition of content knowledge. CCSS authors examined this research and created a document that equally values writing and reading. Writing, according to the CCSS, is needed so that students can express what they know and understand from reading and learning new content, and writing is fundamental to college and career readiness.

A LOOK AT THE INTERDISCIPLINARY STANDARDS

The CCSS authors assert that students should be able to develop the writing skills to produce a wide variety of writing, with a particular emphasis on argumentation:

*For students, writing is a key means of **asserting and defending claims**, **showing what they know about a subject**, and **conveying what they have experienced, imagined, thought, and felt**. To be college and career ready writers, students must take task, purpose, and audience into careful consideration, choosing words, information, structures, and formats deliberately. They need to **know how to combine elements of different kinds of writing**—for example, to use narrative strategies with an argument in explanation within narrative—to produce complex and nuanced writing. They need to be able to **use technology strategically when creating, refining, and collaborating on writing**. They have to become **adept at gathering information, evaluating sources, and citing material accurately**, reporting findings from their research and analysis of sources in a clear and cogent manner. They must **have the flexibility, concentration, and fluency to produce high-quality 1st-draft text** under a tight deadline as well as **the capacity to revisit and make improvements to a piece of writing over multiple drafts** when circumstances encourage or require it.*

(2010, p. 41; emphasis added)

In this chapter, we will explore the major shifts and expectations of the Writing Standards for Literacy in History/Social Studies, Science, and Technical Subjects 6–12 and explore strategies to use in developing curriculum to meet this level of rigor.

CCSS ANCHOR STANDARDS IN WRITING

Like the reading standards, the writing standards comprise ten anchor standards. Each anchor standard is developed into specific skills at each grade level: 6, 7, 8, 9–10, and 11–12 in the Writing Standards for Literacy in History/Social Studies, Science, and Technical Subjects 6–12. As we look at the Common Core State Standards, remember that there are two separate sections of writing standards in the CCSS: English language arts (ELA) and ELA in social studies.

Remember that whether you are a science or a mathematics teacher, the standards that are specific to your content area always link and connect to the major anchor standards. Although things may be worded a bit differently, the literacy skills that are being developed in each content area, Reading and Writing Standards for Literacy in History/Social Studies, Science, and Technical Subjects 6–12, are quite similar.

Text Types and Purposes*

1. Write arguments to support an analysis of substantive topics or texts, using valid reasoning and relevant and sufficient evidence.

2. Write informative/explanatory texts to examine and convey complex ideas and information clearly and accurately through the effective selection, organization, and analysis of content.

3. Write narratives to develop real or imagined experiences or events using effective, well-chosen details, and well-structured event sequences. (Note that standard 3 is not included in the writing standards for Literacy in History/Social Studies, Science, and Technical Subjects 6–12.)

Production and Distribution of Writing

4. Produce clear and coherent writing in which the development, organization, and style are appropriate to task, purpose, and audience.

5. Develop and strengthen writing as needed by planning, revising, editing, rewriting, or trying a new approach.

6. Use technology, including the Internet, to produce and publish writing and to interact and collaborate with others.

Research to Build and Present Knowledge

7. Conduct short as well as more sustained research projects based on focus questions, demonstrating understanding of the subject under investigation.

8. Gather relevant information from multiple print and digital sources, assess the credibility and accuracy of each source, and integrate the information while avoiding plagiarism.

9. Draw evidence from literary or informational texts to support analysis, reflection, and research.

Range of Writing

10. Write routinely over extended time frames (time for research, reflection, and revision) and shorter time frames (a single sitting or a day or two) for a range of tasks, purposes, and audiences.

*These broad types of writing include many subgenres. See CCSS appendix A for definitions of key writing types (CCSS 2010, p. 41).

KEY FEATURES OF THE WRITING STANDARDS

There are a few things to remember as we look at the CCSS writing standards for Literacy in History/Social Studies, Science, and Technical Subjects 6–12. As with the reading standards, there are slight differences in each set of standards, but all relate back to the anchor standards. If we look at the standards for both ELA and the different content areas for sixth through twelfth grade, we can see that similar language is used to describe writing expectations and the kinds of writing for all the different content areas. The Common Core State Standards clearly articulate writing expectations across all content areas. When expectations are articulated in common language across all content areas, student achievement generally increases. This makes sense because all the people involved—teachers, students, parents, and administrators—are talking about the same expectations.

Another important characteristic of CCSS is that types of writing are identified rather than genres of writing. This actually makes a lot of sense because writing by type is more common outside of the ELA classroom. One of the goals of CCSS is to create common and consistent expectations, using common language as a means to foster greater student achievement. You may also notice that the standards do not use the term *thesis*. Instead, the authors use the term *claim*. I have had many conversations with middle school and high school teachers about this particular change. ELA teachers become particularly vocal about this change, since *thesis* is the term traditionally used. We are all familiar with this term from our school experiences. Yet with the shift from genres of writing to types of writing, *claim* is a more appropriate term to use for all of the content areas. There are many types of claims that we know in the different content areas. For example, a claim in an English class or social studies class would be a thesis. But in science, the student would probably use the term *hypothesis*, and in math class a claim could be a theorem or postulate. Unifying the language for interdisciplinary literacy and anchor writing standards through use of the term *claim* fosters consistency in the expectations across all content areas.

Writing Process

The CCSS writing standards emphasize the importance of the writing process: pre-writing, drafting, revising, editing, and publishing. Specifically, standard 5 and standard 10 describe what students need to do routinely to be effective writers. Expectations for planning, revision, and editing become more extensive as students progress through grade levels and achieve greater independence in applying these skills. Anchor standard 10 proposes that students should be able to *"write routinely over extended time frames (time for research, reflection, and revision) and shorter time frames (a single sitting or a day or two)"* (CCSS 2010, p. 18). To meet this expectation, students must write frequently in all content areas and become experts at using the writing process.

The Three Types of Writing

In the CCSS, three types of writing are emphasized: arguments, informative/ explanatory text, and narratives. Note that writing standard 3, which focuses on narrative writing, is not included in the Writing Standards for Literacy in History/Social Studies, Science, and Technical Subjects 6–12. This makes sense since narrative writing is more appropriately part of the English curriculum. As we examine the writing standards for sixth through twelfth grades, rigorous expectations in writing are clearly articulated at each grade level. Students are expected to establish and support claims through evidence and reasoning. At the ninth through twelfth grade levels, students are expected to also provide counterarguments in their writing. The expectation is that students *"produce arguments to support claims in an analysis of substantive topics or texts, using valid reasoning and relevant and sufficient evidence"* (CCSS 2010, p. 45). Specifically, ninth through tenth grade students should develop the following writing skills to meet writing standard 1 (argumentation):

a. *Introduce precise claim(s), distinguish the claim(s) from alternate or opposing claims, and create organization that establishes clear relationships among claim(s), counterclaims, reasons, and evidence.*

b. *Develop claim(s) and counterclaims fairly, supplying evidence for each while pointing out strengths and limitations of both in a manner that anticipates the audience's knowledge level and concerns.*

c. *Use words, phrases, and clauses to link the major sections of the text, create cohesion, and clarify the relationships between claim(s) and reasons, between reasons and evidence, and between claim(s) and counterclaims.*

d. *Establish and maintain a formal style and objective tone while attending to the norms and conventions of the discipline in which they are writing.*

e. *Provide a concluding statement or section that follows from and supports the argument presented.*

In exploring these expectations, we reach the same conclusion: these are highly complex writing skills. Remember, these writing skills are expected at the beginning of high school. How can we meet these expectations? **The most effective**

path in developing these writing skills is to provide substantial practice and opportunities to write through precise and scaffolding instruction. Like reading, the more our students write, the better they become at this skill.

Argumentation

In the CCSS, great emphasis is placed on argumentation in writing throughout the ELA and interdisciplinary writing standards. In the CCSS documents, appendix C for the ELA standards provides exemplars of student writing in argumentation. When student writers are able to argue, or debate, by establishing a claim and explaining and supporting that claim with evidence and reasoning, they are engaging in critical analysis and synthesis of content knowledge. When students reach this level of mastery, they have clearly gained a sophisticated knowledge of the content and are able to express what they know and understand in written text. Teenagers love to argue—we need to let them.

Informational/Explanatory Writing

Informational or explanatory writing is drawn from the work of James Britton and the Write to Learn movement that began in the 1980s. The Write to Learn movement proved that students who were able to write about what they know and understand have higher levels of comprehension. The Write to Learn movement encouraged informational and explanatory writing as a means for the student to convey information accurately. In appendix A of the CCSS, it is explained that informational/explanatory writing is writing that has several related purposes, *"to increase readers' knowledge of a subject, to help readers better understand a procedure or process, or to provide readers with an enhanced comprehension of a concept. The ability of students to express their personal knowledge through writing is strongly connected to the expectations and skills necessary for career and college readiness"* (CCSS 2010, p. 23).

Writing and Technology

The ways in which we read text, write text, use text, and are affected by text have completely changed in the twenty-first century—the information age. Our writing is no longer limited to pen and paper. As I think about the writing I do in a single day, I recall that I did the following:

- ▶ Texted my husband and daughter about dinner
- ▶ Composed and responded to dozens of e-mails (at two different addresses) regarding work and my personal life

- ▶ Sent tweets
- ▶ Posted materials and information about these teaching materials on my public Facebook page (Katie McKnight Literacy)
- ▶ Wrote a blog post for my website that focuses on developing reading comprehension in adolescence
- ▶ Posted some comments about a dress that I purchased online
- ▶ Composed and revised this book chapter
- ▶ Wrote a handwritten grocery list and note to my daughter

There's a vast difference between how I use writing today and my experience as a teenager. Nearly everything I wrote back then was handwritten. Computers were not widely available, and typewritten (not word-processed) papers were not always expected. As I use more technology, I know that my skills as a writer have become more important. We communicate in written text in the twenty-first century at an unprecedented rate. Consequently, I would argue that our classrooms must reflect this change. Students must use many different contexts for writing to be college and career ready, and our classrooms need to reflect this change. We will focus more on the role of technology in developing literacy skills and content knowledge in chapter 7.

Before we dive into strategies that build writing skills in the content area, remember that we use literacy skills like writing to develop content knowledge (and in the previous chapter we focused on reading as a way to do the same thing). Content knowledge is the focus. It's also important to remember that the writing process, which consists of pre-writing, drafting, revising, editing, and publishing, is specifically addressed in standards 5 and 10, which describe what students need to do routinely to become effective writers. What this means for all content areas is that students should always develop and strengthen their writing skills by planning, revising, and editing as they develop content knowledge. You will also notice that the level of planning, revising, and editing becomes even more extensive as students progress from the middle school standards to high school standards. Students should develop even greater independence in applying these writing process skills. This ultimately leads to the summative expectation in anchor standard 10: students should be able to "[w]rite routinely over extended time frames (time for research, reflection, and revision) and in shorter time frames (a single sitting or a day or two) for a range of tasks, purposes, and audiences" (CCSS 2010, p. 63). If students are able to reach this level in their writing, we are definitely meeting the expectations for career and college readiness.

STRATEGIES THAT BUILD WRITING SKILLS IN THE CONTENT AREA

Medium

Easy Hard

Stop and Write

The Stop and Write activity uses a two-column organizer in which students document their thinking about the text and writing. This activity is a well-known Write to Learn strategy that builds both reading skills and writing skills. In the first column, under the heading "What I Know," the student should record simple information about the text. This is the most basic level of comprehension. In the second column, under the heading "What I Think," the student makes predictions about the text. When students are able to discuss the text and make predictions about it, they are reading on a more inferential level, which is a higher level of comprehension. In addition to these important reading comprehension skills, students are also developing writing skills. They are using writing to record details and to document their thinking about a text and what they are learning.

Some Additional Details

When I teach the strategy, I ask students to stop and record what they know and what they're thinking about the reading approximately four to five times. It is important that the students choose when to stop, rather than the teacher making that choice. When students have some kind of choice about their work, they become more engaged and motivated. Leaving this decision up to the student is also a type of formative assessment for us teachers, because if students tend to stop in the same places, that reveals how the students are thinking about the content as it is discussed in the texts.

How Does This Connect to CCSS?

The Stop and Write (figures 3.1a and 3.1b) activity is an example of a Write to Learn activity. Students are expected to use writing to develop thinking and understanding of a text. This activity is most closely aligned with writing standard 2:

Write informative/explanatory texts to examine and convey complex ideas and information clearly and accurately through the effective selection, organization, and analysis of content.

The Stop and Write activity provides a structure for students to examine the text and summarize the most salient information. Summarizing allows students to more deeply analyze the content presented in the text. There are many other similar writing activities that develop the writing skills identified in standard 2. Learning logs, story boards, history trails, and mini-books are a few examples.

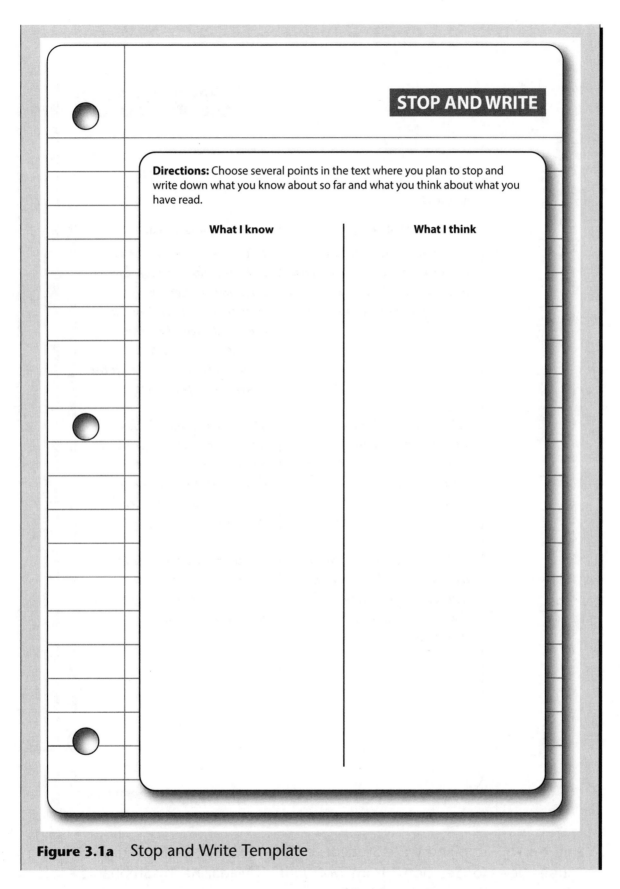

Directions: Choose several points in the text where you plan to stop and write down what you know about so far and what you think about what you have read.

What I know | **What I think**

STOP AND WRITE

Figure 3.1a Stop and Write Template

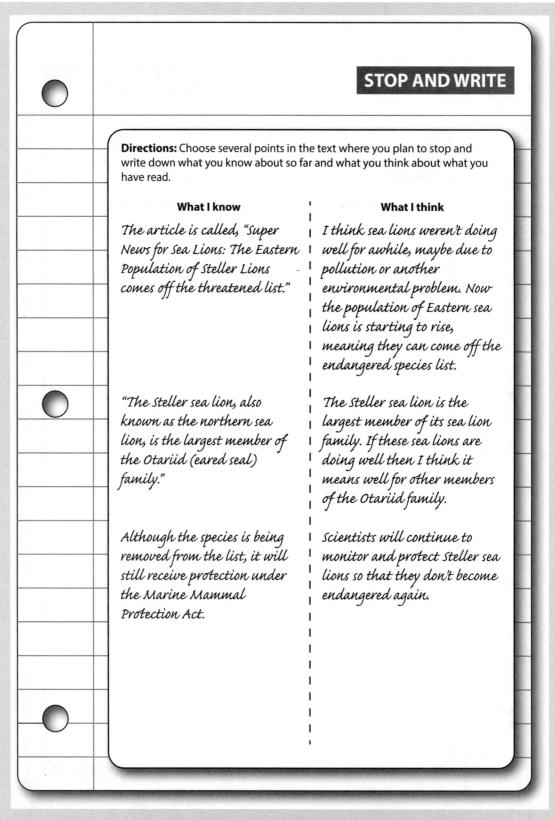

STOP AND WRITE

Directions: Choose several points in the text where you plan to stop and write down what you know about so far and what you think about what you have read.

What I know	What I think
The article is called, "Super News for Sea Lions: The Eastern Population of Steller Lions comes off the threatened list."	I think sea lions weren't doing well for awhile, maybe due to pollution or another environmental problem. Now the population of Eastern sea lions is starting to rise, meaning they can come off the endangered species list.
"The Steller sea lion, also known as the northern sea lion, is the largest member of the Otariid (eared seal) family."	The Steller sea lion is the largest member of its sea lion family. If these sea lions are doing well then I think it means well for other members of the Otariid family.
Although the species is being removed from the list, it will still receive protection under the Marine Mammal Protection Act.	Scientists will continue to monitor and protect Steller sea lions so that they don't become endangered again.

Figure 3.1b Stop and Write Student Sample (Sixth-Grade Student Reading "Super News for Sea Lions" from *TIME for Kids* Magazine, by Stephanie Kraus with AP reporting, October 28, 2013)

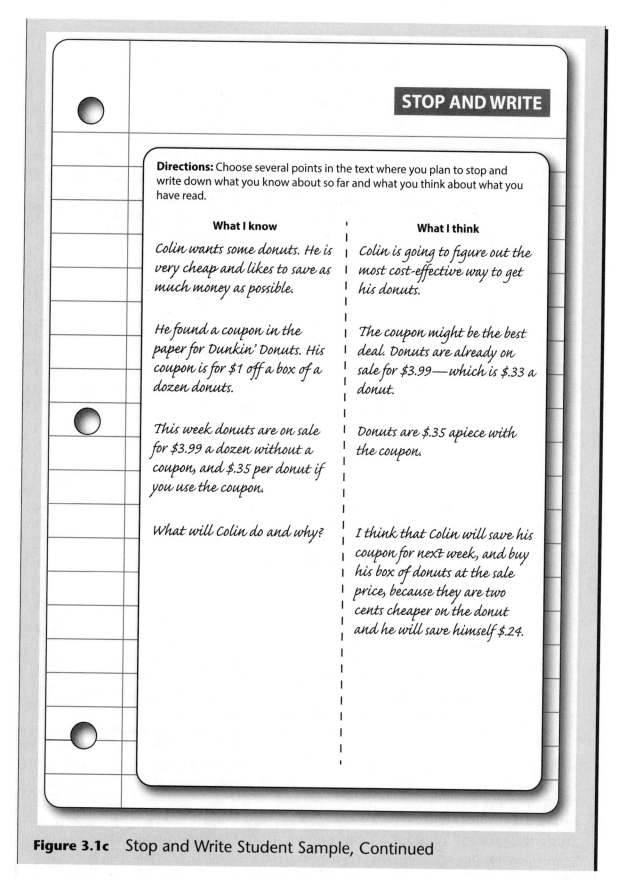

STOP AND WRITE

Directions: Choose several points in the text where you plan to stop and write down what you know about so far and what you think about what you have read.

What I know	**What I think**
Colin wants some donuts. He is very cheap and likes to save as much money as possible.	Colin is going to figure out the most cost-effective way to get his donuts.
He found a coupon in the paper for Dunkin' Donuts. His coupon is for $1 off a box of a dozen donuts.	The coupon might be the best deal. Donuts are already on sale for $3.99—which is $.33 a donut.
This week donuts are on sale for $3.99 a dozen without a coupon, and $.35 per donut if you use the coupon.	Donuts are $.35 apiece with the coupon.
What will Colin do and why?	I think that Colin will save his coupon for next week, and buy his box of donuts at the sale price, because they are two cents cheaper on the donut and he will save himself $.24.

Figure 3.1c   Stop and Write Student Sample, Continued

Stop and Write

National Geographic article—June 2010 "Time for a Sea Change" by Paul Greenberg		
Where did you stop?	What was this about?	What is your personal reaction to what you just read?
Page 79	The author is telling us that all the fisheries in the world will be out of fish if we don't change our ways.	I like the tuna salad sandwich at Subway, so I hope the author is wrong. Also, the picture of the fishing boat is really cool.
Page 81	People are eating more than 4 times the amount of seafood than they did 50 years ago. Most people don't know that it's worse to eat fish from the top of the food chain.	A pound of sardines has a smaller footprint than a pound of tuna. So I should eat sardines. Too bad they look so gross.
Page 83	This picture shows how energy goes up the food chain. It starts with Phytoplankton and Algae and goes all the way up to salmon, tuna, and orange roughy. Herring and anchovies are in the middle.	It says people all over the world eat algae but I've never seen it in my store. It looks slimy.
Page 85	The United Nations scientists think we're in big trouble. But some scientists at the University of Washington think things aren't quite so bad.	I hope we don't really run out of tuna. The picture shows that eating one pound of top predator fish like tuna is the same as eating 1,000 pounds of algae. People could eat a lot of algae, not get hungry, and still get their vitamins. We could eat algae and save tuna for holidays.

Figure 3.2a Stop and Write Student Sample, Continued (Eleventh-Grade Student Reading "Time for a Sea Change" from *National Geographic* Magazine, by Paul Greenberg, October 2010)

Stop and Write

National Geographic article—June 2010 "Time for a Sea Change" by Paul Greenberg		
Where did you stop?	What was this about?	What is your personal reaction to what you just read?
Page 87	These two pictures show where fish is caught and who is eating the fish. The people who are doing the catching aren't always the ones who are doing the eating. Some fish is used to make paint and to feed other animals.	This is complicated! Fixing the problem of overfishing is not going to be easy. I wonder why Chile and Peru catch so much fish but don't eat it?
Page 89	Pauly and Sala, the two scientists don't want us to stop eating fish. They think that if people knew the truth they'd make better decisions. And people should hold their governments responsible for following rules.	I think these scientists are probably right.

Figure 3.2b Stop and Write Student Sample, Continued (Eleventh-Grade Student Reading "Time for a Sea Change" from *National Geographic* Magazine, by Paul Greenberg, October 2010)

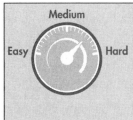

RAFT

This is an engaging writing activity for students since there is opportunity for creative representation. RAFT stands for **role, audience, format**, and **topic**. Table 3.1 lays out the different RAFT elements and some suggestions.

Table 3.1 RAFT Roles and Suggestions

Role	Audience	Format	Topic
Students can take on any role they like, such as that of a scientist or a specific historical figure.	This could be another author, the US Congress, or any real or imaginary group.	Students can choose any format. Here are some suggestions: ▶ Journal or diary ▶ Letter ▶ Job description ▶ Résumé ▶ Interview ▶ Science report ▶ Memo ▶ Poem ▶ Play ▶ Newspaper article ▶ Editorial ▶ Advertisement ▶ Cartoon ▶ Travelogue ▶ Song ▶ Picture book ▶ Science fiction ▶ Fantasy ▶ Fairy tale ▶ Adventure brochure ▶ Book ▶ Television script	This could be one that you assign, or students can select one from assigned material.

Figure 3.3 is a pre-writing graphic organizer or template for students. Once students have brainstormed ideas for a RAFT, they should draft one in narrative form.

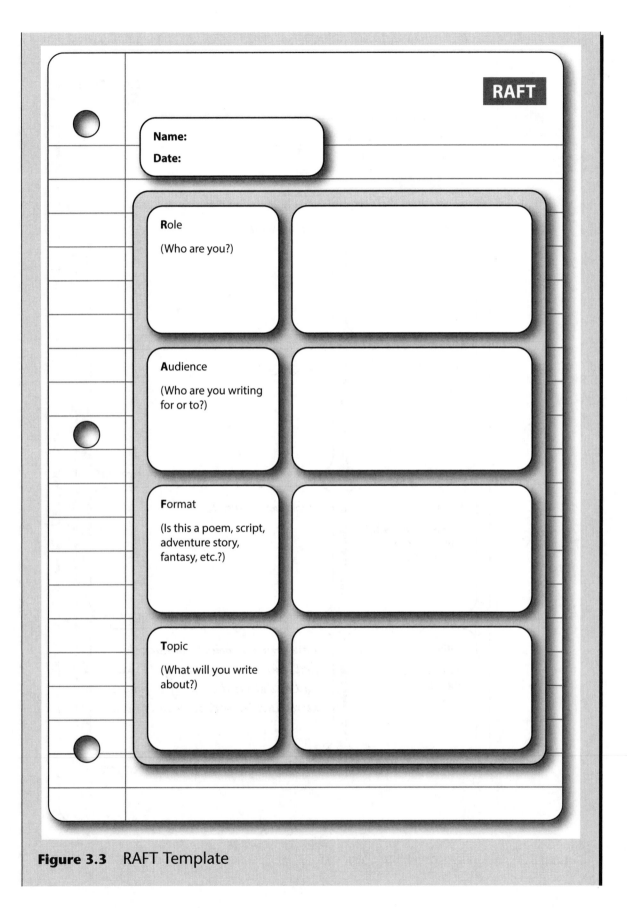

RAFT

Name:

Date:

Role

(Who are you?)

Audience

(Who are you writing for or to?)

Format

(Is this a poem, script, adventure story, fantasy, etc.?)

Topic

(What will you write about?)

Figure 3.3 RAFT Template

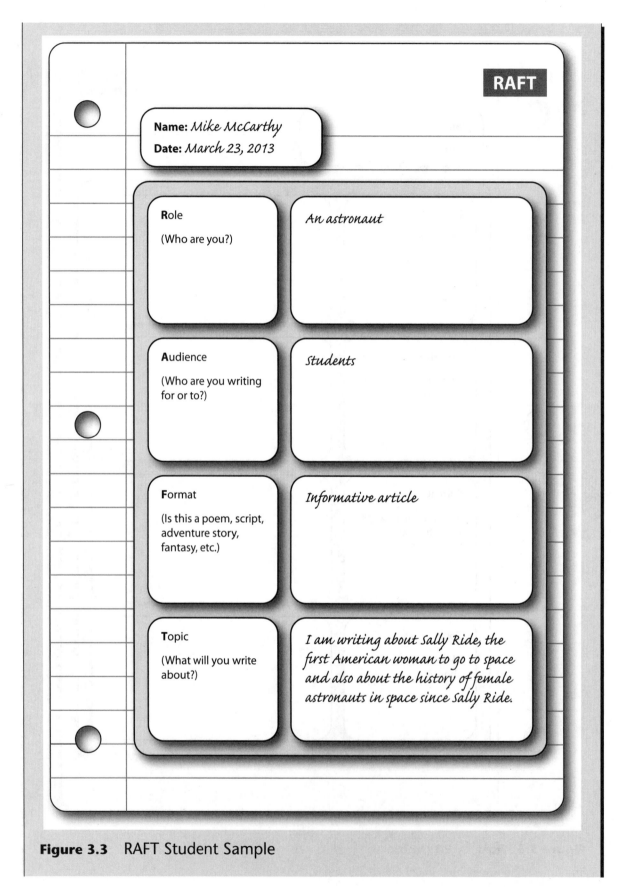

RAFT

Name: Mike McCarthy
Date: March 23, 2013

Role
(Who are you?)

An astronaut

Audience
(Who are you writing for or to?)

Students

Format
(Is this a poem, script, adventure story, fantasy, etc.)

Informative article

Topic
(What will you write about?)

I am writing about Sally Ride, the first American woman to go to space and also about the history of female astronauts in space since Sally Ride.

Figure 3.3 RAFT Student Sample

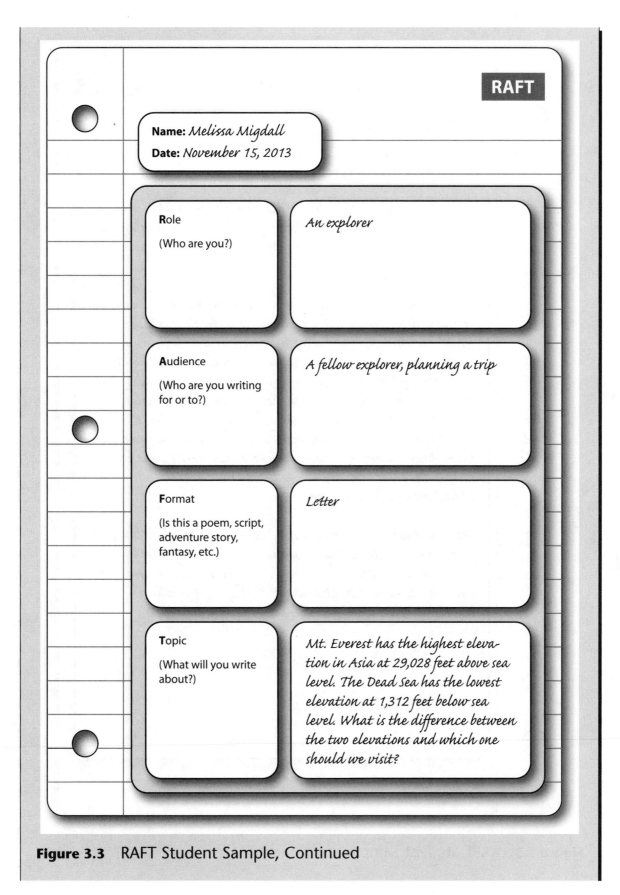

RAFT

Name: *Melissa Migdall*

Date: *November 15, 2013*

Role

(Who are you?)

An explorer

Audience

(Who are you writing for or to?)

A fellow explorer, planning a trip

Format

(Is this a poem, script, adventure story, fantasy, etc.)

Letter

Topic

(What will you write about?)

Mt. Everest has the highest elevation in Asia at 29,028 feet above sea level. The Dead Sea has the lowest elevation at 1,312 feet below sea level. What is the difference between the two elevations and which one should we visit?

Figure 3.3   RAFT Student Sample, Continued

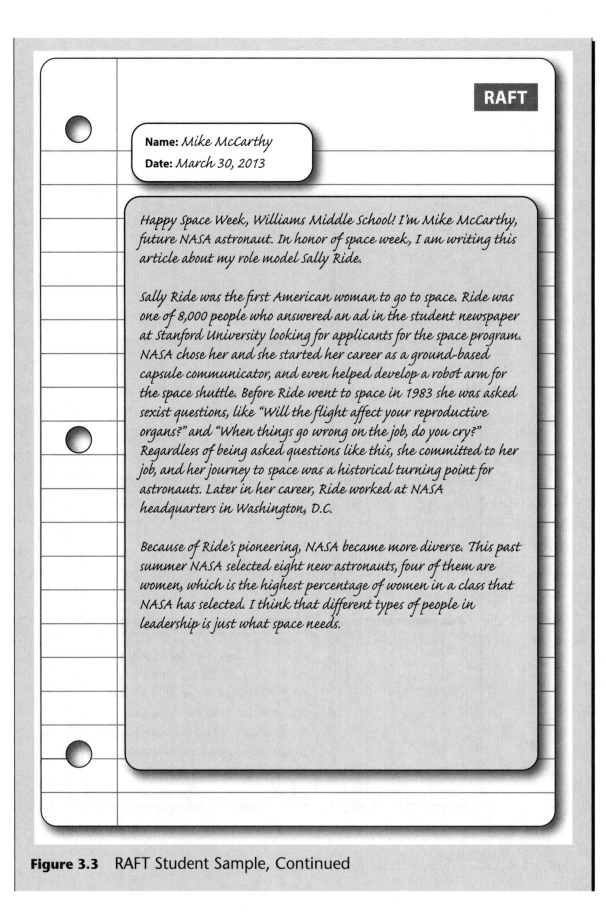

RAFT

Name: Mike McCarthy
Date: March 30, 2013

Happy Space Week, Williams Middle School! I'm Mike McCarthy, future NASA astronaut. In honor of space week, I am writing this article about my role model Sally Ride.

Sally Ride was the first American woman to go to space. Ride was one of 8,000 people who answered an ad in the student newspaper at Stanford University looking for applicants for the space program. NASA chose her and she started her career as a ground-based capsule communicator, and even helped develop a robot arm for the space shuttle. Before Ride went to space in 1983 she was asked sexist questions, like "Will the flight affect your reproductive organs?" and "When things go wrong on the job, do you cry?" Regardless of being asked questions like this, she committed to her job, and her journey to space was a historical turning point for astronauts. Later in her career, Ride worked at NASA headquarters in Washington, D.C.

Because of Ride's pioneering, NASA became more diverse. This past summer NASA selected eight new astronauts, four of them are women, which is the highest percentage of women in a class that NASA has selected. I think that different types of people in leadership is just what space needs.

Figure 3.3   RAFT Student Sample, Continued

RAFT

Name: Melissa Migdall

Date: November 17, 2013

Dear Sean,

I am still considering what location we should choose for our exploration vacation. Today I researched Mt. Everest and The Dead Sea.

Mt. Everest would be quite the challenge. It has the highest elevation in all of Asia, 29,028 feet above sea level. It's the tallest mountain in the world. 4,000 people have tried to climb it, but only 660 people have actually succeeded. Not to freak you out, but 142 people have died trying to climb Mt. Everest.

The Dead Sea would be a different kind of challenge; its elevation is 1,312 feet below sea level. The Dead Sea is so salty that we can easily float in it; it's too salty for fish so we wouldn't have to worry about that. People even go to the Dead Sea for its healing properties.

The difference in elevations between Mt. Everest and The Dead Sea is 30,340 feet.

I think we should take our exploration vacation at the Dead Sea. We can explore, and relax there. Let me know what you think!

Sincerely,

Melissa

Figure 3.3 RAFT Student Sample, Continued

How Does This Connect to CCSS?

RAFTs are an effective learning strategy to develop writing skills along with content knowledge. This writing strategy develops the skills identified in the following standards:

2. *Write informative/explanatory texts to examine and convey complex ideas and information clearly and accurately through the effective selection, organization, and analysis of content.*

3. *Write narratives to develop real or imagined experiences or events using effective technique, well-chosen details, and well-structured event sequences.*

4. *Draw evidence from literary or informational texts to support analysis, reflection, and research.*

Some Additional Details

Sometimes teachers will remark that a RAFT is just a simple story and doesn't develop critical thinking. The RAFT appears simple, but it is a complex strategy that develops writing, content knowledge, and critical thinking skills.

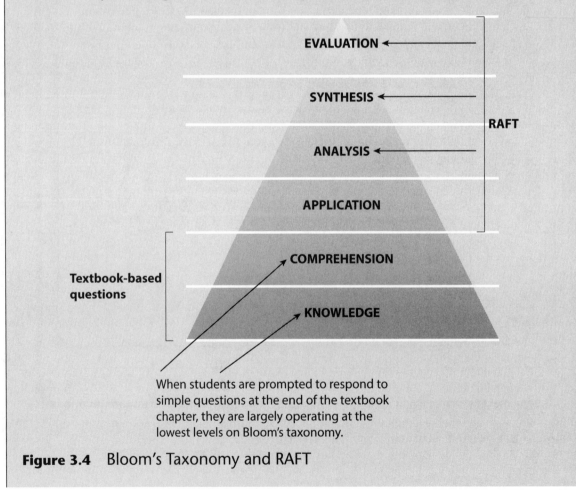

Figure 3.4 Bloom's Taxonomy and RAFT

When students write RAFTs they develop a deeper understanding of the content information as they represent it in a new and original format. The RAFT prompts students to dig more deeply into a text or content information than do many of the end-of-chapter questions requiring written responses. If we apply Bloom's taxonomy of educational objectives to the RAFT activity (figure 3.4), it's apparent that the student must go beyond just knowing the basic facts and content in order to create a RAFT.

People/Content Poem

This people/content poem is adapted to include facts and concepts that focus on particular people, concepts, subjects, places, or events in all content areas. It supports student comprehension and effective summarization of a text.

How Does This Connect to CCSS?

Figure 3.5 is a pre-writing graphic organizer for students. Once the students have brainstormed ideas for a poem, they should draft a more detailed one. This writing strategy develops the skills identified in the following standards:

2. *Write informative/explanatory texts to examine and convey complex ideas and information clearly and accurately through the effective selection, organization, and analysis of content.*

This summative strategy requires students to examine text and content closely in order to create a written representation of the text.

Some Additional Details

Similar to other Write to Learn strategies, it may seem that the people/content poem is a simple activity. However, the ability to summarize content in a succinct format is quite challenging. Like the RAFT, students must progress from a simple, "knowledge" level of understanding to the level of analysis, synthesis, and representation.

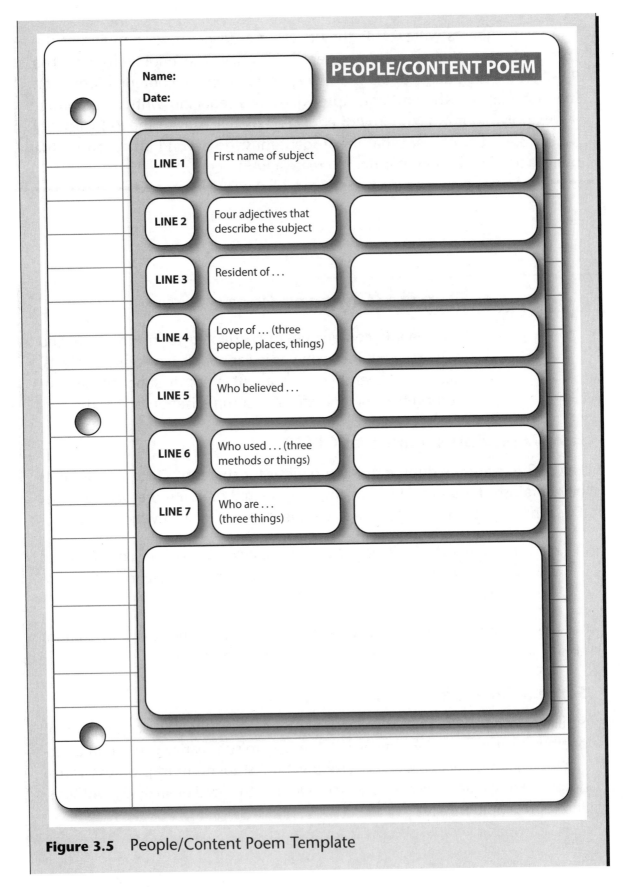

Name:

Date:

PEOPLE/CONTENT POEM

LINE 1	First name of subject	
LINE 2	Four adjectives that describe the subject	
LINE 3	Resident of . . .	
LINE 4	Lover of . . . (three people, places, things)	
LINE 5	Who believed . . .	
LINE 6	Who used . . . (three methods or things)	
LINE 7	Who are . . . (three things)	

Figure 3.5   People/Content Poem Template

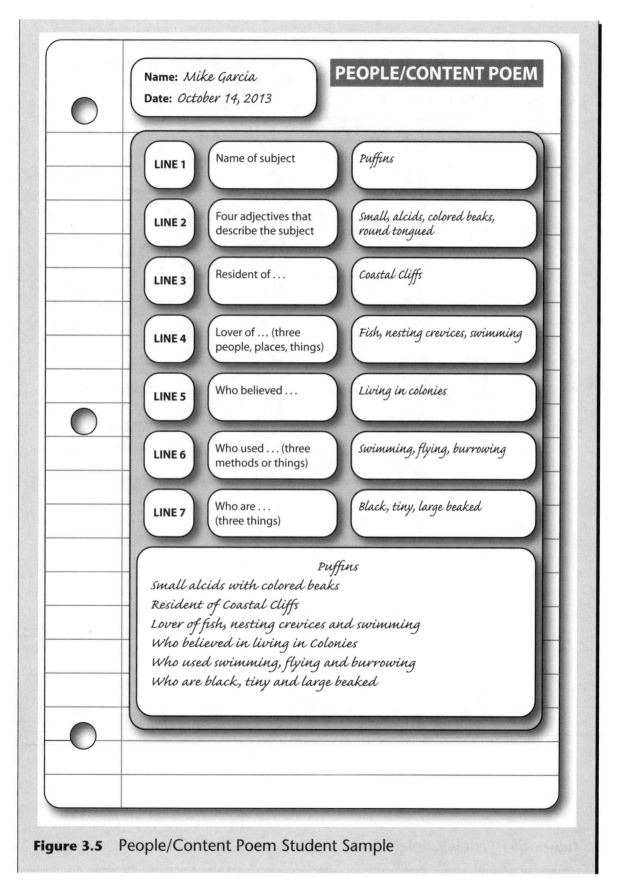

PEOPLE/CONTENT POEM

Name: Mike Garcia
Date: October 14, 2013

LINE 1	Name of subject	Puffins
LINE 2	Four adjectives that describe the subject	Small, alcids, colored beaks, round tongued
LINE 3	Resident of . . .	Coastal Cliffs
LINE 4	Lover of . . . (three people, places, things)	Fish, nesting crevices, swimming
LINE 5	Who believed . . .	Living in colonies
LINE 6	Who used . . . (three methods or things)	Swimming, flying, burrowing
LINE 7	Who are . . . (three things)	Black, tiny, large beaked

Puffins
Small alcids with colored beaks
Resident of Coastal Cliffs
Lover of fish, nesting crevices and swimming
Who believed in living in Colonies
Who used swimming, flying and burrowing
Who are black, tiny and large beaked

Figure 3.5 People/Content Poem Student Sample

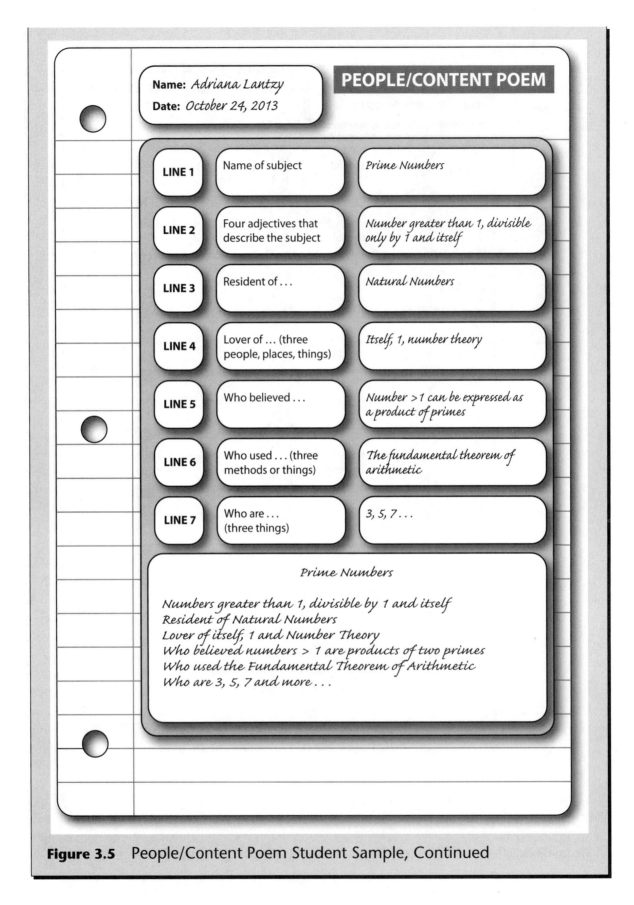

Name: *Adriana Lantzy*
Date: *October 24, 2013*

PEOPLE/CONTENT POEM

LINE 1	Name of subject	*Prime Numbers*
LINE 2	Four adjectives that describe the subject	*Number greater than 1, divisible only by 1 and itself*
LINE 3	Resident of . . .	*Natural Numbers*
LINE 4	Lover of . . . (three people, places, things)	*Itself, 1, number theory*
LINE 5	Who believed . . .	*Number >1 can be expressed as a product of primes*
LINE 6	Who used . . . (three methods or things)	*The fundamental theorem of arithmetic*
LINE 7	Who are . . . (three things)	*3, 5, 7 . . .*

Prime Numbers

Numbers greater than 1, divisible by 1 and itself
Resident of Natural Numbers
Lover of itself, 1 and Number Theory
Who believed numbers > 1 are products of two primes
Who used the Fundamental Theorem of Arithmetic
Who are 3, 5, 7 and more . . .

Figure 3.5 People/Content Poem Student Sample, Continued

Wordless Picture Books

Holly Young, a math trainer for Nevada's Northwest Regional Professional Development Program, created this visualization activity. Many of Holly's innovative, text- and visualization-inspired math lessons can be found on her website: www.makingmathematicians.com.

How Does This Connect to CCSS?

This activity is aligned with writing standard from the 6–12 interdisciplinary standards:

2. *Write informative/explanatory texts to examine and convey complex ideas and information clearly and accurately through the effective selection, organization, and analysis of content.*

Directions

Step 1: Introduce or "read" a book from Alexandra Day's Carl series: *Carl Goes to Daycare, Carl's Snowy Afternoon, Follow Carl!*; any book from the series is appropriate. These books have only a few words at the beginning and end; the rest of the story is told completely in pictures. I've found it's helpful to have five or six different books available for student inspiration.

Step 2: Pass out the Wordless Picture Book Instruction Sheet (figure 3.6). Go over the example clearly explaining which theorems or topics you expect to be addressed in the book that the students are making. It is important that students do not label their book indicating which theorem is which picture! Instead, it's helpful if each student makes up a separate answer sheet for his or her book. The class will guess the theorems as part of the activity.

Step 3: On the day the book is due, pass out the Wordless Picture Book Assessment Sheet (figure 3.7). Students will exchange books and try to guess which theorem is being illustrated by each picture. Encourage students to look at their notes or text to complete this task. When they are finished, have them check their answers with the author.

Wordless Picture Book Instruction Sheet

Using Alexandra Day's *Carl* books as inspiration, you must create a wordless picture book of all the theorems we have reviewed in class. If you choose to work with a partner, you can divide the theorems between the two of you as you see fit. But if your partner flakes, you suffer with him or her.

This is a WORDLESS picture book, so you can't use math words or math symbols! You must show the meaning of the theorem completely through the use of pictures, so you will need to think creatively. DO NOT label the theorems in your picture book. Your classmates will try to guess them later.

You don't have to create a story with a plot, like the actual *Carl* books, but you can if you want to. It's acceptable to have unrelated pictures, one for each theorem.

The goal is to create quality books, so please don't submit crummy pen drawings on lined binder paper.

We'll assemble books in class on this date: _____. Be prepared!

Here is an example of a *good* illustration of the Congruence Theorem:

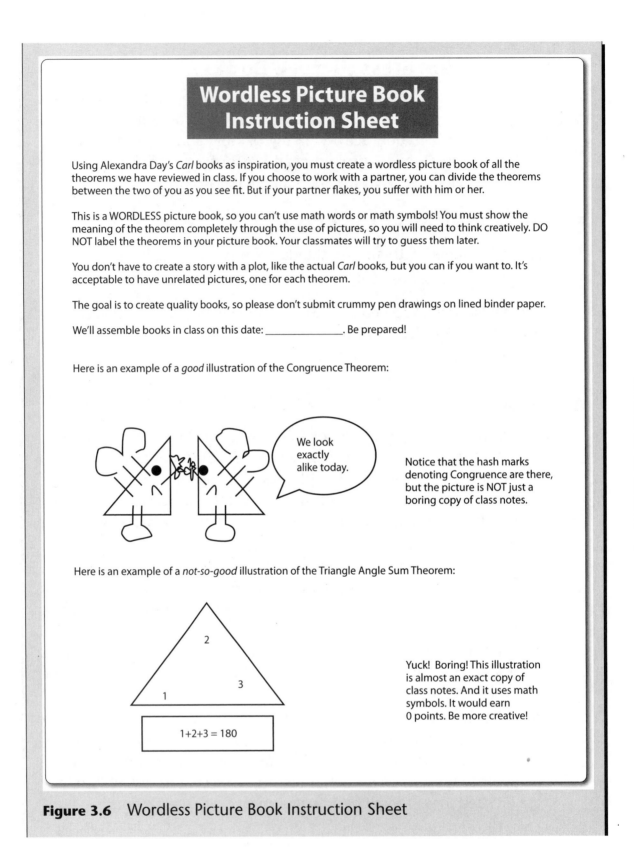

Notice that the hash marks denoting Congruence are there, but the picture is NOT just a boring copy of class notes.

Here is an example of a *not-so-good* illustration of the Triangle Angle Sum Theorem:

Yuck! Boring! This illustration is almost an exact copy of class notes. And it uses math symbols. It would earn 0 points. Be more creative!

Figure 3.6 Wordless Picture Book Instruction Sheet

Wordless Picture Book Assessment Sheet

Assessment by: _____

(This is the name of the person or persons who are assessing the book.)

We are looking at: _____ 's book.

(This is the name of the person or persons who created the book.)

	This is our guess on what theorem the page is showing:	This is why we think so:	This is what the author says it is:
Page 1			
Page 2			
Page 3			
Page 4			
Page 5			
Page 6			
Page 7			
Page 8			
Page 9			
These are some general comments about the quality of the book:			

Figure 3.7 Wordless Picture Book Assessment Sheet

Setting Up and Solving Proportions

This is another integrated-curriculum math lesson from Holly Young. It develops writing, speaking, and listening skills as students apply proportions to a real-life situation. Additional math lessons can be found on Holly's website: www.makingmathematicians.com.

How Does This Connect to CCSS?

This activity is aligned with the following grades 6–12 interdisciplinary writing standards:

1. *Write arguments to support an analysis of substantive topics or texts, using valid reasoning and relevant and sufficient evidence.*
2. *Write informative/explanatory texts to examine and convey complex ideas and information clearly and accurately through the effective selection, organization, and analysis of content.*
7. *Conduct short as well as more sustained research projects based on focus questions, demonstrating understanding of the subject under investigation.*
8. *Gather relevant information from multiple print and digital sources, assess the credibility and accuracy of each source, and integrate the information while avoiding plagiarism.*

Directions

Students are to create their own page from David M. Schwartz's book *If You Hopped Like a Frog*, showing all calculations. Also, they must present to their peers and show a measurement.

Step 1 (20 minutes): Introduce basic proportions to students. I find it's easier to focus on converting measurements (e.g., miles to feet) and solve for an unknown. Allow students to practice sample problems individually or in pairs. For example have students solve for x:

$$48 \text{ inches}/x = 12 \text{ inches}/1 \text{ foot}$$

Step 2 (10 minutes): Read *If You Hopped Like a Frog* aloud to the class. Although this is a children's book, it provides a great summary of ratios and proportions for older students. Work one of the situations created by the author by setting up the proportions for the class.

Step 3 (6–10 minutes): Have the students choose a different problem from the book. Have students work with a partner to generate some information that they would need in order to solve the problem. Open the discussion up to the class. Brainstorm what information is needed to solve the proportion. Check their work.

Step 4 (20 minutes): Break students into groups of four. Each student needs a piece of white paper, a measuring tape, and a glue stick. Assign each group an animal from the Animal Facts sheet (figure 3.8).

Animal facts

Fact: A polar bear travels 30 km a day.
Other information:
A polar bear weighs 400 kg.
Each mile gets multiplied by 1.6 to get km.
There are 2.2 kg per 1 pound.

Fact: Dogs can smell a scent from 1/2 mile away.
Other information:
The average size nose of a dog from start to tip is
.75 inches.
One mile is 5,280 ft.

Fact: Snow leopards jump 45 feet.
Other information:
Snow leopards are about 42 inches long.

Fact: A lion's roar can be heard from 5 miles away.
Other information:
A lion opens its mouth about 7 inches.
There are 5,280 ft. in one mile and 12 inches in a foot.

Fact: A blue whale can make sound at 188 dB (louder than a rock concert), which can be heard 530 miles away.
Other information:
A blue whale is 85 feet long.
A mile is 5,280 ft.

Fact: A hippo eats 100 lbs. of grass in a single night.
Other information:
A hippo weighs 5,000 lbs.

Figure 3.8   Animal Facts Sheet

(It's easier if you have these facts cut into strips before the activity.) Each group will get the facts on one animal. They then have to decide how to use the provided information, set up a problem on their paper, solve the problem, and have each group member ready to explain his or her own work.

Step 5 (15 minutes): As a class, move to an open area like a hallway or courtyard, taking the students' problems and measuring tapes. Each group will present its problem, showing how the members set up the problem and how they solved it. Then they demonstrate their answer for the group. For example, if they were solving a problem about being able to run as fast as a spider, they would need to mark off 10 yards to show everyone that they would be able to run that far in 1 second. I ask each group member to present a different part of the presentation, so no individual student does all the talking.

Extension assignment: Have students research animal facts on their own from a book and write and illustrate their own page from the book.

CERCA: A Framework for Argumentation

CCSS writing anchor standard 1 is one of the most detailed standards and articulates the expectations for argumentation in writing across all content areas:

1. *Write arguments to support claims in an analysis of substantive topics or texts using valid reasoning and relevant and sufficient evidence.*

This standard is further articulated as shown in figure 3.9, with my comments.

The CERCA framework (www.thinkcerca.com), developed by educator Eileen Murphy, promotes the development of the writing and argumentation, and I support THINKCERCA as an advisory board member (see www.thinkcerca.com).

The CERCA framework for argumentative writing provides for the following:

Claim: Make a statement or assertion

Evidence: Provide evidence using text, facts, statistics, or other sources

Reasoning: Explain **how** and **why** the presented evidence proves the claim.

Counterargument: Address other points of view and contrary evidence.

Audience-appropriate language: Construct presentation in language and style appropriate to purpose, audience.

Notice that this framework does not dictate certain "traits" or "elements" or formulas for document creation, like a "hamburger model" or a mandatory paragraph sentence structure. Rather the framework promotes **thinking** and the **creation of logical arguments**. Before students can create an argument in writing, they need to know how to argue. It is no wonder that anchor standards 3 and 4 in speaking and listening identify important verbal skills for argumentation:

3. *Evaluate a speaker's point of view, reasoning, and use of evidence and rhetoric.*

4. *Present information, findings, and supporting evidence such that listeners can follow the line of reasoning and the organization, development, and style are appropriate to task, purpose, and audience.*

Arguing, debating, and articulating our claims in writing is a hallmark of the CCSS ELA writing standards and a necessary skill for college and career readiness.

Claim: Should cell phones be allowed in school? (Students would support one of the following claims: Cell phones should be allowed in school or cell phone should not be allowed in school.)

Evidence: Use textual evidence from articles that examine the use of cell phones for learning in schools.

Reasoning: Explain how the evidence supports and relates to the claim.

Counterargument: Address and debate the opposing claim.

Audience and appropriate language: Shape your argument to suit your audience. For example, is your audience student peers, the principal, or school board? The language that is used in the writing should be appropriate for the selected audience.

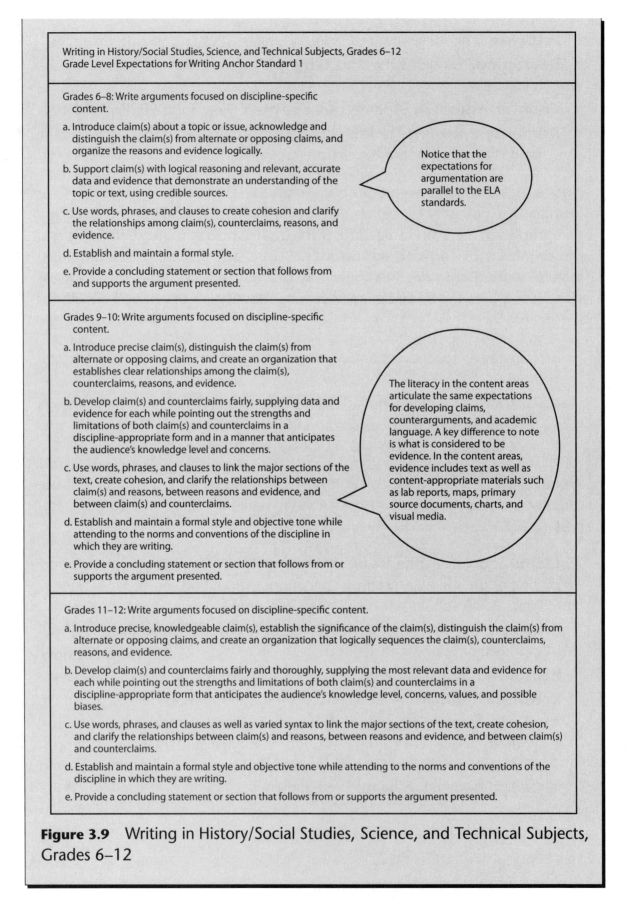

Writing in History/Social Studies, Science, and Technical Subjects, Grades 6–12
Grade Level Expectations for Writing Anchor Standard 1

Grades 6–8: Write arguments focused on discipline-specific content.

a. Introduce claim(s) about a topic or issue, acknowledge and distinguish the claim(s) from alternate or opposing claims, and organize the reasons and evidence logically.

b. Support claim(s) with logical reasoning and relevant, accurate data and evidence that demonstrate an understanding of the topic or text, using credible sources.

c. Use words, phrases, and clauses to create cohesion and clarify the relationships among claim(s), counterclaims, reasons, and evidence.

d. Establish and maintain a formal style.

e. Provide a concluding statement or section that follows from and supports the argument presented.

Notice that the expectations for argumentation are parallel to the ELA standards.

Grades 9–10: Write arguments focused on discipline-specific content.

a. Introduce precise claim(s), distinguish the claim(s) from alternate or opposing claims, and create an organization that establishes clear relationships among the claim(s), counterclaims, reasons, and evidence.

b. Develop claim(s) and counterclaims fairly, supplying data and evidence for each while pointing out the strengths and limitations of both claim(s) and counterclaims in a discipline-appropriate form and in a manner that anticipates the audience's knowledge level and concerns.

c. Use words, phrases, and clauses to link the major sections of the text, create cohesion, and clarify the relationships between claim(s) and reasons, between reasons and evidence, and between claim(s) and counterclaims.

d. Establish and maintain a formal style and objective tone while attending to the norms and conventions of the discipline in which they are writing.

e. Provide a concluding statement or section that follows from or supports the argument presented.

The literacy in the content areas articulate the same expectations for developing claims, counterarguments, and academic language. A key difference to note is what is considered to be evidence. In the content areas, evidence includes text as well as content-appropriate materials such as lab reports, maps, primary source documents, charts, and visual media.

Grades 11–12: Write arguments focused on discipline-specific content.

a. Introduce precise, knowledgeable claim(s), establish the significance of the claim(s), distinguish the claim(s) from alternate or opposing claims, and create an organization that logically sequences the claim(s), counterclaims, reasons, and evidence.

b. Develop claim(s) and counterclaims fairly and thoroughly, supplying the most relevant data and evidence for each while pointing out the strengths and limitations of both claim(s) and counterclaims in a discipline-appropriate form that anticipates the audience's knowledge level, concerns, values, and possible biases.

c. Use words, phrases, and clauses as well as varied syntax to link the major sections of the text, create cohesion, and clarify the relationships between claim(s) and reasons, between reasons and evidence, and between claim(s) and counterclaims.

d. Establish and maintain a formal style and objective tone while attending to the norms and conventions of the discipline in which they are writing.

e. Provide a concluding statement or section that follows from or supports the argument presented.

Figure 3.9 Writing in History/Social Studies, Science, and Technical Subjects, Grades 6–12

More Resources for Developing Argumentation Skills

There are some great resources on argumentation that will support your development of lessons that develop these important skills.

Print

Hillocks Jr., George (2011). *Teaching Argument Writing, Grades 6–12: Supporting Claims with Relevant Evidence and Clear Reasoning*. Portsmouth, NH: Heinemann.

Websites

iDebate: http://idebate.org
Another resource for teaching argumentation and debate.

Mathalicious: http://www.mathalicious.com/
Real-world math lessons help teachers address the Common Core Standards while challenging their students to think critically about the world.

ProCon: http://www.procon.org
Outstanding resource with many materials for teaching argumentation.

Teach Hub: http://www.teachhub.com/video-writing-prompts
Using videos as writing prompts, students can develop an argumentation piece in response to the prompt.

Think CERCA: http://thinkcerca.com/
Help students build college and career readiness skills with engaging real-world ELA, science, and social science topics.

This I Believe: http://www.thisibelieve.com
Templates and reading material for teaching argumentation.

US Library of Congress Primary Source Documents: http://www.loc.gov/teachers/classroommaterials/primarysourcesets/
This is an extensive library of documents and teaching materials to create inquiry and argumentation curriculum.

AN INCREASED FOCUS ON RESEARCH

One of the key features of the Common Core State Standards in the writing strand is the stronger emphasis on research. Specifically, the following writing anchor standards address this emphasis:

7. *Conduct short as well as more sustained research projects based on focused questions, demonstrating understanding of the subject under investigation.*
8. *Gather relevant information for multiple print and digital sources, assess the credibility and accuracy of the source, and integrate while avoiding plagiarism.*
9. *Draw evidence from literary or informational texts to support analysis, reflection, and research.*

These standards establish the expectation that students will be able to research and integrate a wide variety of sources that include technology and digital resources. Not only do we expect students to be able to research competently, they are also expected to use the wide variety of resources in our digital age to clarify, further explore, and document what they know and understand.

Research in the twenty-first century is different. In my travels, I have found that many of our teacher colleagues lament that students don't know how to research anymore. I beg to differ. Teenagers are researching all of the time on their smartphones and computers. Here's an example. Do you know any students who play video games? It's a silly question: I am sure that you do. At the time of writing this book, all of the teenagers I know play *Minecraft*. What do students do when they can't get past a level in the game? They don't give up. They go on the Internet and look for "cheats." As they examine multiple websites and look at different cheats, they analyze and then apply the information (a little Bloom's taxonomy and critical thinking here as well). Once they try out the cheats, they will write their own comments about whether this information worked on some of the very sites they used to research the cheats.

My purpose in bringing up this example is to demonstrate how students already research in our technological age. We can no longer teach that research skills consist of taking handwritten notes on index cards. As proposed in the CCSS, we need more ways to develop research skills using advanced technology. The abundance of information in the twenty-first century is staggering. When I was in school in the 1970s and 1980s, the research challenge was getting my hands on information. I had to scour microfilm, microfiche, and the *Readers' Guide to Periodical Literature*. Today, my university library has more digital than hard copies, and quite honestly I can't recall the last time I had to scour the library stacks for a much-needed volume. It's not good or bad. It's just different.

Here are some ideas for integrating more research opportunities into the teaching of your content area. Remember, research is not limited to a traditional term paper.

Webquests

A great place to start building a technology-infused research project is the website www.webquest.org. An inquiry-oriented pedagogy, a webquest is a research-based activity in which "most or all of the information that learners work with comes from the web. The model was developed by Bernie Dodge at San Diego State University" (home page, accessed August 11, 2013).

Webquests pose a great question that's worthy of investigation and research. For example:

▶ What drives a population to engage in warfare?
▶ Are there limits to freedom?

Using the webquest model, students can examine a wide variety of informational and literary texts in an online web-based platform.

ProCon

The web-based resource www.procon.org was included in the resources for argumentation section, and it is also an excellent tool for research. This site provides plenty of text- and visual-based questions that students can use to research a given topic and develop a written argument. Not only are students developing research skills, they are using their skills in argumentation writing to express what they know and understand.

Integrating Knowledge and Ideas Across Multiple Sources of Information

From www.adlit.org, this video module shows a high school history teacher demonstrating how to use multiple texts to teach about Abraham Lincoln. She develops a learning activity that not only meets the Common Core expectation that students should be able to read and navigate multiple texts, but also meets the expectations established in standards 7 and 8.

SOME FINAL THOUGHTS

Developing students' literacy skills, and writing skills in particular, is a shared responsibility within a school. **If students realize that a claim, thesis, hypothesis, theorum, or postulate all refer to the same thing, they may realize the value of writing to convey, convince, and share what they know and understand.** As students articulate what they think in written text, they are developing the skills they need to take their place as adults in a democratic society **and** to become college and career ready.

CHAPTER FOUR

Speaking and Listening in the Content Area

I'm sure you have heard educators refer to speaking and listening as the forgotten literacy. More classroom time has been invested in developing students' abilities to write well-composed essays than helping them master well-constructed oral presentations. And encouraging students to recognize arguments, evidence, and conclusions when they **read** has taken precedence over teaching them to **listen** for those same things. This is true in English language arts as well as all content areas.

Yet if our students are going to succeed as literate twenty-first-century citizens, it's imperative that they master both forms of **receptive** language (reading and listening), as well as both forms of **expressive** language (writing and speaking).

How can we develop speaking and listening skills so that students can better represent content that they know and understand?

Like the language strand, the speaking and listening strand is included in the ELA standards but **not** in the standards for Literacy in History/Social Studies, Science, and Technical Subjects 6–12. We use oral language, as we do writing, to express what we know and understand. As teachers, we develop our students' literacy skills in reading and writing as well as in speaking and listening and language while developing content knowledge.

A LOOK AT THE SPEAKING AND LISTENING STANDARDS

As with the reading and writing strands, we are going to use the speaking and listening anchor standards to develop our overall understanding of the skill development expectations for this literacy strand.

Comprehension and Collaboration

1. *Prepare for and participate effectively in a range of conversations and collaborations with diverse partners, building on others' ideas and expressing their own clearly and persuasively.*
2. *Integrate and evaluate information presented in diverse media and formats, including visually, quantitatively, and orally.*
3. *Evaluate a speaker's point of view, reasoning, and use of evidence and rhetoric.*

Presentation of Knowledge and Ideas

4. *Present information, findings, and supporting evidence such that listeners can follow the line of reasoning and the organization, development, and style are appropriate to task, purpose, and audience.*
5. *Make strategic use of digital media and visual displays of data to express information and enhance understanding of presentations.*
6. *Adapt speech to a variety of contexts and communicative tasks, demonstrating command of formal English when indicated or appropriate.*

Here's what content teachers need to know about the speaking and listening standards.

TECHNOLOGY

The standards establish the expectation that students use technology to enhance their presentations. This expectation makes sense because we use technology and digital media every day in college and our careers. The standards state the expectation this way: *"make strategic use of data to express information and enhance understanding of presentations"* (CCSS 2010, p. 48).

According to the CCSS, middle school and high school students are expected to be "strategic" and use the speaking and listening skills to "enhance" their presentations. In the past, technology was often an afterthought or included in a separate list of standards. In the Common Core era, technology is recognized as a valuable tool for enhancing a student's ability to analyze information and support claims, and technology is prominently featured in the speaking and listening standards.

The number of opportunities to engage in speaking and listening is greatly increased through use of technology. Content area teachers need to actively consider different technology tools that will support students in meeting the expectations of the speaking and listening standards.

PowerPoint and Prezi are examples of digital tools that can enhance a presentation with visual representation of information. Here are some additional Web 2.0 tools that students may consider using to enhance presentations:

- **Prezi**: Think of a three-dimensional PowerPoint.
- **PresentMe**: Creates a split screen to allow a speaker to discuss a PowerPoint presentation. I see many uses for children who are learning how to read.
- **Vocaroo**: A recording site
- **Audioboo**: A recording site where you create "boos" that can be uploaded to sites and e-mailed
- **Fotobabble**: Great tool for digital storytelling
- **Vialogues**: A Web 2.0 tool providing a platform for asynchronous discussions centered around videos
- **Viewbix**: Site where videos from multiple sites or apps can be featured on a platform. This is a great tool for creating "flipped classroom" experiences for students.
- **Webdoc**: A site that resembles a digital scrapbook or an interactive, enhanced blog
- **Mixbook**: A site where students can create e-books in a digital storytelling platform
- **SlideShare**: A web-based tool for sharing digital content

Technology does change rapidly, and I am sure that you have other Web 2.0 tools that can be added to this list.

In the twenty-first century, we use technology to enhance communication, including speaking and listening.

New technologies have broadened and expanded the role that speaking and listening play in acquiring and sharing knowledge and have tightened their link to other

*forms of communication. The Internet has accelerated the speed at which connec-
tions between speaking, listening, reading, and writing can be made, requiring that
students be ready to use these modalities nearly simultaneously. Technology itself is
changing quickly, creating a new urgency for students to be adaptable in response
to change.*

(CCSS 2010, p. 48)

The simultaneous nature supports the role of active learning in developing adolescent students with strong literacy skills.

The importance of using technology to build literacy skills and content knowledge is recognized in the CCSS. Later in this chapter, we will explore examples of
how to integrate technology, speaking and listening, and content study in science,
math, and technical subjects.

SMALL AND LARGE GROUP DISCUSSIONS

The standards require students to engage in a variety of small and large group
discussions. The CCSS authors explain that in order for students to become
college and career ready, they must have substantial opportunities to participate
in meaningful conversations in varied contexts: as a whole class, in small groups,
or with a partner. Academic conversations are critical because these experiences
allow students to compare, contrast, and integrate ideas. Additionally, the CCSS
speaking and listening standards also emphasize the importance of students
being able to listen attentively so that *"they are able to build on others' meritorious
ideas while expressing their own clearly and persuasively"* (CCSS 2010, p. 48). To meet
these expectations, we need to create contexts in which students actually talk
and discuss ideas in class.

Any teacher of teenagers is also well aware that listening is an area in which
students usually need additional modeling and practice. Listening and speaking
are inextricably connected skills, and in order to be an effective communicator,
students must develop both skills. For example, the CCSS authors state that students should be able to listen to a newscast and determine whether the reasoning
might be faulty or off message: *"evaluate a speaker's point of view, reasoning, and use
of evidence and rhetoric, identifying any fallacious reasoning or exaggerated or distorted evidence"* (CCSS 2010, p. 50).

DEVELOPING ARGUMENTATION SKILLS THROUGH SPEAKING AND LISTENING

Like the CCSS writing standards, the speaking and listening standards place particular emphasis on argumentation. In the ninth through tenth and eleventh through twelfth grade speaking and listening standards, students are expected to orally present information that clearly demonstrates their ability to support a well-thought-out claim with evidence and reasoning, using a logical structure or sequence. In chapter 3, I provided the CERCA framework for teaching argumentation in writing. This framework is also excellent for the development of oral argumentation skills. This is a model in which a speaker or writer does the following:

Claim: Make a statement or assertion

Evidence: Provide evidence using text, facts, statistics, or other sources

Reasoning: Explain how and why the presented evidence proves the claim

Counterargument: Address other points of view and contrary evidence

Audience-appropriate language: Construct presentation in language and style as *"appropriate to purpose, audience"* (CCSS speaking and listening standard 4)

Argumentation is fundamental to what the Common Core State Standards define as career and college readiness. Its placement in speaking and listening is appropriate and requires us to create opportunities for students to develop these skills in both written **and** oral communications. There are some excellent sites for argumentation that English and social studies teachers might find particularly useful:

▶ **iDebate**: www.IDebate.com
▶ **ProCon**: www.Procon.org
▶ **Library of Congress primary sources website**: http://www.loc.gov /teachers/classroommaterials/primarysourcesets/

WHAT DO THE STANDARDS MEAN FOR SCIENCE AND MATHEMATICS TEACHERS?

As we begin to look at specific strategies and ideas for the integration of speaking and listening strategies for these content areas, I want to reiterate that the speaking and listening standards in the CCSS are "officially" included only for the

English language arts content area, not the science, math, and technical subject content area. As I mentioned in the introduction, I consider this an oversight. The CCSS authors make the case for an integrated model of literacy, in which content area teachers are an active part of successful efforts to develop these skills in all students. Students definitely need to learn how to use reading and writing to understand content information. To omit speaking and listening (and language, which we'll address in chapter 5) from this design, in my view, is not sensible. Students must develop speaking and listening skills in all content areas. Just as teachers in the content areas other than English are charged with the task of developing reading and writing skills, these teachers must also be expected to develop students' skills in the areas of speaking and listening and language. I also have no doubt that, along with English language arts teachers, there are plenty of science, math, and technical subject teachers who develop students' speaking and listening skills while teaching content.

Instructional Ideas for Speaking and Listening in the English and Social Studies Content Areas

Say Something, Ask Something is a strategy that is effective for building large and small group instruction interactivity. Once students have discussed a topic in either a large group or a small group, instruct the students to make a statement about what they learned: "Say Something." Next, instruct the students to develop a question based on what they learned in the large or small group discussion: "Ask Something." Not only is this an effective metacognitive strategy, prompting students to analyze and synthesize what they have learned, it also is a check for understanding. Based on the students' responses, teachers have a formative assessment that they can use to modify future lessons.

Think-Pair-Share was one of the first teaching strategies that I learned more than twenty-five years ago. It is also probably one of the most common speaking and listening strategies that I see in the classroom. It's a simple and effective means for students to express what they know and understand about a specific topic, and it also gives teachers the opportunity to check for their understanding. Briefly, Think-Pair-Share is a strategy in which the students briefly turn to another classmate and respond to a teacher prompt, question, or statement. The students share their thinking. A Think-Pair-Share session is brief. It should not last more than two to three minutes.

Audio and video recordings are effective tools for the development of student listening skills. The listening skills that are identified in anchor standards 2 and 3 can be effectively met with the use of audio and video recordings.

2. *Integrate and evaluate information presented in diverse media and formats, including visually, quantitatively, and orally.*
3. *Evaluate a speaker's point of view, reasoning, and use of evidence and rhetoric.*

I am certain that there are plenty of science, math, and technical subject teachers who use recordings in class. For example, teachers could show different video recordings from Mythbusters and the Discovery channel. YouTube is a great source for these videos. It's always particularly interesting to show students a variety of presentations on a specific topic so that they can analyze different points of view, reasoning, and evidence (speaking and listening standard 3).

Computerphile is a British learning channel that offers entertaining YouTube videos about computers, coding, programming, and other topics. It's a sister channel of the popular Numberphile.

Crash Course is a YouTube channel put together by brothers Hank and John Green (popularly known as the vlogbrothers). They offer short courses in biology, chemistry, ecology and psychology, as well as literature and world history.

MinutePhysics and MinuteEarth offer concise, one-minute lessons about "cool physics and other sweet science" and "our awesome planet." These lessons are also available in Spanish as MinutoDeFisica and MinutoDeLaTierra.

Numberphile is a British learning channel about numbers—prime numbers, number lines, the Ulam spiral, transcendental numbers, and various mathematical concepts. It's supported by the Mathematical Sciences Research Institute.

SciShow discusses science news, science history and scientific concepts with equal parts skepticism and enthusiasm. Hank Green, who works with his brother on Crash Course, produces SciShow.

SmarterEveryDay explores the world using science. Creator and host, Destin, strives to create intelligent, original, respectful content. His videos are on YouTube; his ever-growing collection of infographics can be found at http://smartereveryday.tumblr.com/

TED is a nonprofit organization devoted to spreading ideas, usually in the form of short, powerful talks (eighteen minutes or less). TED began in

1984 as a conference where technology, entertainment, and design converged, and today it covers almost all topics—from science to business to global issues. http://www.ted.com/

Vsauce features internet personality Michael Stevens. The program originally focused on video games. The wide-ranging videos, available on YouTube, now address such intriguing questions as these: Is your red the same as my red? How high can we build? Who owns the moon? What is the brightest thing in the universe?

Consider pairing these content sources with some of the Web 2.0 tools for digital recording discussed earlier, including Audioboo and Vocaroo. Students can create newscasts, narratives, and presentations with voiceovers to demonstrate what they know about content.

Listening to a text or watching a video supplement supports the development of listening skills and content knowledge. Focused questions can be developed to foster effective discussions.

As the Parabola Opens: Vocabulary Project

This vocabulary project is one of Holly Young's inspired lessons, which successfully integrates literacy skills while developing content knowledge in mathematics. Holly works as a mathematics teacher, education consultant, and math trainer for Nevada's Northwest Regional Professional Development Program. More examples of her creative lessons can be found on her website: www.making mathematicians.com.

How Does This Connect to CCSS?

This vocabulary project is aligned with the following speaking and listening standards:

1. *Prepare for and participate effectively in a range of conversations and collaborations with diverse partners, building on others' ideas and expressing their own clearly and persuasively.*

2. *Integrate and evaluate information presented in diverse media and formats, including visually, quantitatively, and orally.*

6. *Adapt speech to a variety of contexts and communicative tasks, demonstrating command of formal English when indicated or appropriate.*

It is also aligned with language standard 3:

3. *Apply knowledge of language to understand how language functions in different contexts, to make effective choices for meaning or style, and to comprehend more fully when reading or listening.*

Directions

Students write and perform a scene from a soap opera. The basic plot of each scene is listed below. Each scene corresponds to a section number from the book. In the scene the students may introduce characters and appropriate situations using the vocabulary and main ideas from their section. Students need to use each vocabulary word as it applies to math. As Holly explains to her class, "In other words you can't name a dog Triangle and have him running around doing dog things; he would need to always turn 180 times before lying down, for example, or only have three legs. You may also include props that have math meaning. This does not mean having a parabola on the wall and think that you don't have to mention it."

Each scene can use other class members, not just those in the assigned group. And all group members need not perform. But they must be involved in some way—by writing, typing, staging, and so on.

A final copy of each script is due immediately after the performance. Students' scripts must include all vocabulary and main ideas from their section. The vocabulary words need to be underlined in red.

The sample scene list that follows could be easily adapted for other subject matter, and scenes could correspond to any textbook chapters or classroom lessons.

"As the Parabola Opens": Sample Scene List

Scene 1 (corresponds to textbook section 5.1)—*Basic plot:* Mr. Para Bola and Miss Parab LA meet for the first time.

Scene 2 (corresponds to textbook section 5.2)—*Basic plot:* Mr. Para Bola and Miss Parab LA get married, but the wedding gets interrupted and they don't marry.

Scene 3 (corresponds to textbook section 5.3)—*Basic plot:* Miss Parab LA is kidnapped by evil Dr. FacTor and is taken to his hidden tropical island.

Scene 4: (corresponds to textbook section 5.4)—Basic plot: Miss Parab LA is rescued by C.T. Square, a private detective hired by Mr. Para Bola. A love triangle forms.

Scene 5 (corresponds to textbook section 5.5)—*Basic plot:* Miss Parab LA and C.T. Square attend an opera, and Mr. Para Bola catches them together.

Scene 6 (corresponds to textbook section 5.6)—*Basic plot:* Mr. Para Bola starts dating his ex-girlfriend ComPlex, and both couples go to the same restaurant and try to make each other jealous.

Scene 7 (corresponds to textbook section 5.8)—*Basic plot:* Miss Parab LA walks through the park and reminisces about the olden days with Mr. Para Bola. She realizes she wants Mr. Para Bola more than C.T. Square, so she finds him and they live happily ever after.

A FEW WORDS ABOUT ENGLISH LANGUAGE LEARNERS

English language proficiency isn't just about developing verbal skills in everyday life. Developing speaking and listening skills in school is critical for English language learners as they embark on college and career readiness. Although CCSS does not specifically address English language learners, we know as classroom teachers that speaking and listening opportunities facilitate the ability to express content knowledge in a second language.

SOME FINAL THOUGHTS

As I mentioned in the opening of this chapter, the speaking and listening skills are listed only in the English language arts standards. However, speaking and listening skills need to be developed in all content areas, including math, science, and technical subjects.

CHAPTER FIVE

Developing Academic Language

Why does language matter in the teaching and learning of content? How can we support students who speak more than one dialect or language to become career and college ready?

As a high school student many years ago, I was often assigned long lists of vocabulary words in my English and social studies classes and instructed to write each word three times, along with its definition. Sometimes I was asked to write a sentence or paragraph using the new vocabulary words. Three easy steps, and I would know the words forever! Of course I didn't remember many words—maybe a few—and I certainly didn't master the new vocabulary. Today, we know through extensive research (National Institute for Literacy, 2007) in the teaching of vocabulary that this method was among the most ineffective ways to teach students new vocabulary, because it's largely a passive experience for students.

Just as I did with vocabulary lists, I struggled with grammar because I didn't have many writing assignments. I was assigned copious grammar worksheets but rarely had the opportunity to apply what I understood about grammatical structures in writing. I certainly could tell you that a noun is a person, place, or thing, but I did not possess the confidence to use language effectively in writing.

What we know today is that language learning, particularly in vocabulary and grammar, is most effective when it is active, student centered, and engaging. Students must understand how grammar and vocabulary supports writing, reading, and speaking and listening.

Language development, as suggested in the CCSS, is an ongoing process. Like all literacy skills we seek to develop, language should not be limited to a curriculum, and the development of language continues throughout our lives.

As middle school and high school teachers, we should expect to see increasingly complex writing in all content areas, not just in English class. The reality is that many of our students fall short of these expectations when they enter middle school and high school. Teaching students about grammar and vocabulary is challenging. Yet content study and language skills are connected. When we involve all of our colleagues from the different content areas, we offer our students many opportunities to practice language skills **while teaching our content**. Content area teachers are the most effective models for students as they develop their language skills.

A LOOK AT THE CCSS ANCHOR STANDARDS IN LANGUAGE

Like the speaking and listening strand, the language strand is exclusive to the English language arts standards and is not included in the literacy in science and technical subjects. However, I think it is absolutely essential to discuss the language strand, like the speaking and listening strand, within the context of science and mathematics content study. As we examine the language strand, it becomes easier to relate these language skills and expectations to the teaching of all content areas.

In the introduction to the language standards, the six anchor standards are divided into three categories.

Conventions of Standard English

1. *Demonstrate command of the conventions of standard English grammar and usage when writing or speaking.*
2. *Demonstrate command of the conventions of standard English capitalization, punctuation, and spelling when writing.*

Knowledge of Language

3. *Apply knowledge of language to understand how language functions in different contexts, to make effective choices for meaning or style, and to comprehend more fully when reading or listening.*

Vocabulary Acquisition and Use

4. *Determine or clarify the meaning of unknown and multiple-meaning words and phrases by using context clues, analyzing meaningful word parts, and consulting general and specialized reference materials, as appropriate.*

5. *Demonstrate understanding of figurative language, word relationships, and nuances in word meanings.*

6. *Acquire and use accurately a range of general academic and domain-specific words and phrases sufficient for reading, writing, speaking, and listening at the college and career readiness level; demonstrate independence in gathering vocabulary knowledge when considering a word or phrase important to comprehension or expression.*

Generally the language standards contain a strong focus on the ability to effectively use Standard English through a wide variety of tasks and contexts. This includes writing lab reports in science class or explaining mathematics principles as applied to a specific context, for example. Vocabulary development is expected in the language standards. Both of these expectations support the development of student literacy skills **and** content knowledge. The introduction to the sixth through twelfth grade language standards explains these expectations in greater detail:

> *To be college and career ready in language, **students must have firm control over the conventions of standard English**.... They must also have extensive vocabularies, built through reading and study, enabling them **to comprehend complex texts and engage in purposeful writing about and conversations around content**. They need to become skilled in determining or clarifying the meaning of words and phrases they encounter, choosing flexibly from an array of strategies to aid them. **They must learn to see an individual word as part of a network of other words**—words, for example, that have similar denotations but different connotations. **The inclusion of language standards in their own strand should not be taken as an indication that skills related to conventions, effective language***

use, and vocabulary are unimportant to reading, writing, speaking, and listening; indeed, they are inseparable from such contexts. (emphasis added)

(CCSS 2010, p. 51)

I contend that, like the speaking and listening strand, language development should be included in Common Core State Standards for all content areas and disciplines.

THE IMPACT OF THE LANGUAGE STRAND ON CONTENT INSTRUCTION

The CCSS Conventions of Standard English (grammar) standards require students to **demonstrate and understand** how to use grammatical structures. Being able to identify the rules of grammar and define the parts of speech is not a CCSS requirement. Instead, students are expected to actually use and apply their knowledge of grammatical structures and Standard English. You'll notice that this expectation is also articulated in the next section of standards, Knowledge of Language. Again, the CCSS authors indicate that **it is the contextual application of language skills that matters, not the knowledge of rules**.

It is no longer enough for students to know that a noun is a person, place, thing, or idea. To meet CCSS expectations, students must be able to apply what they know and understand how language functions in multiple contexts. Students need to be able to demonstrate their increasing mastery of the functions of language, which requires a deeper understanding of language. As you can see from this level of expectation, this effort cannot be isolated to the ELA classroom. This expectation must be reinforced throughout the entire academic experience.

With these new expectations, I think some additional clarifications are necessary. Through my inclusion of the language strand in this book, I am **not** making the argument that science and mathematics teachers, along with ELA teachers, should teach grammatical structures to their students. ELA teachers will continue to teach grammatical structures, but math, science, and technical subject teachers should be models of Standard English in oral and written work as they develop student knowledge and skills in their content area. Specifically, all teachers should require effective language use (as identified in the CCSS language anchor standards) for all academic work in their classrooms. Not only does this requirement give students more practice in developing language proficiency, the requirement also creates a school culture that supports the development of Standard English and academic vocabulary.

What Do the Vocabulary Standards Mean for Content Teachers?

The CCSS Vocabulary Acquisition and Use standards (a subset of the language strand) clarify that students are expected to develop a deep understanding of words. Memorization of word lists is not sufficient; students should determine the meaning of unfamiliar words and phrases through effective and appropriate strategies. You may already know that the development of a strong academic and domain-specific vocabulary is essential for college and career readiness. We also know through the work of Robert J. Marzano that a strong academic and content-specific vocabulary leads to greater comprehension and student achievement.

STRATEGIES TO BUILD LANGUAGE SKILLS IN CONTENT AREAS

When I present to teachers from all disciplines, they often comment that students need to build language skills in academic English and vocabulary. When we support the development of language skills in our content area or discipline, we are offering students greater experiences with language and they are experiencing how language works in different content areas. We will start with mini-lessons as a means to develop grammatical knowledge and then move to strategies for the development of vocabulary, which is more pressing for science and mathematics teachers. When appropriate, you should consider teaching grammar mini-lessons as it relates to mathematics and science content.

Medium

Easy | Hard

Teaching Grammatical Structures: Mini-Lessons

Creating Effective Mini-Lessons

The acquisition of writing skills is developmental. A one-size-fits-all approach and the use of formulas do not always lead to successful student writing. What leads to successful student writing skills is the opportunity for students to learn and develop writing through individualized and authentic experiences. The mini-lesson is an instructional writing tool that builds on what students already

---

know so that they can improve and develop writing skills through experience and discovery. The writing mini-lesson is a proven strategy for individualized writing instruction that meets the developmental needs of students as they improve their writing skills.

When I entered the teaching profession in the late 1980s, the writing workshop became a new paradigm for writing instruction. Process was advocated over product, and mini-lessons were an integral tool in the writing workshop paradigm. Today, thanks to writing gurus like Nancie Atwell, Linda Reif, and Constance Weaver, the mini-lesson has become an important component of effective writing and language instruction.

Tips for Creating Effective Mini-Lessons

Determine Content Need. As teachers, we often see patterns in our students' writing. Document the skills that the students have mastered and what they still need to master.

Keep the Mini-Lessons Short and Simple. Mini-lessons should take ten minutes or less to complete. Break down the mini-lessons into the smallest component. For example, maybe one mini-lesson should cover one or two comma rules instead of all seven. Think of "chunking" the information students need to learn about writing in the smallest morsels possible.

Engage the Students and Provide for Interaction. These are important points to stress. Worksheets and drill sheets are not the most effective means to teach writing skills. Instead, consider the students' experiences and what they already know about language. Create activities that provide for multimodal interactions.

Practice! Once you introduce a new writing skill, give the students ample time to practice.

Ask "What's Next?" One of my favorite questions to ask students is "What did you learn, and why is it important?" This question is also relevant for teachers as they consider what their students are learning. Once a mini-lesson is completed, we need to ask, "What's next?" What have the students mastered, and what do they need to learn next?

How Does This Connect to CCSS?

Language anchor standards 1, 2, and 3 identify expectations for students' developing mastery of Standard English:

1. *Demonstrate command of the conventions of standard English grammar and usage when writing or speaking.*

2. *Demonstrate command of the conventions of standard English capitalization, punctuation, and spelling when writing.*

3. *Apply knowledge of language to understand how language functions in different contexts, to make effective choices for meaning or style, and to comprehend more fully when reading or listening.*

These standards are further articulated at each grade level (CCSS 2010, p. 52); see tables 5.1 (Grades 6–8) and 5.2 (Grades 9–12).

Table 5.1 Language Standards, Grades 6–8

Grade 6 Students: Conventions of Standard English	Grade 7 Students: Conventions of Standard English	Grade 8 Students: Conventions of Standard English

1. Demonstrate command of the conventions of standard English grammar and usage when writing or speaking.
 	
  a. Ensure that pronouns are in the proper case (subjective, objective, possessive).
 	
  b. Use intensive pronouns (e.g., myself, ourselves).
 	
  c. Recognize and correct inappropriate shifts in pronoun number and person.
 	
  d. Recognize and correct vague pronouns (i.e., ones with unclear or ambiguous antecedents).
 	
  e. Recognize variations from standard English in their own and others' writing and speaking, and identify and use strategies to improve expression in conventional language.
	1. Demonstrate command of the conventions of standard English grammar and usage when writing or speaking.
	
	  a. Explain the function of phrases and clauses in general and their function in specific sentences.
	
	  b. Choose among simple, compound, complex, and compound-complex sentences to signal differing relationships among ideas.
	
	  c. Place phrases and clauses within a sentence, reorganizing and correcting misplaced and dangling modifiers.
	
	2. Demonstrate command of the conventions of standard English capitalization, punctuation, and spelling when writing.
		1. Demonstrate command of the conventions of standard English grammar and usage when writing or speaking.
		
		  a. Explain the function of verbals (gerunds, participles, infinitives) in general and their function in particular sentences.
		
		  b. Form and use verbs in the active and passive voice.
		
		  c. Form and use verbs in the indicative, imperative, interrogative, conditional, and subjunctive mood.
		
		  d. Recognize and correct inappropriate shifts in verb voice and mood.
		
		2. Demonstrate command of the conventions of standard English capitalization, punctuation, and spelling when writing.

Table 5.1 Continued

Grade 6 Students: Conventions of Standard English	Grade 7 Students: Conventions of Standard English	Grade 8 Students: Conventions of Standard English

2. Demonstrate command of the conventions of standard English capitalization, punctuation, and spelling when writing.
 	
  a. Use punctuation (commas, parentheses, dashes) to set off nonrestrictive/parenthetical elements.
 	
  b. Spell correctly.
	a. Use a comma to separate coordinate adjectives (e.g., It was a fascinating, enjoyable movie but not He wore an old[,] green shirt).
	
	b. Spell correctly.
		a. Use punctuation (comma, ellipsis, dash) to indicate a pause or break.
		
		b. Use an ellipses to indicate an omission.
		
		c. Spell correctly.

3. Use knowledge of language and its conventions when writing, speaking, reading, or listening.
 	
  a. Vary sentence patterns for meaning, reader/listener interest, and style.
 	
  b. Maintain consistency in style and tone.
	3. Use knowledge of language and its conventions when writing, speaking, reading, or listening.
	
	  a. Choose language that expresses ideas precisely and concisely, recognizing and eliminating wordiness and redundancy.
		3. Use knowledge of language and its conventions when writing, speaking, reading, or listening.
		
		  a. Use verbs in the active and passive voice and in the conditional and subjunctive mood to achieve particular effects (e.g., emphasizing the actor or the action; expressing uncertainty or describing a state contrary to fact).

Table 5.2 Language Standards, Grades 9–12

Grades 9–10 Students: Conventions of Standard English	Grades 11–12 Students: Conventions of Standard English
1. *Demonstrate command of the conventions of standard English grammar and usage when writing or speaking.*	1. *Demonstrate command of the conventions of standard English grammar and usage when writing or speaking.*
a. *Use parallel structure.*	a. *Apply the understanding that usage is a matter of convention, can change over time, and is sometimes contested.*
b. *Use various types of phrases (noun, verb, adjectival, adverbial, participial prepositional, absolute) and clauses (independent, dependent; noun, relative, adverbial) to convey specific meanings and add variety and interest to writing or presentations.*	b. *Resolve issues of complex or contested usage, consulting references (e.g., Merriam-Webster's Dictionary of English Usage, Garner's Modern American Usage) as needed.*
2. *Demonstrate command of the conventions of standard English capitalization, punctuation, and spelling when writing.*	2. *Demonstrate command of the conventions of standard English capitalization, punctuation, and spelling when writing.*
a. *Use a semicolon (and perhaps a conjunctive adverb) to link two or more closely related independent clauses.*	a. *Observe hyphenation conventions.*
b. *Use a colon to introduce a list or quotation.*	b. *Spell correctly.*
c. *Spell correctly.*	
3. *Apply knowledge of language to understand how language functions in different contexts, to make effective choices for meaning or style, and to comprehend more fully when reading or listening.*	3. *Apply knowledge of language to understand how language functions in different contexts, to make effective choices for meaning or style, and to comprehend more fully when reading or listening.*
a. *Write and edit work so that it conforms to the guidelines in a style manual (e.g., MLA Handbook, Turabian's A Manual for Writers) appropriate for the discipline and writing type.*	a. *Vary syntax for effect, consulting references (e.g., Tufte's Artful Sentences) for guidance as needed: apply an understanding of syntax to the study of complex texts when reading).*

Sample Mini-Lessons

The mini-lessons in this section are examples of ways to develop student understanding of grammatical structures and conventions. These mini-lessons were originally published in my earlier book *Teaching Writing in the Inclusive Classroom* (coauthored with Roger Passman).

Knowing Nouns and Venturing about Verbs

Knowing Nouns and Venturing about Verbs is an interactive lesson that builds student understanding of how nouns and verbs function in language. This exercise is designed to develop students' innate understanding of nouns and verbs.

I developed this lesson and often use it to determine what students already know about grammar and more specifically the parts of speech. Definitions such as "a noun is a person, place, or thing" are not very helpful for student writers. Far better is for students to articulate how nouns, verbs, and other parts of speech work in the language. This hands-on lesson actively engages students as they build on their understanding of nouns.

In this lesson, students articulate their reasons for identifying nouns as nouns. For example, students may develop rules such as the following: Most nouns can be turned into plurals by adding "s" or "es" at the end. A noun can have "a," "an," or "the" in front of it. (The latter definition can be a great introduction to articles in addition to determining noun rules.)

Usually, through class discussion, we come up with five or six rules like these by the end of the lesson. Thus, we prompt the students to examine the ways in which language works and how we use it to express ideas. This gives them a far more specific understanding than when they merely regurgitate the familiar definitions. Student writers can tell us a ton about language if we provide them with opportunities to do so; from there, students can build on their previous knowledge about language. This activity takes about ten minutes.

Materials

You will need poster paper or large sticky notes, markers, and envelopes. Before you begin, make photocopies of figure 5.1. Cut the words contained in the exhibit into individual strips and put them in envelopes. There should be one envelope for every group of three to five students, and each envelope should include all of the words contained in the exhibit. Write the following directions on the outside of each envelope: "Dump the contents of this envelope onto a desk, and based on what you already know about the parts of speech, divide these words into two separate groups: nouns and verbs."

Procedure

Step 1. Divide the students into groups of three to five. Give each group one envelope.

Step 2. Direct the students to read and follow the directions on the outside of the envelope.

Step 3. Repeat the directions verbally. Tell students to divide the words into two groups: nouns and verbs.

Step 4. Circulate among the groups and monitor the students' progress. Ask students, "How did you divide the words?" Encourage the students to articulate why they divided the words as they did. Ask the students to label each list. The students may develop labels such as "nouns and verbs," "nonaction words and action words," or "things and moving words." All of these are fine, because they will trigger a discussion about what makes a noun a noun and what makes a verb a verb.

Step 5. Once the students have divided their words, distribute poster paper and markers. Instruct the students to write down the group's reasons for dividing the words as they chose. This should take about five minutes.

Step 6. Conduct a whole group discussion about the students' lists and create a combined class list that identifies the characteristics of nouns and verbs.

book	birthday cake	answered
walking	ran	flower
computer	music	drove
sings	cutting	oregano
pencil	sandwich	sent
played	growing	paper clip
video game	homework	wrote
cooking	cleaning	box
map	envelope	listening
prepared	painted	refrigerator
studied	compact disk	hears
sports car	questioned	house
leaped	concert	jumped
milkshake		

Figure 5.1   Knowing Nouns and Venturing about Verbs Handout

Postcards from the Past

This mini-lesson explores verb tenses and how this part of speech can convey time and can create a mood or tone. This mini-lesson specifically meets language anchor standard 1, as articulated for students in grade 8.

1. *Demonstrate command of the conventions of standard English grammar and usage when writing or speaking.*
   a. *Explain the function of verbals (gerunds, participles, infinitives) in general and their function in particular sentences.*
   b. *Form and use verbs in the active and passive voice.*
   c. *Form and use verbs in the indicative, imperative, interrogative, conditional, and subjunctive mood.*
   d. *Recognize and correct inappropriate shifts in verb voice and mood.*

Postcards from the Past is a mini-lesson designed to develop students' understanding of time in their writing. This lesson builds on students' innate understanding of verbs in determining time. Verbs are not only action words—they are also time determiners. In this case, they describe past actions. This activity takes about fifteen to twenty minutes.

Material

You will need postcards with pictures of various tourist destinations, poster paper, and markers.

Procedure

Step 1. Begin a discussion about postcards. Ask the students why people send postcards.

What do people write on postcards? Model a postcard that you have written to someone.

Then distribute postcards and invite the students to think about the picture on theirs. Ask the students to pretend they've visited the site on the picture and ask them to describe what they did there to a friend at home.

Step 2. Give the students about five minutes to write their postcards.

Step 3. Collect the postcards, so you can read some aloud, or read them together in class.

Once you have read three or so postcards, ask the students to write down the verbs—or action words—or time determiners. Then read a few more postcards.

Step 4. Ask the students to share their list of verbs and compile a class list. A pattern will form that will be dominated by verbs in the past tense.

Step 5. Conduct a whole group discussion about past-tense verbs and how these words are time determiners.

Who? What? A World Without Pronouns

This mini-lesson focuses on pronoun use. It aligns with anchor standards 1, 2, and 3. It specifically meets anchor standard 1 as it is articulated for grade 6 students.

1. *Demonstrate command of the conventions of standard English grammar and usage when writing or speaking.*
   a. *Ensure that pronouns are in the proper case (subjective, objective, possessive).*
   b. *Use intensive pronouns (e.g., myself, ourselves).*
   c. *Recognize and correct inappropriate shifts in pronoun number and person.*
   d. *Recognize and correct vague pronouns (i.e., ones with unclear or ambiguous antecedents).*
   e. *Recognize variations from standard English in their own and others' writing and speaking, and identify and use strategies to improve expression in conventional language.*

This exercise is designed to help students understand the purposes of pronouns in writing.

The students will articulate their reasons for using pronouns in writing. Again, this lesson builds on their innate understanding of the parts of speech. This activity generally takes about ten minutes.

Materials

You will need sheets of paper or large sticky notes, markers, and envelopes containing text samples with some words, including pronouns, missing. Choose samples from literature that your students have read. On the envelopes, write the following directions: "Read the enclosed passage and fill in the blank spaces with words of your choice."

Procedure

Step 1. Divide the students into groups of three to five.

Step 2. Instruct the students to read and follow the directions on the outside of the envelope.

Step 3. Give the students about five minutes to read the passage and write words in the blank spaces.

Step 4. Once the students have completed the passage, ask them the following questions about the words that they chose to complete the passage: What words did you use? What do these words have in common?

Step 5. Conduct a whole group discussion about what the students wrote, and create a combined class list that identifies the characteristics of the parts of speech that they used to complete the passage. Put particular emphasis on pronouns.

Capitalizing Capitalization

Capitalizing Capitalization is a mini-lesson that develops student understanding and application of correct capitalization in English. Language anchor standard 2 addresses language conventions, and this lesson specifically meets language anchor standard 2 as it is articulated for students in grades 9–12.

Grades 9–10

2. *Demonstrate command of the conventions of standard English capitalization, punctuation, and spelling when writing.*

   a. *Use a semicolon (and perhaps a conjunctive adverb) to link two or more closely related independent clauses.*

   b. *Use a colon to introduce a list or quotation.*

   c. *Spell correctly.*

Grades 11–12

2. *Demonstrate command of the conventions of standard English capitalization, punctuation, and spelling when writing.*

   a. *Observe hyphenation conventions.*

   b. *Spell correctly.*

In Capitalizing Capitalization, students identify the instances where capitalization is needed for proper nouns and create a list of rules for doing so. This activity takes about ten minutes.

Materials

You will need a blindfold, a large box or bag, and items that can spark discussion about capitalization.

Here's a list of possible items:

▶ Map with a city or location circled
▶ Newspaper or magazine
▶ Soup label with the name of the kind of soup (not the brand name) circled
▶ Soup label with the brand name (not the type of soup) circled
▶ Book with the title circled
▶ Spiral notebook
▶ Compact disc with the artist's name circled
▶ Stapler
▶ Compass, with the directions North, South, East, and West capitalized
▶ DVD
▶ Picture of a famous person
▶ CD
▶ Pencil with the brand name circled
▶ Notebook with the brand name circled
▶ Calendar or datebook

For fun, label the box "To Capitalize or Not! That Is the Question."

Procedure

Step 1. Blindfold a student and instruct him or her to remove an item from the box.

Step 2. After retrieving an item, have the student remove the blindfold and determine whether the name of the item should be capitalized. The student must also explain why the item should be capitalized or not.

Step 3. Have another student record the item and the capitalization on chart paper or the chalkboard.

Step 4. Repeat steps 1 through 3, with the remaining students taking turns being blindfolded while the observing student records their choices and explanations for why they capitalized the item or not.

Defragging Sentence Fragments

This mini-lesson supports the CCSS focus on the development of language understanding and applying grammatical structures for more effective verbal and written communication. This activity specifically addresses language anchor standard 3.

3. *Apply knowledge of language to understand how language functions in different contexts, to make effective choices for meaning or style, and to comprehend more fully when reading or listening.*

This activity is designed to provide practice and application for students to identify and correct sentence fragments. Like apostrophes, sentence fragments and run-ons can be difficult concepts for student writers to grasp. Students need experience with these concepts; they must be taught many times. As students correct their sentences, they will also improve their understanding of a complete sentence structure. This activity takes about fifteen minutes.

Materials

You will need ruled sheets of paper, a large envelope or other container (such as a cookie jar), one set of fragment slips made by photocopying figure 5.2 and cutting apart the individual phrases, and an overhead transparency made from figure 5.3. (You may also want to make copies of figure 5.5; see step 4.)

Directions: Cut out each phrase as a separate slip of paper. Put the slips into a container, such as an envelope or a cookie jar, and distribute to the students. Make sure there are enough slips so that each student receives one.

I would like
a large cheese pizza
for dinner
Her little brother loves to play
with different toy trains
almost every day
My favorite music
is often what is played
on the radio
My parents love to tell
me stories
about their youth
Does anyone
like to eat cheese
with crackers
My favorite cartoon
characters are
usually dogs

Figure 5.2   Defragging Sentence Fragments: Phrase Slips

Sentence Fragment	What Do I Need to Know?	Complete Sentence
My favorite story in the book	What about the story? Is there a title? What is the story about?	My favorite story in the book is called "My Little Puppy."
Walking to the store	Did something happen when walking to the store? Was there a reason for walking to the store?	Walking to the store, I tripped on a stone.
Wanted to go to an amusement park	Who wanted to go to an amusement park?	I wanted to go to an amusement park.
Thought that looked	Who? What?	I thought that looked delicious.
Very good too	Was something very good too? Or was someone very good too?	My little sister was very good too.

Figure 5.3   Defragging Sentence Fragments: Part 1

Procedure

Step 1. Ask your students, "What makes a sentence fragment a sentence fragment?" Using figure 5.3 as a guide, brainstorm with the students as a whole group about the characteristics of sentence fragments. Here are some possible prompts and discussion points:

As you look at these examples, ask yourself, "What's missing? What don't I know from reading this sentence fragment? How can I add information so that I understand the entire meaning of the possible sentence?"

Point out that sentence fragments are poor writing because they create confusion for the reader.

Step 2. Discuss with the students the requirements of a complete sentence (refer to figure 5.4). Point out to the students that the sentence (larger ring) encompasses a subject and a predicate (smaller components).

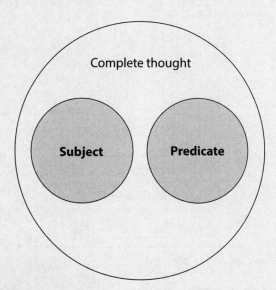

Figure 5.4   What a Sentence Needs

Step 3. Explain the rules for this activity. Each student is to take one slip of paper from your container. Then the students circulate and find another student or students with whom to combine slips of paper to create a complete sentence. Students must combine at least two slips of paper and can combine as many as three slips of paper. Students should add punctuation and capitalization to form a complete sentence. When they have a complete sentence, they should stand with the other students with whom they are combining slips and raise their hands.

Step 4. Copy figure 5.5 on the chalkboard or on chart paper, or distribute the copies you have made as handouts. Once all students have created their sentence slips of paper, complete figure 5.5 with the sentences that they created.

Directions: Write this on a chalkboard or on chart paper, or make copies for all students. Ask the students to fill in the blanks with you.

Fragment	*Fragment*	*Fragment*

Created Sentence

Example

Fragment	*Fragment*	*Fragment*
the newspaper	was not delivered	last week

Created Sentence

Last week, the newspaper was not delivered.

The newspaper was not delivered last week.

Figure 5.5 Defragging Sentence Fragments: Part 2

Vocabulary Strategies

The following strategies build student vocabulary acquisition as well as content knowledge. We know that the content areas are rich with discipline-specific vocabulary, and it is generally agreed that students must be exposed to vocabulary through increased reading. It's not just about increasing the amount of reading; to develop a strong vocabulary, students should encounter a variety of texts (which is the expectation of reading anchor standard 10). When encountering new vocabulary in their reading, adolescents need strategies that help them to interact with words. When students possess a variety of strategies and learn how to manipulate and play with words, students can internalize the new vocabulary.

The strategies that follow will support your students' academic vocabulary development.

Vocabulary Slides

We know that students learn vocabulary most effectively when they manipulate words in a variety of ways. Vocabulary Slides are graphic representations of words that prompt students to use new words and terminology in a variety of ways. The following figures 5.6, 5.7, 5.8, and 5.9 are four vocabulary slide formats. Downloadable versions of these templates are available on the publisher's website (see appendix A of this book for more details).

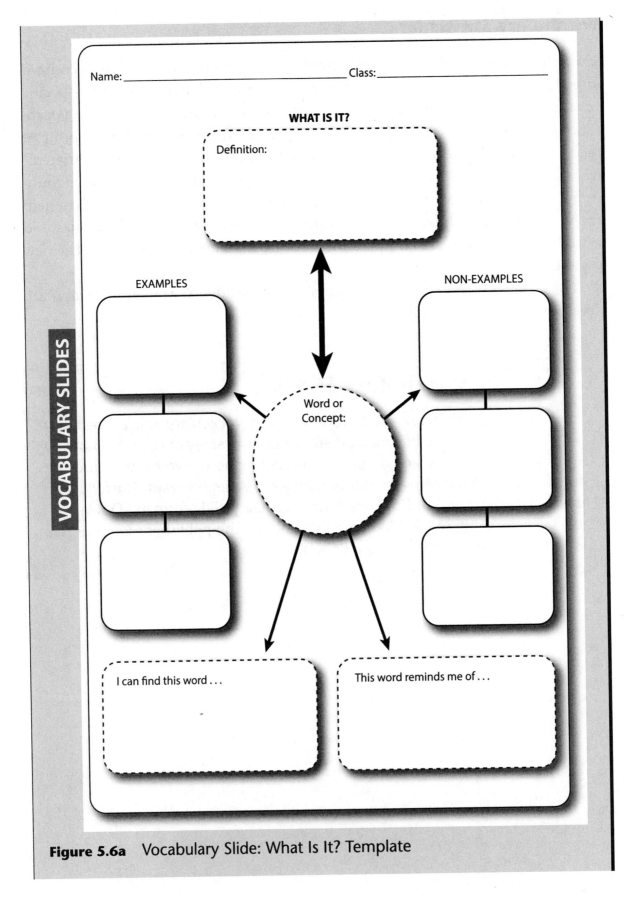

VOCABULARY SLIDES

Name: _____ Class: _____

WHAT IS IT?

Definition:

EXAMPLES

NON-EXAMPLES

Word or Concept:

I can find this word . . .

This word reminds me of . . .

Figure 5.6a   Vocabulary Slide: What Is It? Template

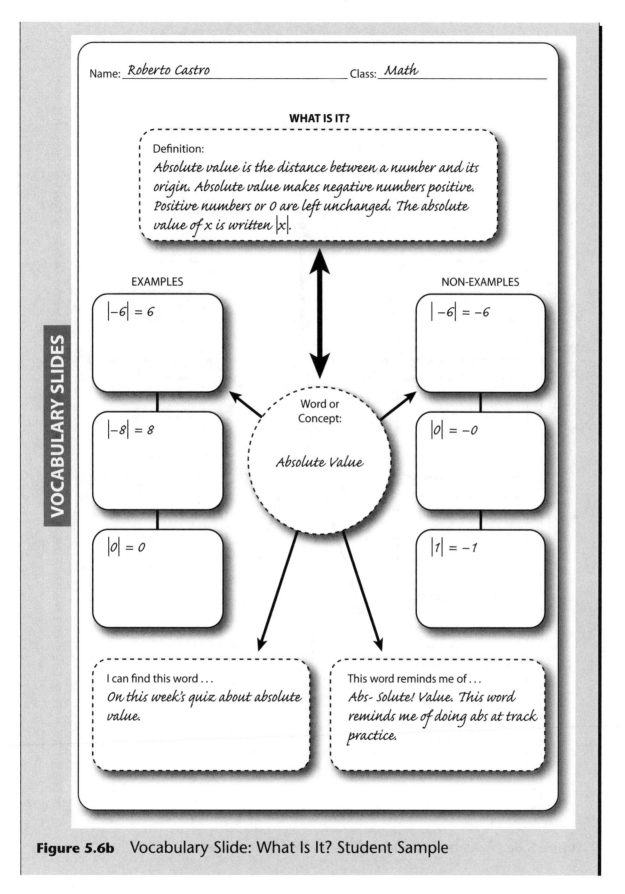

VOCABULARY SLIDES

Name: _Roberto Castro_   Class: _Math_

WHAT IS IT?

Definition:
Absolute value is the distance between a number and its origin. Absolute value makes negative numbers positive. Positive numbers or 0 are left unchanged. The absolute value of x is written |x|.

EXAMPLES

$|-6| = 6$

$|-8| = 8$

$|0| = 0$

Word or Concept:

Absolute Value

NON-EXAMPLES

$|-6| = -6$

$|0| = -0$

$|1| = -1$

I can find this word . . .
On this week's quiz about absolute value.

This word reminds me of . . .
Abs- Solute! Value. This word reminds me of doing abs at track practice.

Figure 5.6b Vocabulary Slide: What Is It? Student Sample

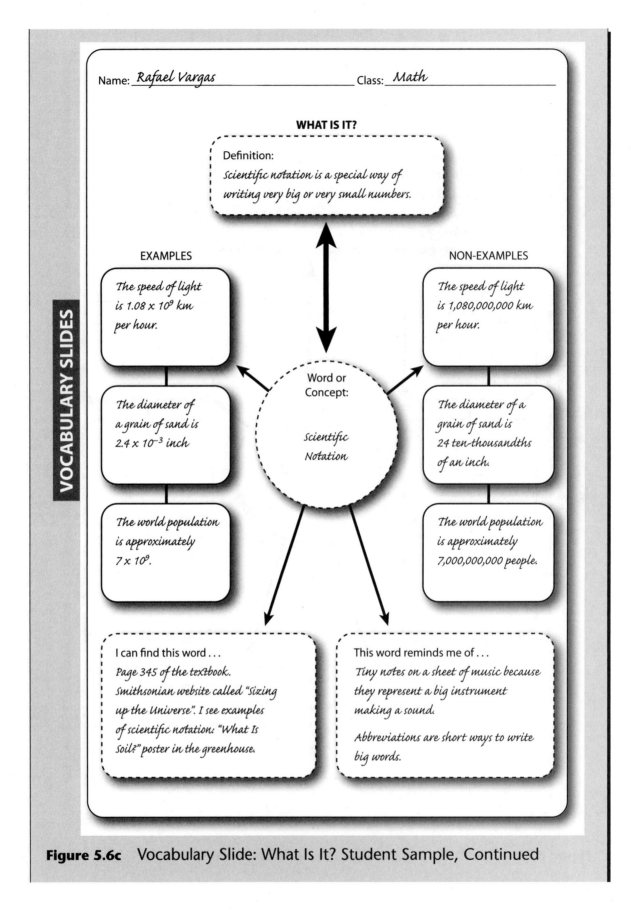

VOCABULARY SLIDES

Name: *Rafael Vargas* Class: *Math*

WHAT IS IT?

Definition:
Scientific notation is a special way of writing very big or very small numbers.

EXAMPLES

The speed of light is 1.08×10^9 km per hour.

The diameter of a grain of sand is 2.4×10^{-3} inch

The world population is approximately 7×10^9.

Word or Concept:

Scientific Notation

NON-EXAMPLES

The speed of light is 1,080,000,000 km per hour.

The diameter of a grain of sand is 24 ten-thousandths of an inch.

The world population is approximately 7,000,000,000 people.

I can find this word . . .
Page 345 of the textbook. Smithsonian website called "Sizing up the Universe". I see examples of scientific notation: "What Is Soil?" poster in the greenhouse.

This word reminds me of . . .
Tiny notes on a sheet of music because they represent a big instrument making a sound.

Abbreviations are short ways to write big words.

Figure 5.6c Vocabulary Slide: What Is It? Student Sample, Continued

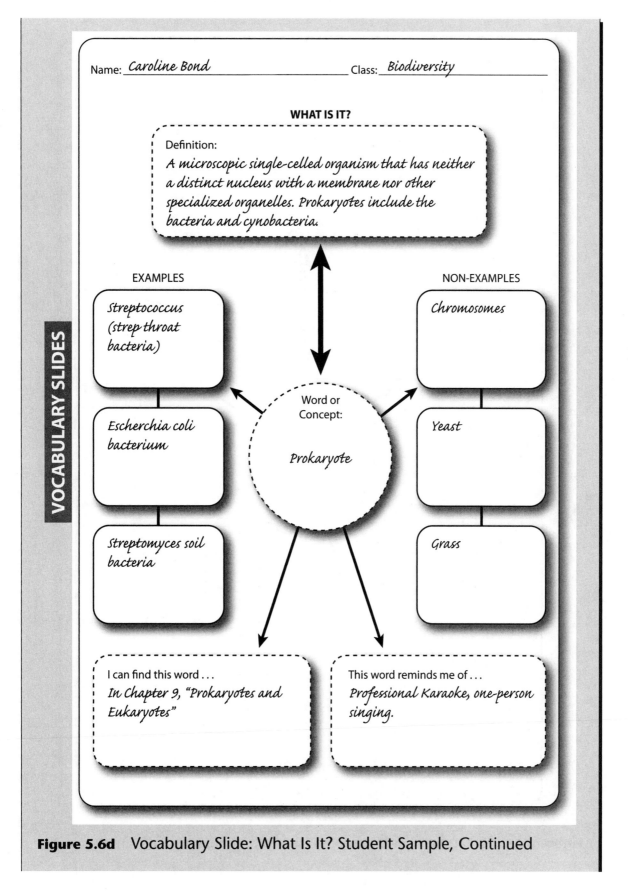

VOCABULARY SLIDES

Name: Caroline Bond   Class: Biodiversity

WHAT IS IT?

Definition:
A microscopic single-celled organism that has neither a distinct nucleus with a membrane nor other specialized organelles. Prokaryotes include the bacteria and cynobacteria.

EXAMPLES

Streptococcus (strep throat bacteria)

Escherchia coli bacterium

Streptomyces soil bacteria

Word or Concept:

Prokaryote

NON-EXAMPLES

Chromosomes

Yeast

Grass

I can find this word . . .
In Chapter 9, "Prokaryotes and Eukaryotes"

This word reminds me of . . .
Professional Karaoke, one-person singing.

Figure 5.6d Vocabulary Slide: What Is It? Student Sample, Continued

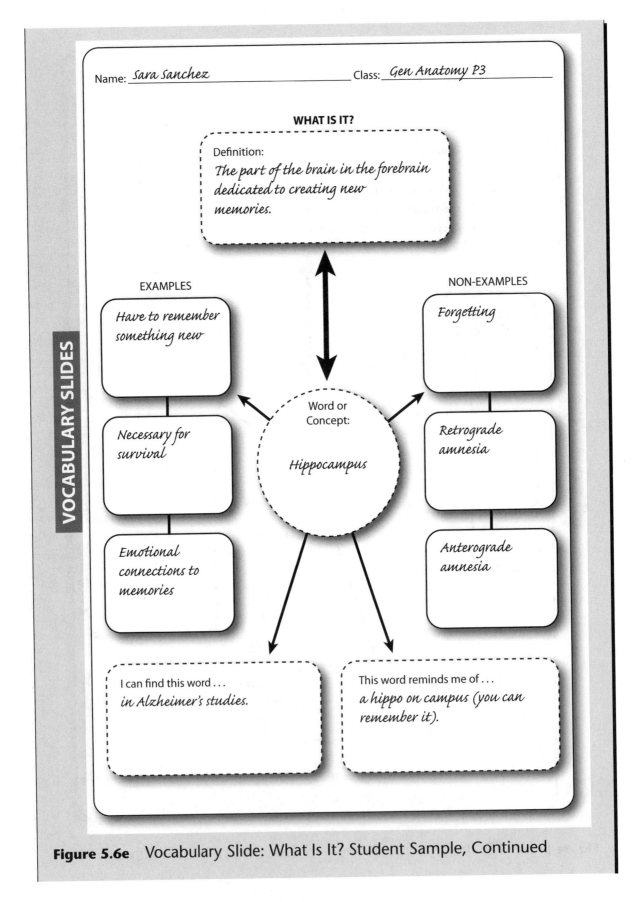

Figure 5.6e Vocabulary Slide: What Is It? Student Sample, Continued

VOCABULARY SLIDES

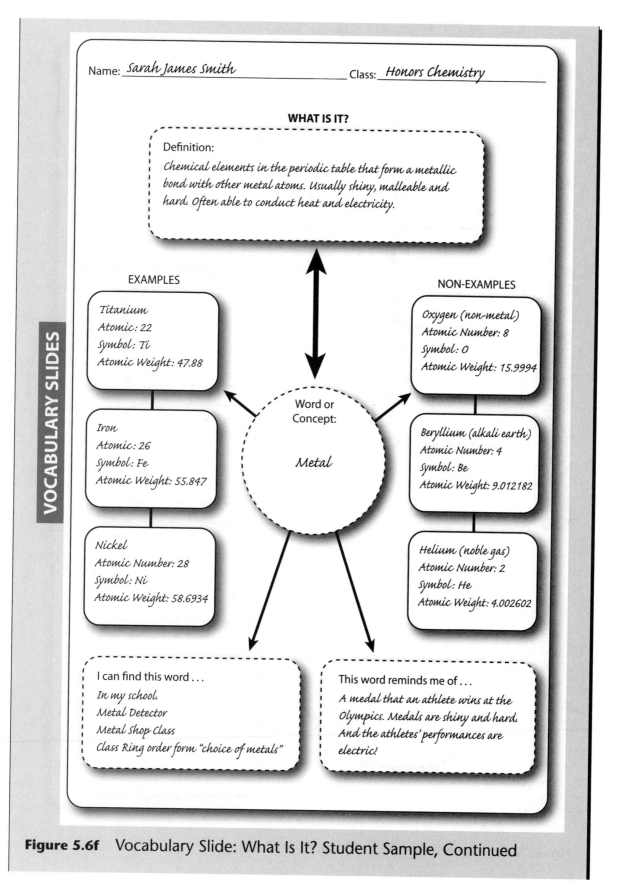

Name: _Sarah James Smith_   Class: _Honors Chemistry_

WHAT IS IT?

Definition:
Chemical elements in the periodic table that form a metallic bond with other metal atoms. Usually shiny, malleable and hard. Often able to conduct heat and electricity.

EXAMPLES

Titanium
Atomic: 22
Symbol: Ti
Atomic Weight: 47.88

Iron
Atomic: 26
Symbol: Fe
Atomic Weight: 55.847

Nickel
Atomic Number: 28
Symbol: Ni
Atomic Weight: 58.6934

Word or Concept:

Metal

NON-EXAMPLES

Oxygen (non-metal)
Atomic Number: 8
Symbol: O
Atomic Weight: 15.9994

Beryllium (alkali earth)
Atomic Number: 4
Symbol: Be
Atomic Weight: 9.012182

Helium (noble gas)
Atomic Number: 2
Symbol: He
Atomic Weight: 4.002602

I can find this word . . .
In my school.
Metal Detector
Metal Shop Class
Class Ring order form "choice of metals"

This word reminds me of . . .
A medal that an athlete wins at the Olympics. Medals are shiny and hard. And the athletes' performances are electric!

Figure 5.6f   Vocabulary Slide: What Is It? Student Sample, Continued

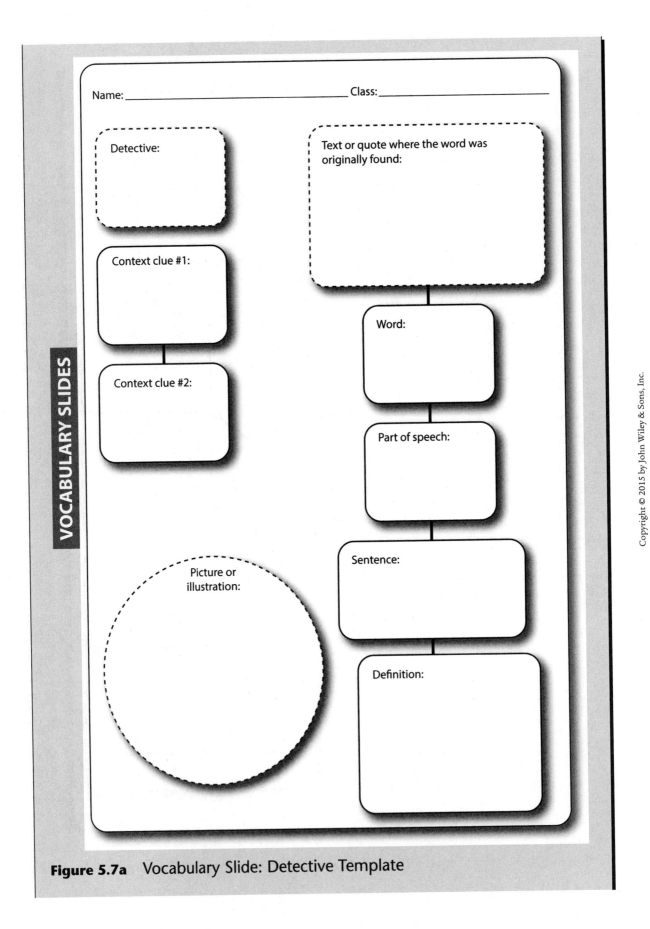

VOCABULARY SLIDES

Name: _____ Class: _____

Detective:

Text or quote where the word was originally found:

Context clue #1:

Context clue #2:

Word:

Part of speech:

Picture or illustration:

Sentence:

Definition:

Figure 5.7a Vocabulary Slide: Detective Template

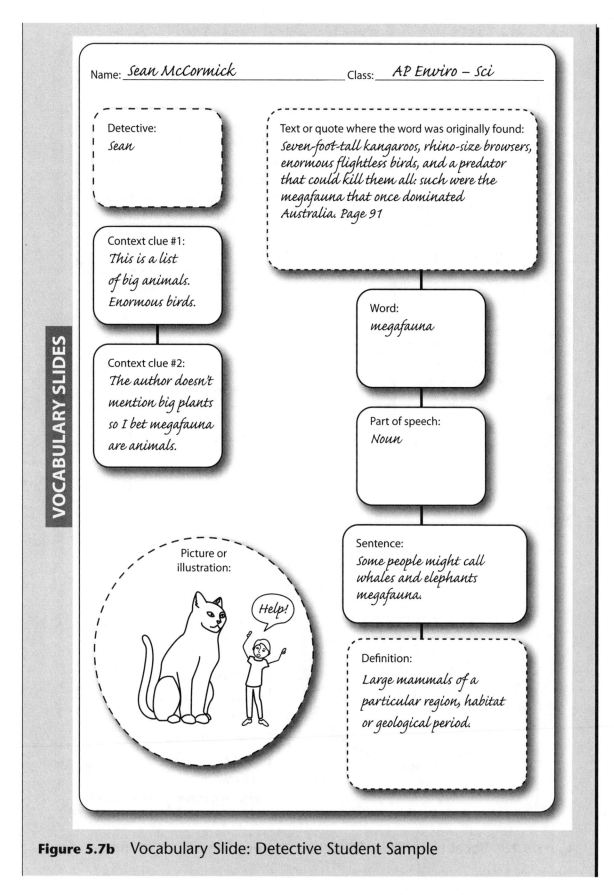

VOCABULARY SLIDES

Name: _Sean McCormick_   Class: _AP Enviro – Sci_

Detective:
Sean

Context clue #1:
This is a list
of big animals.
Enormous birds.

Context clue #2:
The author doesn't
mention big plants
so I bet megafauna
are animals.

Text or quote where the word was originally found:
Seven-foot-tall kangaroos, rhino-size browsers,
enormous flightless birds, and a predator
that could kill them all: such were the
megafauna that once dominated
Australia. Page 91

Word:
megafauna

Part of speech:
Noun

Sentence:
Some people might call
whales and elephants
megafauna.

Picture or
illustration:

Help!

Definition:
Large mammals of a
particular region, habitat
or geological period.

Figure 5.7b   Vocabulary Slide: Detective Student Sample

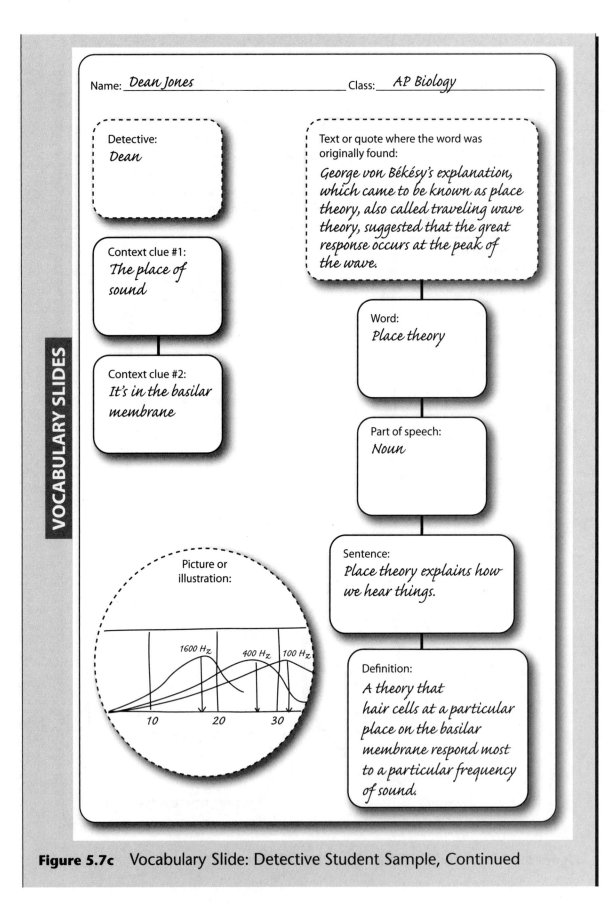

Figure 5.7c Vocabulary Slide: Detective Student Sample, Continued

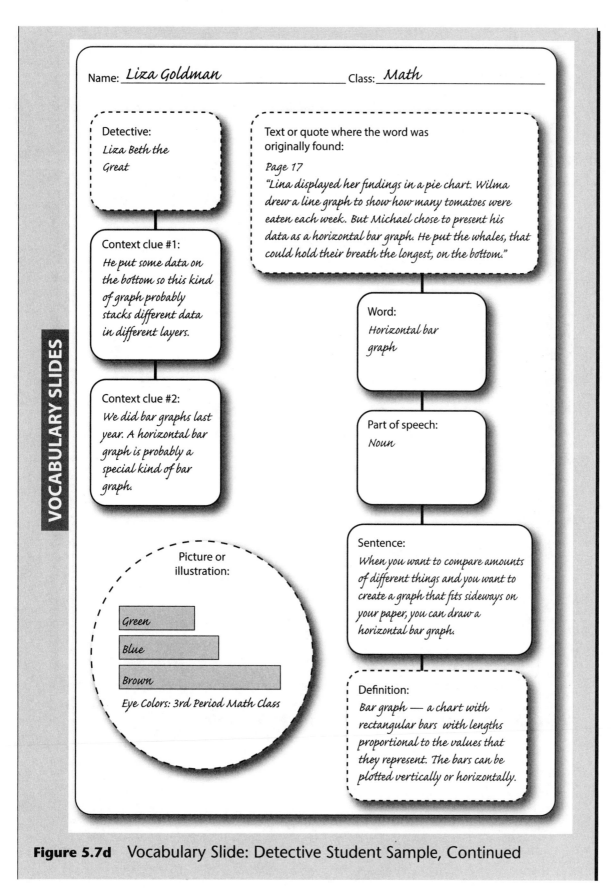

VOCABULARY SLIDES

Name: *Liza Goldman* Class: *Math*

Detective:
Liza Beth the Great

Context clue #1:
He put some data on the bottom so this kind of graph probably stacks different data in different layers.

Context clue #2:
We did bar graphs last year. A horizontal bar graph is probably a special kind of bar graph.

Text or quote where the word was originally found:

Page 17
"Lina displayed her findings in a pie chart. Wilma drew a line graph to show how many tomatoes were eaten each week. But Michael chose to present his data as a horizontal bar graph. He put the whales, that could hold their breath the longest, on the bottom."

Word:
Horizontal bar graph

Part of speech:
Noun

Sentence:
When you want to compare amounts of different things and you want to create a graph that fits sideways on your paper, you can draw a horizontal bar graph.

Picture or illustration:

Green
Blue
Brown

Eye Colors: 3rd Period Math Class

Definition:
Bar graph — a chart with rectangular bars with lengths proportional to the values that they represent. The bars can be plotted vertically or horizontally.

Figure 5.7d Vocabulary Slide: Detective Student Sample, Continued

VOCABULARY SLIDES

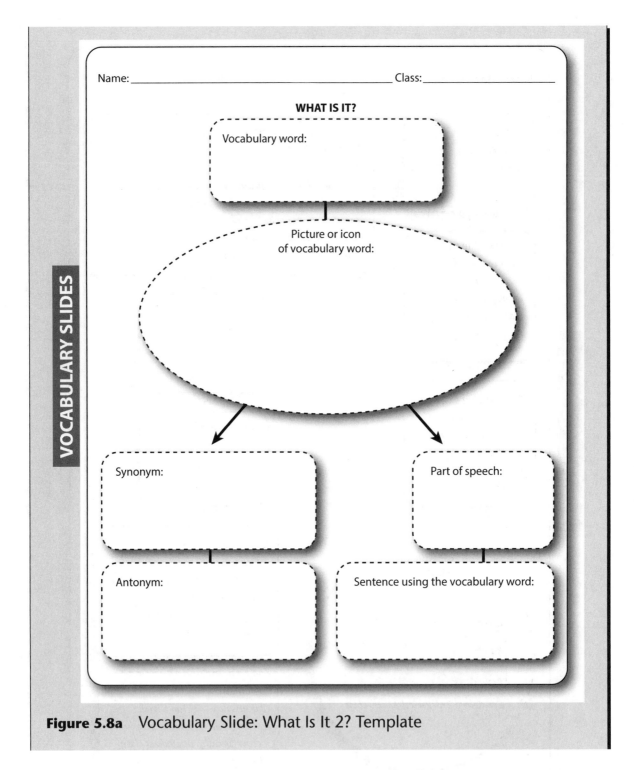

Name: _____   Class: _____

WHAT IS IT?

Vocabulary word:

Picture or icon
of vocabulary word:

Synonym:

Part of speech:

Antonym:

Sentence using the vocabulary word:

Figure 5.8a   Vocabulary Slide: What Is It 2? Template

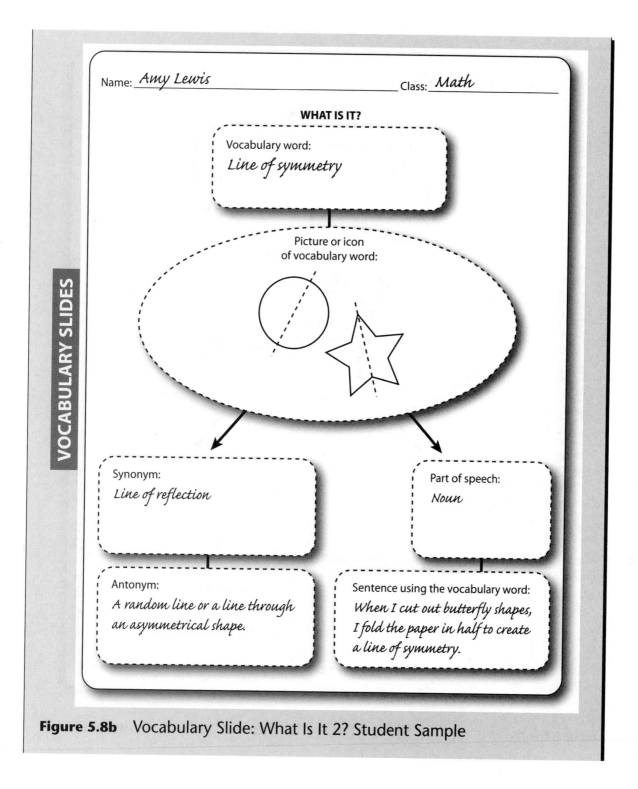

WHAT IS IT?

Vocabulary word:

Line of symmetry

Picture or icon
of vocabulary word:

Synonym:

Line of reflection

Part of speech:

Noun

Antonym:

A random line or a line through an asymmetrical shape.

Sentence using the vocabulary word:

When I cut out butterfly shapes, I fold the paper in half to create a line of symmetry.

Name: *Amy Lewis*   Class: *Math*

VOCABULARY SLIDES

Figure 5.8b   Vocabulary Slide: What Is It 2? Student Sample

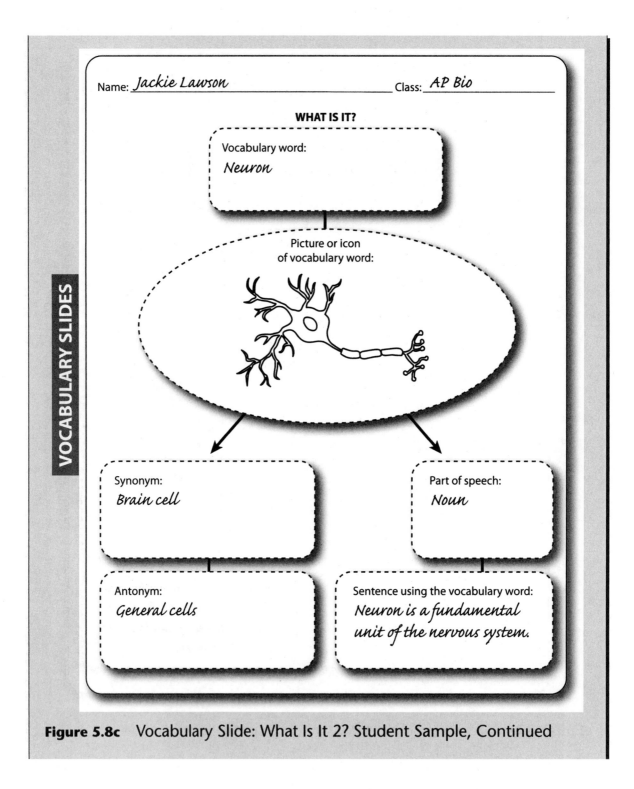

WHAT IS IT?

Name: *Jackie Lawson*   Class: *AP Bio*

Vocabulary word:
Neuron

Picture or icon
of vocabulary word:

Synonym:
Brain cell

Antonym:
General cells

Part of speech:
Noun

Sentence using the vocabulary word:
*Neuron is a fundamental
unit of the nervous system.*

Figure 5.8c Vocabulary Slide: What Is It 2? Student Sample, Continued

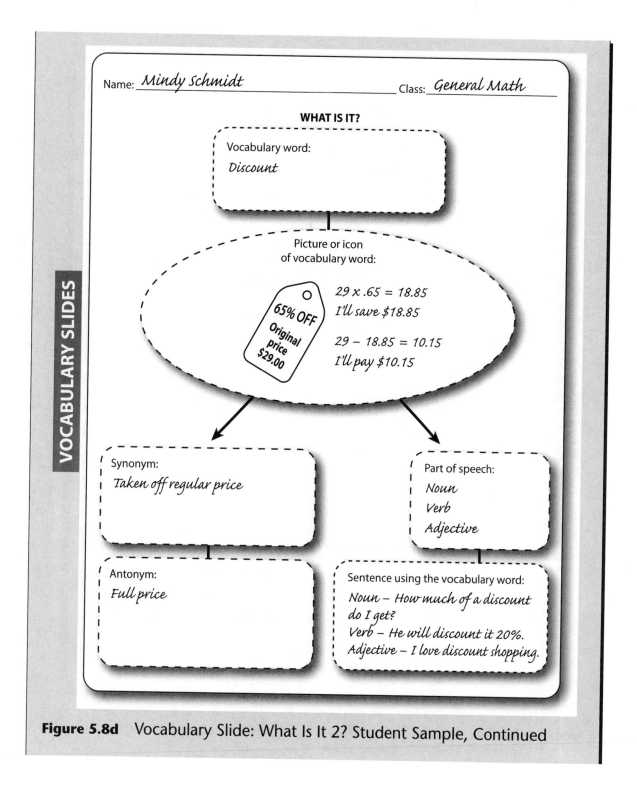

VOCABULARY SLIDES

Name: _Mindy Schmidt_   Class: _General Math_

WHAT IS IT?

Vocabulary word:

Discount

Picture or icon
of vocabulary word:

65% OFF
Original
price
$29.00

_29 x .65 = 18.85_
I'll save $18.85

_29 − 18.85 = 10.15_
I'll pay $10.15

Synonym:
Taken off regular price

Part of speech:
Noun
Verb
Adjective

Antonym:
Full price

Sentence using the vocabulary word:
Noun – How much of a discount do I get?
Verb – He will discount it 20%.
Adjective – I love discount shopping.

Figure 5.8d   Vocabulary Slide: What Is It 2? Student Sample, Continued

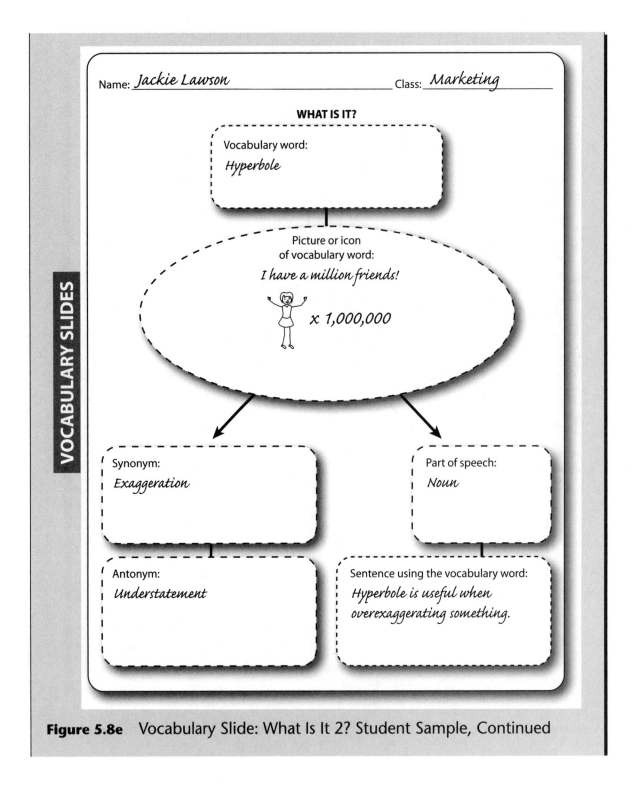

VOCABULARY SLIDES

Name: *Jackie Lawson*   Class: *Marketing*

WHAT IS IT?

Vocabulary word:
Hyperbole

Picture or icon
of vocabulary word:
I have a million friends!

x 1,000,000

Synonym:
Exaggeration

Part of speech:
Noun

Antonym:
Understatement

Sentence using the vocabulary word:
Hyperbole is useful when overexaggerating something.

Figure 5.8e   Vocabulary Slide: What Is It 2? Student Sample, Continued

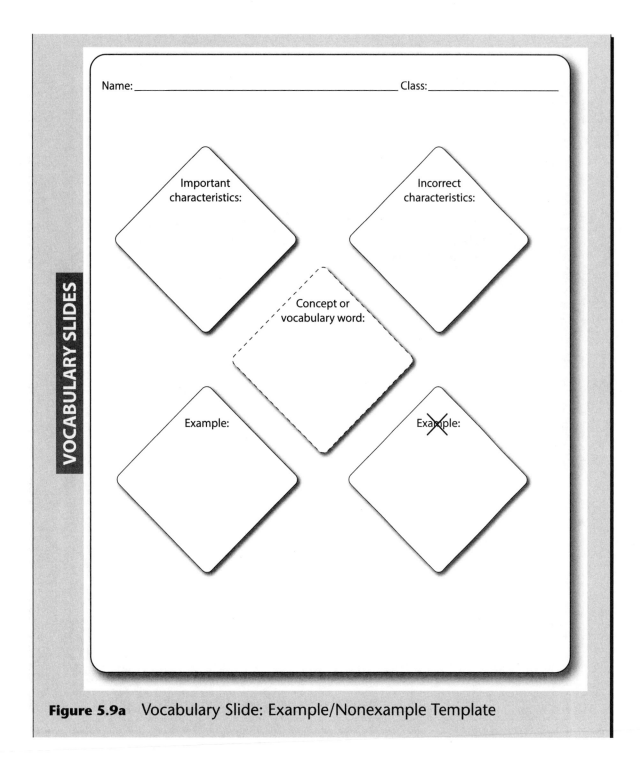

Name: _____ Class: _____

Important characteristics:

Incorrect characteristics:

Concept or vocabulary word:

Example:

Example:

Figure 5.9a Vocabulary Slide: Example/Nonexample Template

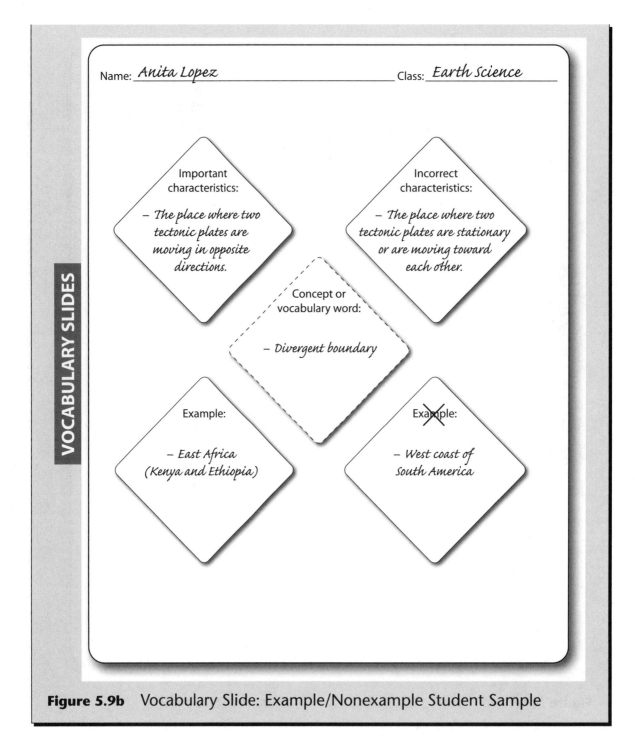

Name: _Anita Lopez_   Class: _Earth Science_

Important characteristics:

– The place where two tectonic plates are moving in opposite directions.

Incorrect characteristics:

– The place where two tectonic plates are stationary or are moving toward each other.

Concept or vocabulary word:

– Divergent boundary

Example:

– East Africa (Kenya and Ethiopia)

Example:

– West coast of South America

Figure 5.9b   Vocabulary Slide: Example/Nonexample Student Sample

Vocabulary Organizer

The Vocabulary Organizer is a learning log that catalogues vocabulary words and terminology. This is particularly helpful when students encounter many new words and terms (for instance, *polygons*, *systems of government*, or *cell structure*). This activity can be the basis for a learning center, with students working together in groups to come up with synonyms, antonyms, and pictures for each new word. A handout you can use follows in figure 5.10. Again, you can find a downloadable version of this template on the publisher's website; check appendix A for access information.

Name: _____ Class: _____

WORD/TERM	DEFINITION	SYNONYM	ANTONYM	PICTURE OF WORD

VOCABULARY ORGANIZER

Figure 5.10a Vocabulary Organizer Template

Name: _Frank Johnson_   Class: _Anatomy and Physiology_

VOCABULARY ORGANIZER

WORD/TERM	DEFINITION	SYNONYM	ANTONYM	PICTURE OF WORD
placebo	treatment that contains no active ingredient but produces an effect	false treatment	treatment/ medicine with an ingredient	pill with no ingredient
independent variable	variable manipulated by researcher in an experiment	items that are changed/ altered	dependent variable	independent dependent
mean	measure of central tendency, that is, the average inset of data	average	maximum	1 2 (3) 4 5
dendrite	neuron fiber that receives signals from axons	messenger for the cell	message blocker	
axon	neuron fiber that carries signals from neuron to other neuron	neuron messenger	message blocker	
glial cell	cell in nervous system that holds neurons together	neuron glue	drugs and alcohol	GLUE
myelin	fatty substance that wraps around some axons and increases the speed of action potential	blanket	speed decreaser	
synapse	tiny gap between neurons across which they communicate	communication gap	close contact; no communication	
central nervous system	parts of the nervous system encased in bone (i.e., brain and spine)	control of body	nonresponsive	
motor systems	parts of nervous system that influence muscles to respond to environment	movement control	stagnant	
reflex	involuntary reaction in form of swift movements	automatic reaction	purposeful movement	

Figure 5.10b   Vocabulary Organizer Student Sample

Name: _Jackson Miller_   Class: _Math_

WORD/TERM	DEFINITION	SYNONYM	ANTONYM	PICTURE OF WORD
quantitative data	measures of values or counts	measurable	qualitative data	How many lemons are in the lemonade?
qualitative	measures of "types"	conditional or dependent	quantitative	Is it lemonade? ☒ yes ☐ no
outlier	value that lies outside most others in set	aberration or quirk	normal	outlier
median	middle value in a list of #s		average mean	1, 3, ⑦, 9, 10,

Figure 5.10c   Vocabulary Organizer Student Sample, Continued

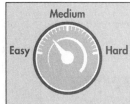

List-Group-Label

Drawing meaningful connections between words helps students to understand and learn new vocabulary. Here's how the activity works (see figure 5.11):

1. Have students read a selected passage.

2. Instruct the students to **list** all of the words they think are important from the passage.

3. Direct students, in pairs or groups of three to four, to **group** similar words.

4. Once students have grouped the words, instruct students to provide a **label** for each group that reveals the reasoning behind the grouping.

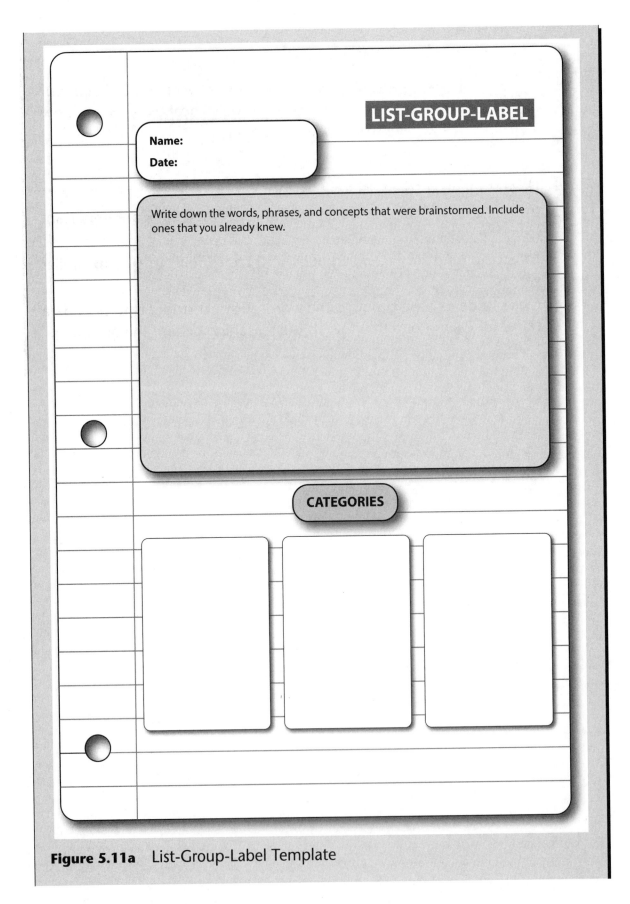

Figure 5.11a List-Group-Label Template

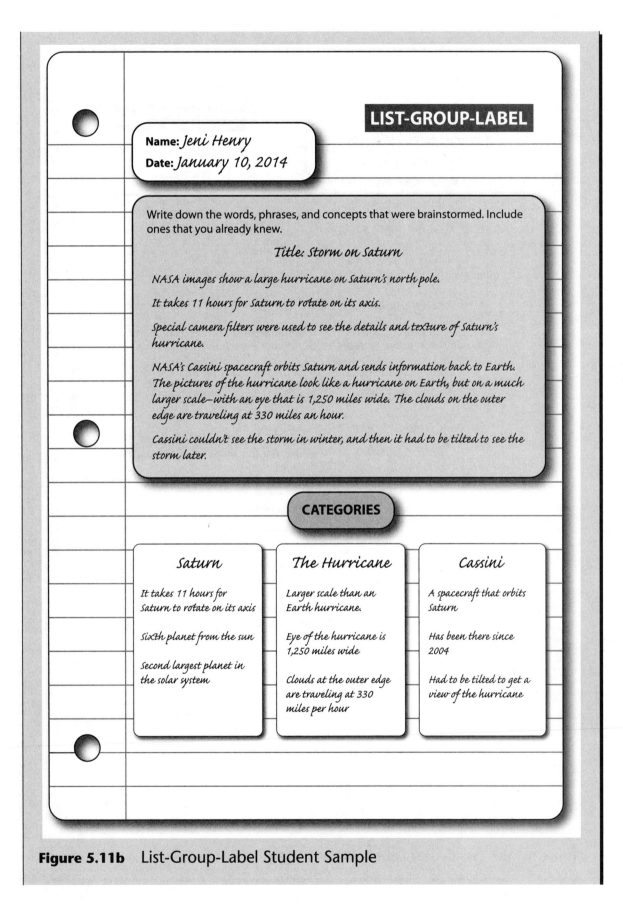

LIST-GROUP-LABEL

Name: *Jeni Henry*
Date: *January 10, 2014*

Write down the words, phrases, and concepts that were brainstormed. Include ones that you already knew.

Title: Storm on Saturn

NASA images show a large hurricane on Saturn's north pole.

It takes 11 hours for Saturn to rotate on its axis.

Special camera filters were used to see the details and texture of Saturn's hurricane.

NASA's Cassini spacecraft orbits Saturn and sends information back to Earth. The pictures of the hurricane look like a hurricane on Earth, but on a much larger scale—with an eye that is 1,250 miles wide. The clouds on the outer edge are traveling at 330 miles an hour.

Cassini couldn't see the storm in winter, and then it had to be tilted to see the storm later.

CATEGORIES

Saturn	*The Hurricane*	*Cassini*
It takes 11 hours for Saturn to rotate on its axis	*Larger scale than an Earth hurricane.*	*A spacecraft that orbits Saturn*
Sixth planet from the sun	*Eye of the hurricane is 1,250 miles wide*	*Has been there since 2004*
Second largest planet in the solar system	*Clouds at the outer edge are traveling at 330 miles per hour*	*Had to be tilted to get a view of the hurricane*

Figure 5.11b   List-Group-Label Student Sample

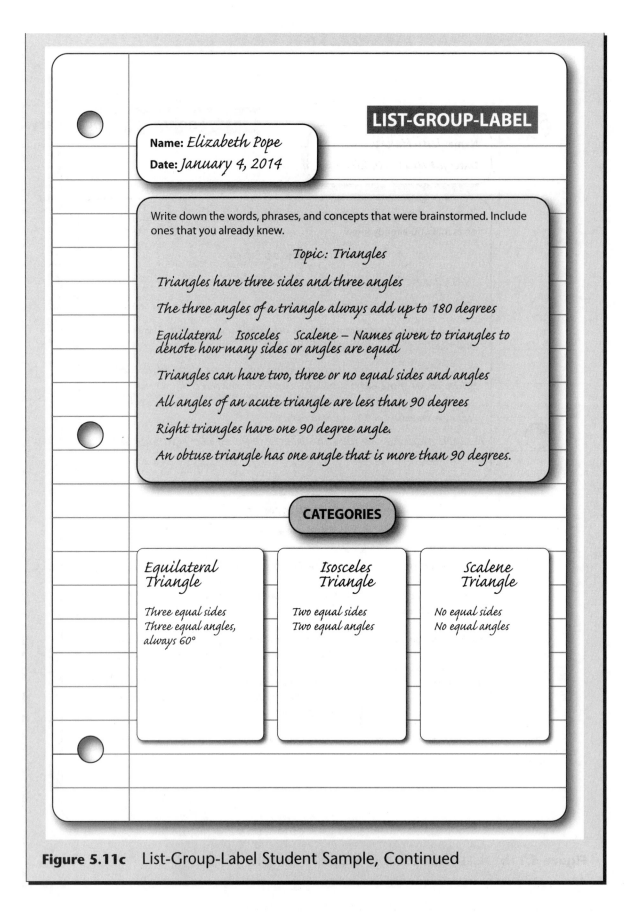

LIST-GROUP-LABEL

Name: Elizabeth Pope
Date: January 4, 2014

Write down the words, phrases, and concepts that were brainstormed. Include ones that you already knew.

Topic: Triangles

Triangles have three sides and three angles

The three angles of a triangle always add up to 180 degrees

Equilateral   Isosceles   Scalene – Names given to triangles to denote how many sides or angles are equal

Triangles can have two, three or no equal sides and angles

All angles of an acute triangle are less than 90 degrees

Right triangles have one 90 degree angle.

An obtuse triangle has one angle that is more than 90 degrees.

CATEGORIES

Equilateral
Triangle

Three equal sides
Three equal angles,
always 60°

Isosceles
Triangle

Two equal sides
Two equal angles

Scalene
Triangle

No equal sides
No equal angles

Figure 5.11c List-Group-Label Student Sample, Continued

WHY VISUALIZATION MATTERS

Visualizing words and their meanings is critical to the internalization of new language. It gets particularly challenging to internalize new vocabulary when students are learning high-level discipline-specific terminology and vocabulary. Mathematics and science content is rich in this kind of vocabulary and terminology. Making understanding and comprehension visible supports a student's internalization of new material. I am sure that you noticed that many of the vocabulary strategies in this chapter require students to create nonlinguistic, or visual, representations of discipline-specific meanings and the concepts. Brooke McCray, a middle school teacher in Indianapolis, uses many vocabulary visualizations in the teaching of her content area, biology.

McCray often remarks that the students have to possess a deep understanding of the vocabulary in order to create a visualization. In the following examples, she and her students were studying organelles and cells. She often requires her students to draw and create analogies about the new concepts and vocabulary. It provides a perfect opportunity to check students' grasp of the material, uncover misunderstandings, and improve communication.

In figure 5.12, the student demonstrated an understanding of the role of endoplasmic reticulum. Mini-lessons like Capitalizing Capitalization and Defragging Sentences would empower this student to create a project that clearly communicates that comprehension to a wider audience.

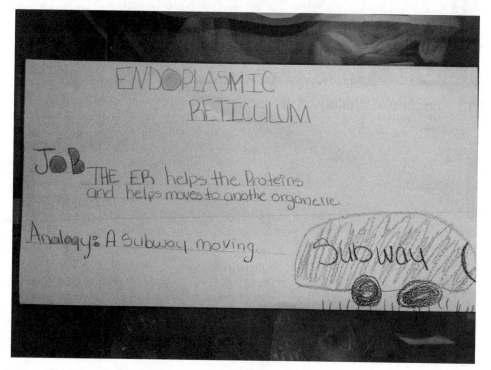

Figure 5.12   Organelle Analogy: Endoplasmic Reticulum

Sometimes the student's choice of analogy is unclear. Does this student who drew figure 5.13 really understand the role of lysosomes? In order to use this exercise as an effective formative assessment, the teacher will want to ask for clarification. For example, a compost container or recycling bin can be said to function like lysosomes, while a container of nonrecyclables, destined for a landfill, serves a different function. If the student's understanding is imprecise, further explanation is in order. A mini-lesson in sentence structure (see figures 5.2 to 5.4), punctuation, and capitalization would help the student communicate with more precision.

Figure 5.13   Organelle Analogy: Lysosomes

The student who drew figure 5.14 clearly understands Golgi apparatus and its function. Notice the cartoon illustration of a "Peanut Burglar" trying to look casual while packing up stolen goods and removing them. The combination of humor and specificity is an indication of solid comprehension. Encouraging this student to use spelling resources like dictionaries, textbook glossaries, and online sources would help him or her communicate even more clearly. This could easily be accomplished as part of a Vocabulary Slide exercise (see figures 5.6 to 5.9)

Figure 5.14   Organelle Analogy: Golgi Apparatus

The student's choice of analogy in figure 5.15 is unclear. Does the student think the knife or the halved sandwich is analogous to the function of centrioles? Or does he or she believe that the *action* of cutting the sandwich into two evenly sized pieces and the *action* of the river flowing into two branches are accurate representations of a centrioles function? Because this is a complicated concept for students to grasp, the teacher will want to confirm accurate understanding. If this student continues to explore his or her assigned word through one of the Vocabulary Slides (see figures 5.6 to 5.9), there's a good chance he or she will catch the spelling error in figure 5.15 before doing a final draft.

Figure 5.15   Organelle Analogy: Centrioles

Figure 5.16 is a great example of combining visualization and the writing of narrative text in a content area class. In this two-part exercise, the student shows an understanding of the parts of a cell and illustrates it through a hand-drawn graphic (figure 5.16a). The student's narrative paragraph (figure 5.16b) provides ample opportunity to

▶ *Demonstrate command of the conventions of standard English grammar and usage when writing or speaking. (CCR.L.1)*

▶ *Demonstrate command of the conventions of standard English capitalization, punctuation, and spelling when writing. (CCR.L.2)*

▶ *Acquire and use accurately a range of general academic and domain-specific words and phrases sufficient for reading, writing, speaking, and listening at the college and career readiness level; demonstrate independence in gathering vocabulary knowledge when considering a word or phrase important to comprehension or expression. (CCR.L.6)*

▶ *Write narratives to develop real or imagined experiences or events using effective technique, well-chosen details, and well-structured event sequences. (CCR.W.3)*

▶ *Produce clear and coherent writing in which the development, organization, and style are appropriate to task, purpose, and audience. (CCR.W.4)*

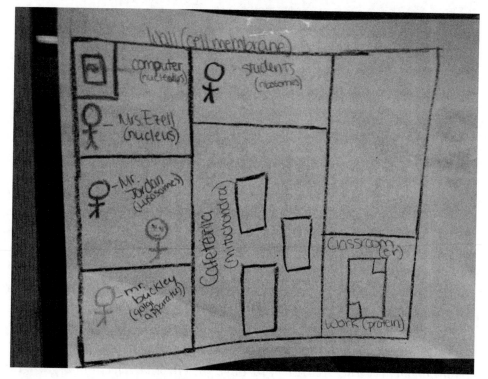

Figure 5.16a   Cell/School Analogy

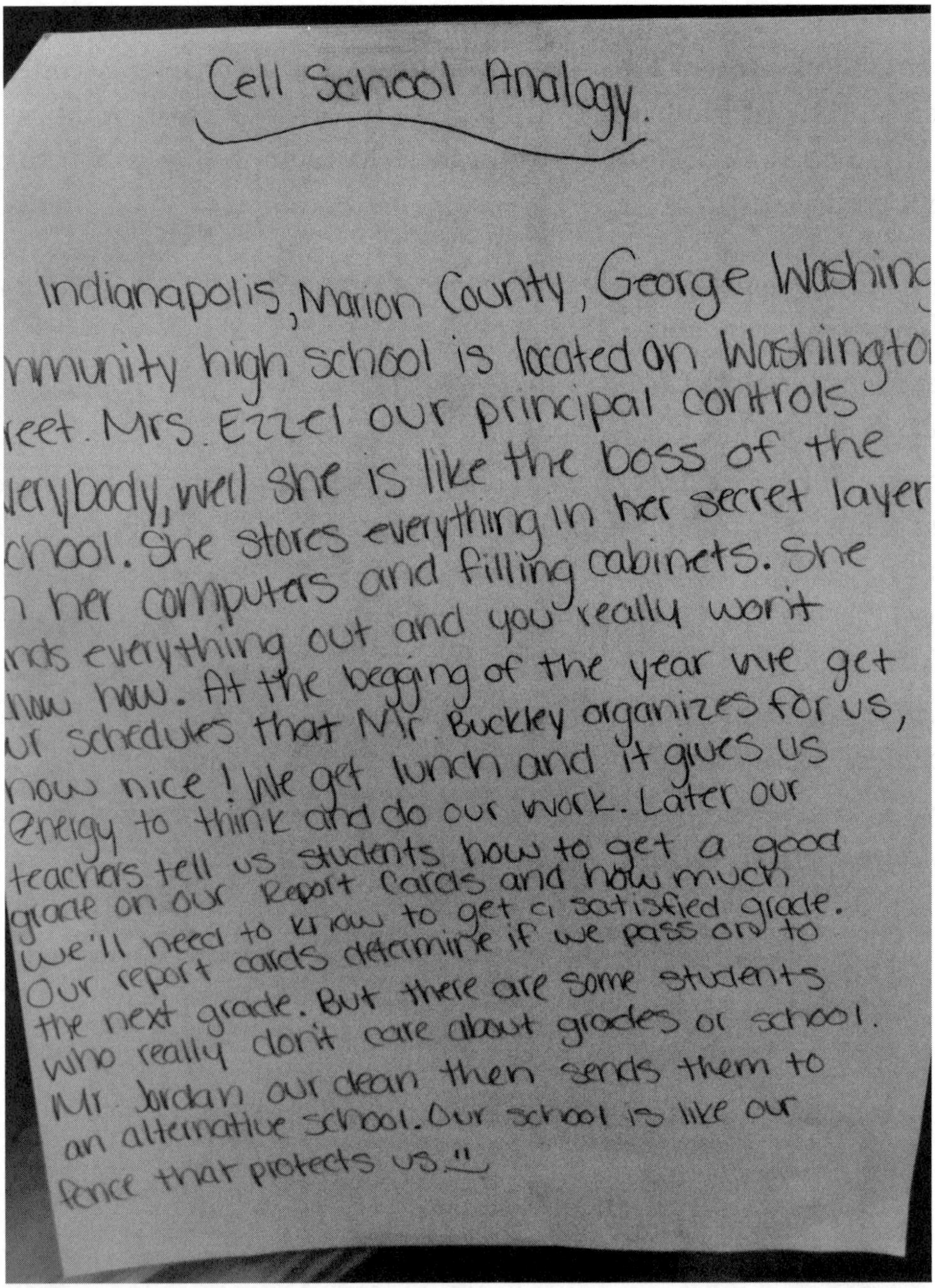

Cell School Analogy.

Indianapolis, Marion County, George Washing[ton] [Co]mmunity high school is located on Washingto[n] [St]reet. Mrs. Ezzel our principal controls [ev]erybody, well she is like the boss of the [s]chool. She stores everything in her secret layer [i]n her computers and filling cabinets. She [se]nds everything out and you really won't [kn]ow how. At the begging of the year we get [o]ur schedules that Mr. Buckley organizes for us, how nice! We get lunch and it gives us energy to think and do our work. Later our teachers tell us students how to get a good grade on our Report Cards and how much we'll need to know to get a satisfied grade. Our report cards determine if we pass on to the next grade. But there are some students who really don't care about grades or school. Mr. Jordan our dean then sends them to an alternative school. Our school is like our fence that protects us."

Figure 5.16b   Cell/School Analogy

Figure 5.17 is another example using visualization in conjunction with literacy skill development in a content area class. By limiting the writing requirement to one or two sentences, both the teacher and student have time to focus on mastery of content *and* address the student's ability to

▶ *Write informative/explanatory texts to examine and convey complex ideas and information clearly and accurately through the effective selection, organization, and analysis of content. (CCR.W.2)*

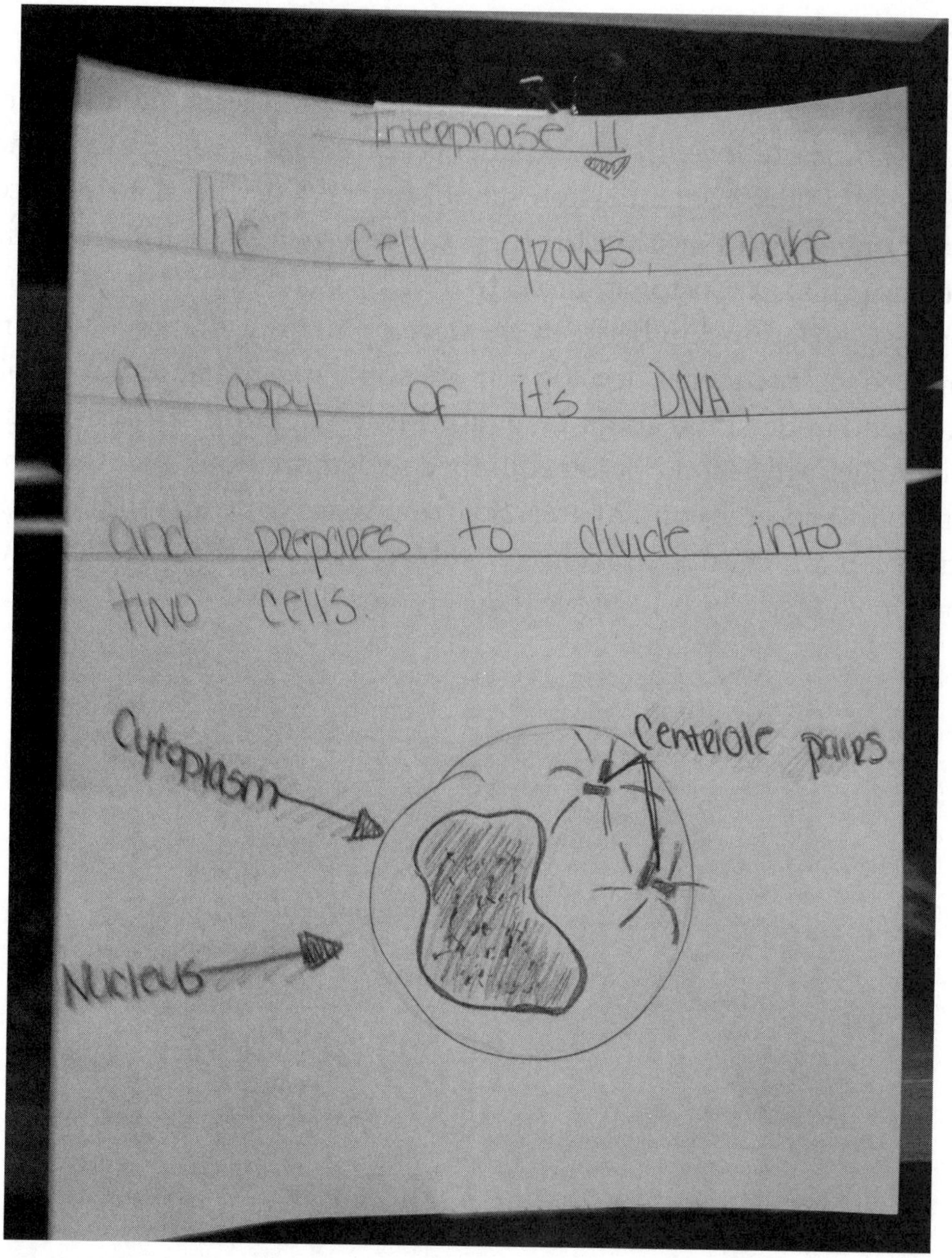

Figure 5.17 Cell Division Stage: Interphase

▶ *Demonstrate command of the conventions of standard English grammar and usage when writing or speaking. (CCR.L.1)*

▶ *Demonstrate command of the conventions of standard English capitalization, punctuation, and spelling when writing. (CCR.L.2)*

▶ *Acquire and use accurately a range of general academic and domain-specific words and phrases sufficient for reading, writing, speaking, and listening at the college and career readiness level; demonstrate independence in gathering vocabulary knowledge when considering a word or phrase important to comprehension or expression. (CCR.L.6)*

SOME FINAL THOUGHTS

I make no apologies that I want students to enjoy and learn about the content area that I so dearly love. In my experience, one of the top reasons that people become middle school and high school teachers is that they want to share their knowledge of and passion for their content area. I get it. Developing student literacy skills is a way for students to develop that content knowledge. There is a synergistic relationship between the development of literacy skills and content knowledge. If students develop a more sophisticated ability to apply what they know and understand about language through grammatical structures and vocabulary, they will become better equipped to demonstrate what they know and understand in a specific content area. So if you yearn for your students to appreciate science, mathematics, or technical subjects, one of the best things you can do is to help your students improve their literacy skills.

CHAPTER SIX

Learning Centers and Student-Centered Activities

In my work with schools and districts all over the United States as we transition to the Common Core State Standards, the comment I hear most often is, "The Common Core will change everything. Our classrooms are going to look completely different!"

Our classrooms must reflect these new expectations—particularly the expectation for students to apply literacy skills independently as a means to learn and deepen content knowledge and to express what they know and understand.

Yet the CCSS authors do not identify any specific strategy or curriculum as a means to meet the CCSS expectations. As a teacher, I crave **real** models. I need to know what a CCSS-friendly classroom looks like and what strategies are most effective in meeting these new demands.

What does a CCSS-friendly, twenty-first-century classroom look like? This question is exactly what this chapter is all about.

Although the CCSS authors do not identify specific instructional strategies or curriculum, several strategies are conducive to developing the skills that Common Core advocates for, including learning centers, literature circles, and text groups.

LEARNING CENTERS

We often think of learning centers as stations in K–3 classrooms. Learning centers are a valuable instructional strategy to build literacy skills and content knowledge with differentiated instructional support (Doyle, 2011).

I have used centers in middle school and high school classrooms in nearly every demographic context you could imagine: rural, urban, suburban, inclusive classrooms, self-contained classrooms for students with special needs, gifted, high-poverty, and ethnically diverse. Here's what I've discovered.

▶ When teenagers work in a center, they become more engaged.
▶ Students with special needs report that they feel "safer" in a small group. They like working with their classmates and are more willing to ask questions and participate. The students reveal that it's easier to focus and they enjoy and learn from their peers.

When I co-teach with the classroom teachers to demonstrate centers, they make comments like these:

▶ "I'm surprised at how focused the students have become."
▶ "We're able to cover more content and skill development in centers."
▶ "I can work individually with students in centers."

Honestly, even after using learning centers with middle and high school students for more than a decade, I'm continually amazed at what an effective strategy this can be for the classroom.

How to Get Started with Learning Centers

In my work in developing centers in multiple contexts, I've learned (the hard way) a few things that I'd like to share.

Group size: Keep groups to three to five students. Placing more than five students in a group will create some distraction and potential obstacles for the group.

Choice: At each center, when possible, give the students a choice. For example, at vocabulary centers, I provide two to three activities from which the students may choose.

Timing: Timing is often difficult, but I try to keep the work at the centers between ten and fifteen minutes long. Balancing the same amount of time at each center is challenging. This challenge led me to create a "makeup" station.

Makeup center: The makeup center is the last center for all of the students. It's not a location; it's a state of mind. Once students have completed all of the centers, they review, revise, and complete any unfinished center work. It has been my experience that students work at different paces, and we need to accommodate this reality.

Procedures: As middle school and high school teachers, we are well aware that adolescents' listening skills aren't the strongest. It's part of teenagers' charm. In response to this reality, it is advantageous to display written directions for each center. I also like to use posters at each center, and I have included some samples in this chapter.

Teach students how to move between the centers. When I introduce centers, I spend about five minutes on the first day directing students to practice movement between centers.

Suggestions for Centers

► **Vocabulary**: At this center, provide students with an activity where they can manipulate and work with words. For example, students can create Vocabulary Slides or use the List-Group-Label activity.

► **Reading**: Provide students with a variety of texts to read at this center. When possible, provide a variety of texts for the students to read. They can read silently, read together, or work on a reading strategy like SQ3R at this station.

► **Visualization**: We already know about the strong connections between visualization and comprehension (McKnight, 2010). Students can work on graphic organizers or create story boards or sequence trails at this center.

► **Listening or viewing center**: Use videos, audio recordings, and other media-based materials to teach students about content and to develop their skills in critical viewing.

As I suggested earlier, groups for the centers should be no larger than five students. Figure 6.1 shows some sample centers.

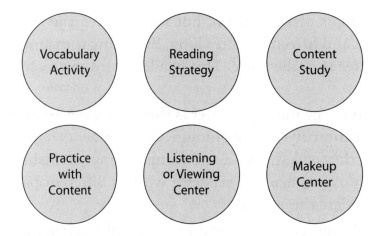

Figure 6.1   Sample Learning Centers

Figures 6.2 through 6.16 show examples of centers that I have used in classrooms. These templates are typically printed out, poster size, and hung around the classroom where students are meeting. (On this book's accompanying web page, www.wiley.com/go/ccliteracy2, you can download these templates to print them out for use in your own classroom.)

Learning Center Station: Vocabulary

Directions: Write or draw the vocabulary word in the center circle, and then follow the prompts to fill out the vocabulary map.

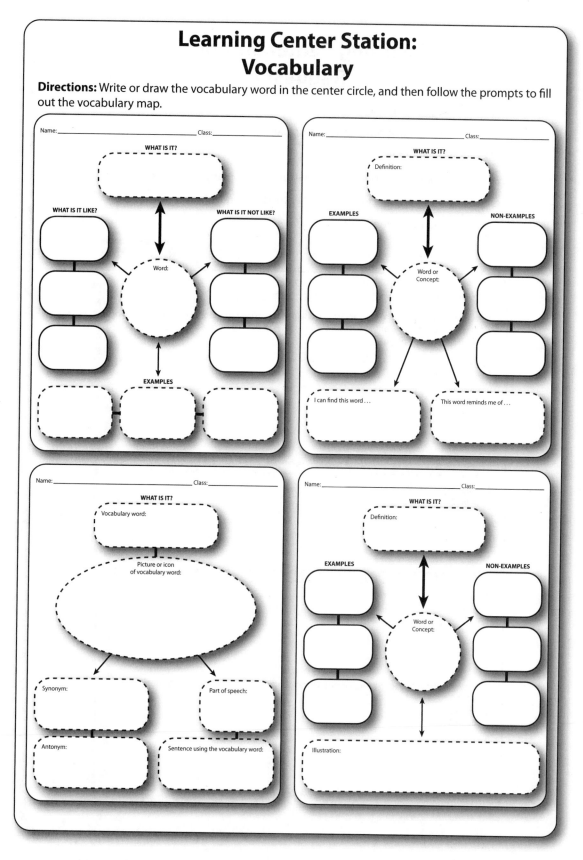

Figure 6.2 Learning Center Station: Vocabulary

Learning Center Station: Request

1. Preview text prior to reading.

2. Discuss background information and vocabulary.

3. Ask questions about the text.

4. Read to stopping point. Next, write down and ask as many questions as you can.

5. Close your book, it's time for your teacher to ask you questions.

6. Repeat for each stopping point.

REQUEST

Name: _____ Class: _____

Directions: Read the assigned text and stop reading as requested by your teacher. At each stopping point you will create questions to ask your teacher. Write down as many questions as you can. Do this for each stopping point.

Stopping point 1

Stopping point 2

Stopping point 3

Stopping point 4

Figure 6.3 Learning Center Station: Request

Learning Center Station:
Postcards

Directions: On the front of your postcard, illustrate a scene that you think is important. On the back of your postcard, explain what happened in the scene, and why you think it is important.

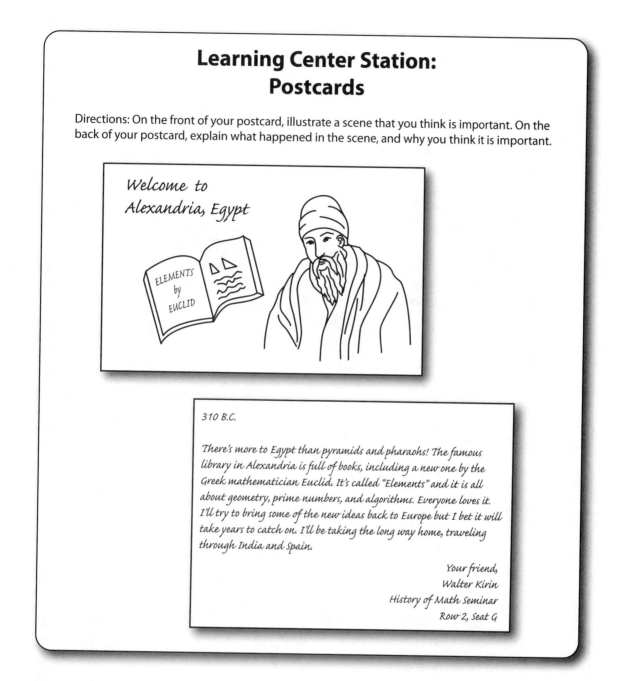

Figure 6.4a   Learning Center Station: Postcards Student Sample

Learning Center Station: Postcards

Directions: On the front of your postcard, illustrate a scene that you think is important. On the back of your postcard, explain what happened in the scene, and why you think it is important.

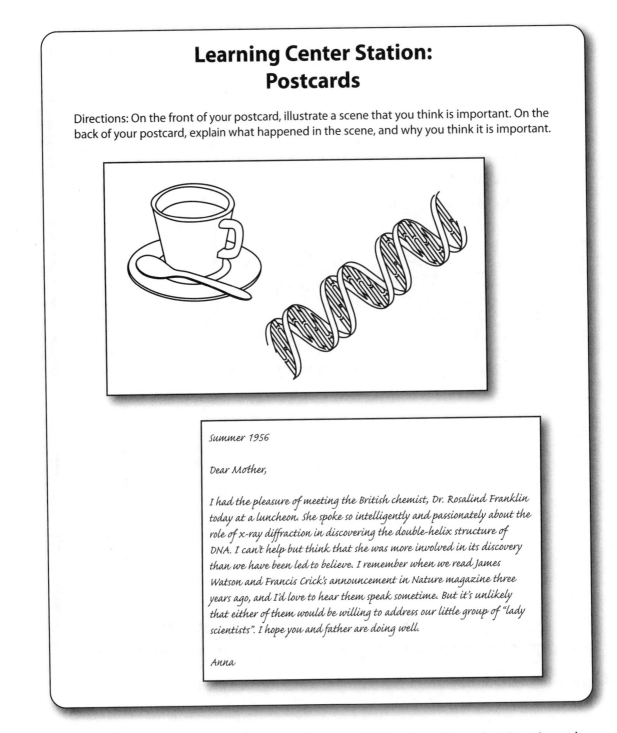

Summer 1956

Dear Mother,

I had the pleasure of meeting the British chemist, Dr. Rosalind Franklin today at a luncheon. She spoke so intelligently and passionately about the role of x-ray diffraction in discovering the double-helix structure of DNA. I can't help but think that she was more involved in its discovery than we have been led to believe. I remember when we read James Watson and Francis Crick's announcement in Nature magazine three years ago, and I'd love to hear them speak sometime. But it's unlikely that either of them would be willing to address our little group of "lady scientists". I hope you and father are doing well.

Anna

Figure 6.4b Learning Center Station: Postcards Student Sample, Continued

Learning Center Station: DRTA

The directed reading and thinking activity develops your purpose for reading a text.

This activity helps us become more active readers as questions are considered during reading.

When students use this activity, especially while reading textbooks, we can focus on the content, main ideas, and concepts.

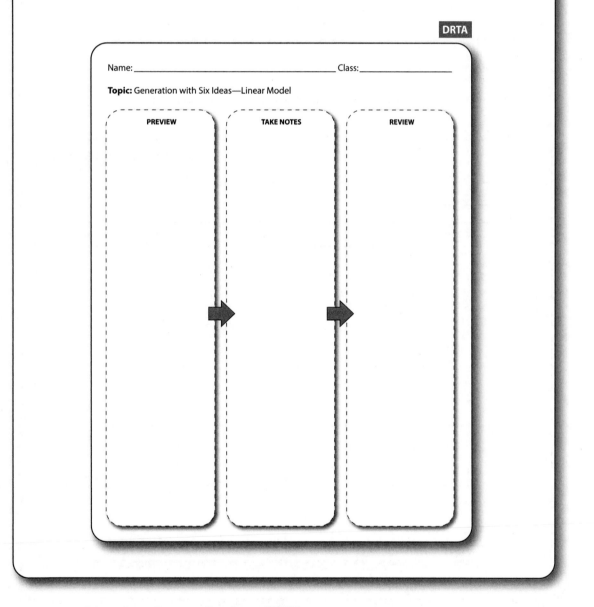

Figure 6.5 Learning Center Station: DRTA

Learning Center Station:
Inquiry Chart

The inquiry chart (I-chart) is a strategy that enables you to ask meaningful questions about a topic, and to organize your writing.

You will integrate prior knowledge or thoughts about the topic with additional information found in several sources.

The I-chart procedure is organized into three phases:

1. Planning
2. Interacting
3. Integrating/Evaluating

Each phase consists of activities designed to engage you in evaluating a topic.

INQUIRY CHART (I-CHART)

Name: _____ Date: _____

Topic: _____

	Question 1	Question 2	Question 3	Question 4	Other Interesting Facts	New Questions
What We Know						
Source 1						
Source 2						
Source 3						
Summaries						

Figure 6.6 Learning Center Station: Inquiry Chart

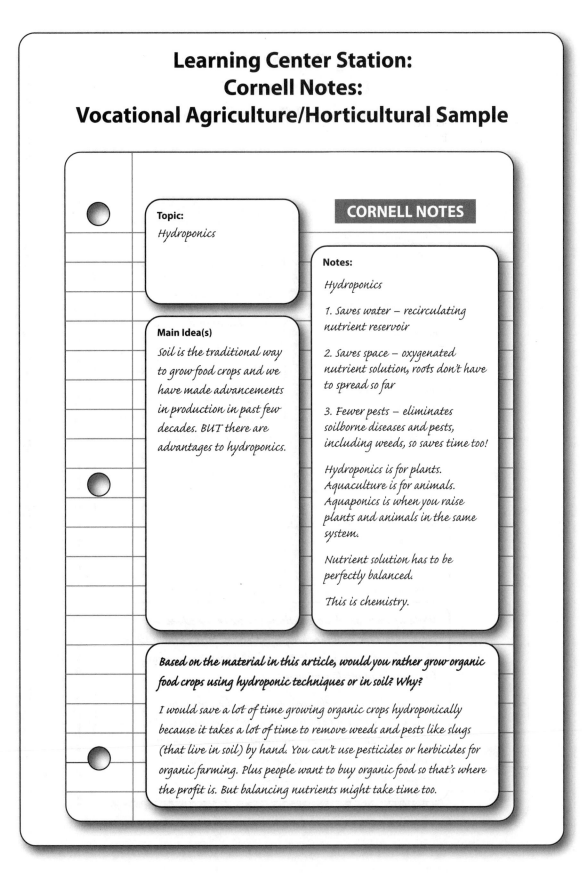

Learning Center Station:
Cornell Notes:
Vocational Agriculture/Horticultural Sample

Topic:
Hydroponics

CORNELL NOTES

Main Idea(s)
Soil is the traditional way to grow food crops and we have made advancements in production in past few decades. BUT there are advantages to hydroponics.

Notes:
Hydroponics

1. Saves water – recirculating nutrient reservoir

2. Saves space – oxygenated nutrient solution, roots don't have to spread so far

3. Fewer pests – eliminates soilborne diseases and pests, including weeds, so saves time too!

Hydroponics is for plants. Aquaculture is for animals. Aquaponics is when you raise plants and animals in the same system.

Nutrient solution has to be perfectly balanced.

This is chemistry.

Based on the material in this article, would you rather grow organic food crops using hydroponic techniques or in soil? Why?

I would save a lot of time growing organic crops hydroponically because it takes a lot of time to remove weeds and pests like slugs (that live in soil) by hand. You can't use pesticides or herbicides for organic farming. Plus people want to buy organic food so that's where the profit is. But balancing nutrients might take time too.

Figure 6.7 Learning Center Station: Cornell Notes Student Sample

Learning Center Station:
Cornell Notes:
Proportions and Ratios Sample

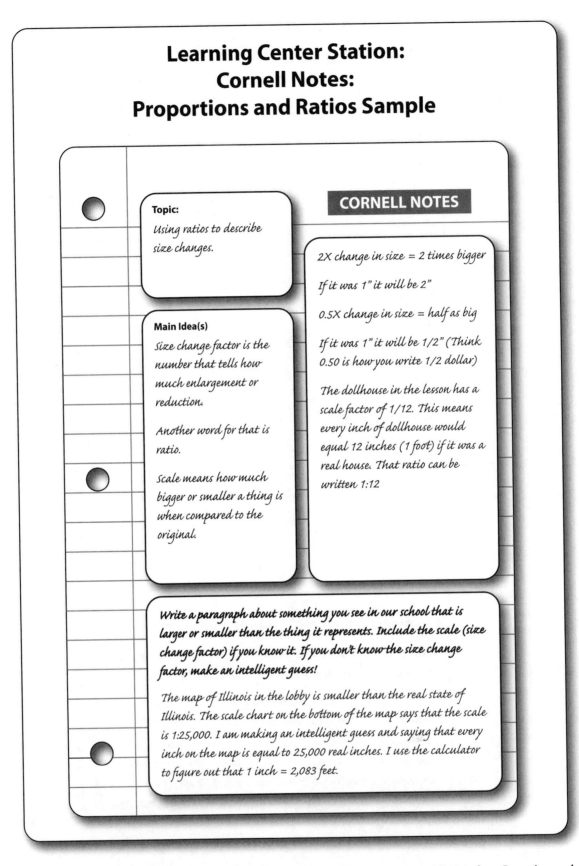

CORNELL NOTES

Topic:
Using ratios to describe size changes.

Main Idea(s)
Size change factor is the number that tells how much enlargement or reduction.

Another word for that is ratio.

Scale means how much bigger or smaller a thing is when compared to the original.

2X change in size = 2 times bigger

If it was 1" it will be 2"

0.5X change in size = half as big

If it was 1" it will be 1/2" (Think 0.50 is how you write 1/2 dollar)

The dollhouse in the lesson has a scale factor of 1/12. This means every inch of dollhouse would equal 12 inches (1 foot) if it was a real house. That ratio can be written 1:12

Write a paragraph about something you see in our school that is larger or smaller than the thing it represents. Include the scale (size change factor) if you know it. If you don't know the size change factor, make an intelligent guess!

The map of Illinois in the lobby is smaller than the real state of Illinois. The scale chart on the bottom of the map says that the scale is 1:25,000. I am making an intelligent guess and saying that every inch on the map is equal to 25,000 real inches. I use the calculator to figure out that 1 inch = 2,083 feet.

Figure 6.8   Learning Center Station: Cornell Notes Student Sample, Continued

Learning Center Station:
Text, Think, Connect

1. Text Facts
In this column you will record important information. This information could include direct quotes or words and phrases that interest the reader.

2. What do you think about the text?
In this column, record what you think about the text and the author's message. Record your impressions and make efforts to interpret the text.

3. Connections
When we read, we make personal connections with the text. We connect the text to our personal experiences, knowledge, and beliefs. In this column, record what this text reminds you of in your personal life.

TTC

Name: _____ Class: _____

Topic: Text, Think, Connect (TTC)

Directions: Use this graphic organizer to record information from your reading and how this information connects to your personal experiences.

Text facts	What do you think about the text?	Connections: how does this information connect to what you already know?

Figure 6.9   Learning Center Station: Text, Think, Connect

Learning Center Station: Concept Sort

What is it?

The Concept Sort introduces you to the vocabulary of a new topic or book.

Directions

You are given a list of terms or concepts from reading material.

Place the words into different categories based on each word's meaning.

Categories can be defined by you or your teacher.

When used before reading, concept sorts provide an opportunity to see what you already know about the given content.

Figure 6.10 Learning Center Station: Concept Sort

Learning Center Station: Makeup Station

Use this checklist to revise and reflect on your work.

Check if completed:

☐ All of the activities from each center are completed.

☐ I've reviewed my work and I have the following questions:

_____

_____

☐ I think my best work is _____ because

_____ .

☐ The most challenging activity was _____ because

_____ .

Figure 6.11   Learning Center Station: Makeup Station

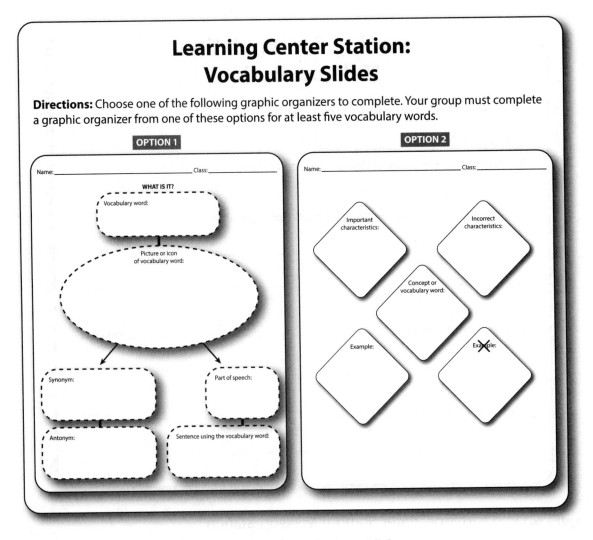

Figure 6.12   Learning Center Station: Vocabulary Slides

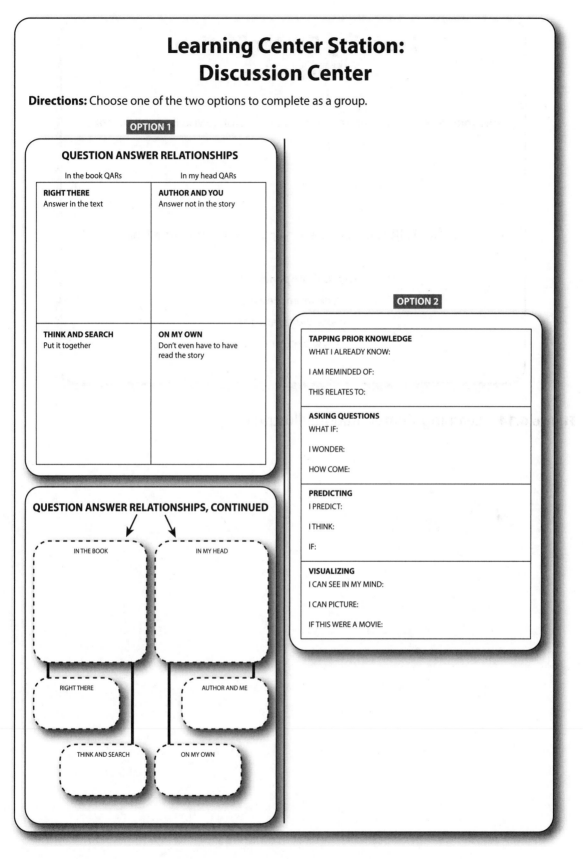

Learning Center Station: Discussion Center

Directions: Choose one of the two options to complete as a group.

OPTION 1

QUESTION ANSWER RELATIONSHIPS

In the book QARs   In my head QARs

RIGHT THERE
Answer in the text

AUTHOR AND YOU
Answer not in the story

THINK AND SEARCH
Put it together

ON MY OWN
Don't even have to have read the story

OPTION 2

TAPPING PRIOR KNOWLEDGE
WHAT I ALREADY KNOW:

I AM REMINDED OF:

THIS RELATES TO:

ASKING QUESTIONS
WHAT IF:

I WONDER:

HOW COME:

PREDICTING
I PREDICT:

I THINK:

IF:

VISUALIZING
I CAN SEE IN MY MIND:

I CAN PICTURE:

IF THIS WERE A MOVIE:

QUESTION ANSWER RELATIONSHIPS, CONTINUED

IN THE BOOK

IN MY HEAD

RIGHT THERE

AUTHOR AND ME

THINK AND SEARCH

ON MY OWN

Figure 6.13 Learning Center Station: Discussion Center

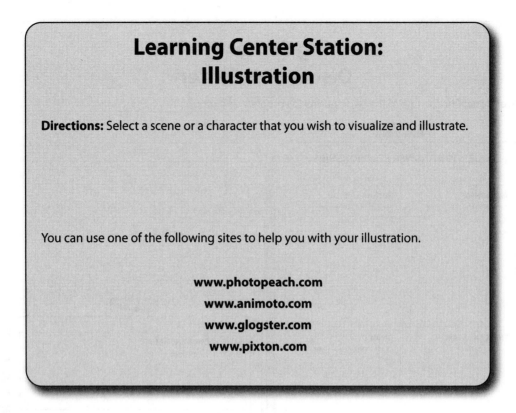

Figure 6.14   Learning Center Station: Illustration

Learning Center Station: Listening Station

Directions: Read your assigned selection as a group.
Take turns reading out loud.

As you listen, use sticky notes to record your Questions, Comments, and
Connections (QCC).

Figure 6.15 Learning Center Station: Listening Station

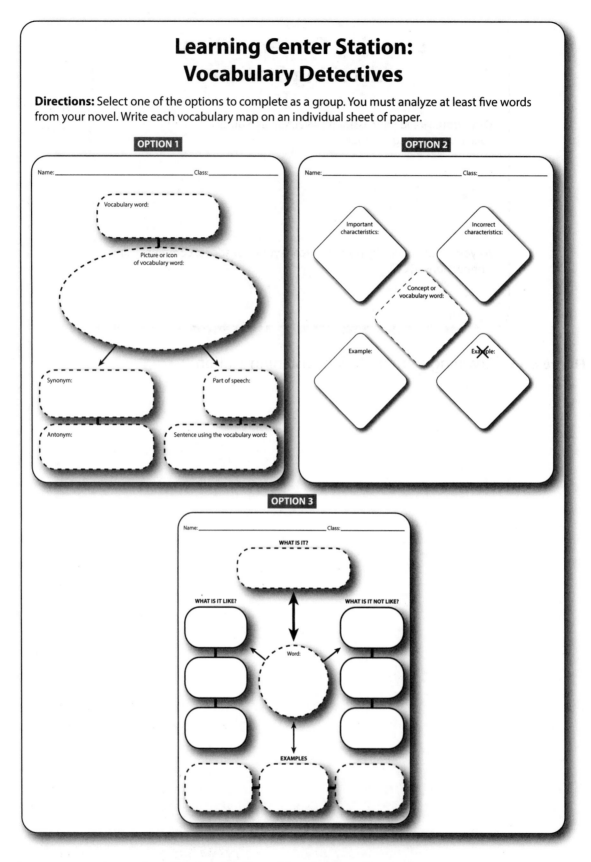

Figure 6.16   Learning Center Station: Vocabulary Detectives

Some Additional Advice About Centers

As I mentioned earlier, center groups should be no larger than five students. The chart in table 6.1 will help you plan for your centers.

If you have more than thirty students in a class, make duplicate stations and create two groups (like grocery store checkout lines) to ease demands for planning and preparation (see table 6.2).

As I suggested earlier, time your centers to be within the range of 10–15 minutes each. If you are teaching within a block schedule where the class time range is 75–90 minutes, you'll be able to complete a full center rotation with your students in one class period. If the school schedule is structured into 40–50 minute periods, it will take two class periods to complete a center rotation.

How Often Should I Use Centers in the Classroom?

Centers are another instructional strategy in our teacher toolbox. We wouldn't use centers every single day; we might use them every other week or a few times a month.

Table 6.1 Suggested Number and Types of Centers

Class Size	Suggested Number of Centers	Suggested Types of Centers
15–20 students	4+ makeup	vocabulary, reading, visualization, and video/audio
21–25	5+ makeup	vocabulary, reading, visualization, video/audio, practicing with content
26–30	6+ makeup	vocabulary, reading, visualization, video/audio, practicing with content, and writing/short response

Table 6.2 Suggested Centers for Larger Classes

Class Size	Suggested Number of Centers	Suggested Types of Centers (create two of the same center and assign students to either Group A or Group B for the center rotation)
31–39 students	3+ makeup	**Group A**: vocabulary, reading, visualization **Group B**: vocabulary, reading, visualization

TEXT DISCUSSION GROUPS

In addition to learning centers, text discussion groups are effective student-centered instructional tools for the development of literacy skills and content knowledge. Modeled after Harvey "Smokey" Daniels's (Daniels and Steineke, 2004) literature circles, this strategy is effective for reading in other content areas. For mathematics and science teachers, this is also a valuable instructional strategy. It creates a context for students to read a wide variety of texts (CCSS reading anchor standard 10) and is by nature a student-centered strategy that is compatible with differentiation. For the purposes of this discussion, I refer to these as "text circles," since this is a more generalizable term across different content areas. Appendix B of this book is a "mini-guide" that provides information about literature circles and text circles along with step-by-step procedures. There are also several videos on this book's accompanying web page that walk you through various aspects of literature circles. See appendix A of this book for more details.

ADVANTAGES OF CENTERS AND TEXT CIRCLES

Each of the student-centered strategies discussed in this chapter meets the expectations of the CCSS. Reading anchor standard 10 promotes the rigorous expectation that students must read a wide variety of increasingly complex texts independently. In addition, writing anchor standard 10 promotes the rigorous expectation that students are able to create a variety of context-appropriate written texts. Student-centered strategies such as learning centers and text circles are contexts where students can develop important literacy skills while gaining content knowledge and learning how to develop and apply these skills and knowledge with increasing independence.

SCIENCE LABS AND THE COMMON CORE

A well-planned, well-executed science lab helps students achieve many of the same goals as learning centers. In fact, a lab *is* a type of learning center. And by its very nature, a good science lab aligns with and echoes the CCSS goals.

Consider this statement in the National Science Teachers Association position paper (2007):

A school laboratory investigation (also referred to as a lab) is defined as an experience in the laboratory, classroom, or the field that provides students with opportunities to interact directly with natural phenomena or with *data collected by others* using tools, materials, data collection techniques, and models (NRC, 2006, p. 3; emphasis added). Throughout the process, students should have opportunities to design investigations, engage in scientific reasoning, manipulate equipment, record data, analyze results, and *discuss their findings*. These skills and knowledge, fostered by laboratory investigations, are an important part of inquiry—the process of asking questions and conducting experiments as a way to understand the natural world (NSTA 2004; emphasis added).

How do students interact with the "data collected from others"? For the most part, they read it. How do students "discuss their findings"? They do it through speaking with and presenting to teachers and peers, of course, but also through lab reports. These formulaic presentations of scientific findings are one of the most obvious places in which science teachers can incorporate literacy standards into their classes. Typically, lab reports are written in complete sentences, except for material lists, charts, and graphs. Student scientists are instructed to write lab reports in the third person, while observing the protocols of correct spelling and punctuation. Great emphasis is placed on avoiding plagiarism. Requiring student scientists to read and interpret others' lab reports and write their own lab reports helps them achieve many of the CCSS literacy goals.

Reading Standards

1. *Read closely to determine what the text says explicitly and to make logical inferences from it; cite specific textual evidence when writing or speaking to support conclusions drawn from the text.*

7. *Integrate and evaluate content presented in diverse formats and media, including visually and quantitatively, as well as in words.*

Writing Standards

1. *Write arguments to support claims in an analysis of substantive topics or texts, using valid reasoning and relevant and sufficient evidence.*

2. *Write informative/explanatory texts to examine and convey complex ideas and information clearly and accurately through the effective selection, organization, and analysis of content.*

4. *Produce clear and coherent writing in which the development, organization, and style are appropriate to task, purpose, and audience.*

7. *Conduct short as well as more sustained research projects based on focused questions, demonstrating understanding of the subject under investigation.*

8. *Gather relevant information from multiple print and digital sources, assess the credibility and accuracy of each source, and integrate the information while avoiding plagiarism.*

Language Standards

1. *Demonstrate command of the conventions of standard English grammar and usage when writing or speaking.*

2. *Demonstrate command of the conventions of standard English capitalization, punctuation, and spelling when writing.*

3. *Apply knowledge of language to understand how language functions in different contexts, to make effective choices for meaning or style, and to comprehend more fully when reading or listening.*

Student lab reports are clearly a valuable component of an integrated literacy curriculum. Efforts should be made to introduce them early in a student's educational career. Figure 6.17 is an example of a graphic organizer that was designed to help grade 6 students prepare for the rigor of high school science labs.

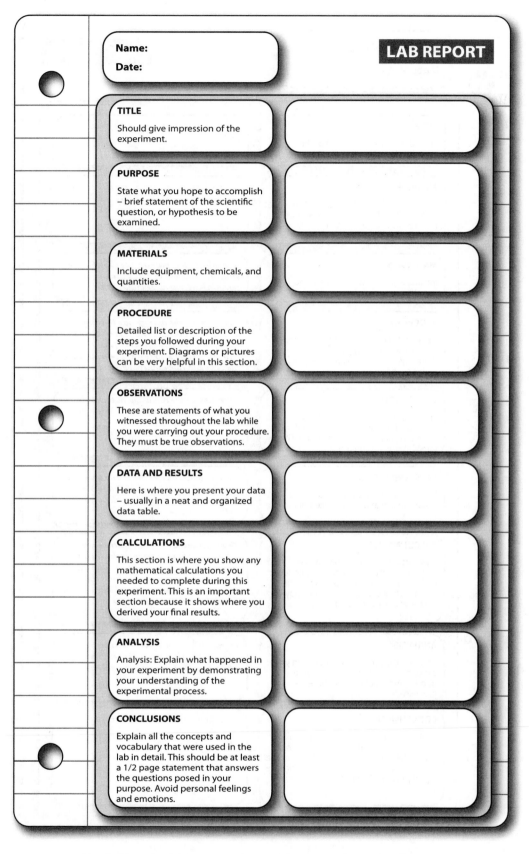

Figure 6.17a Sixth-Grade Science Lab Preparation Template

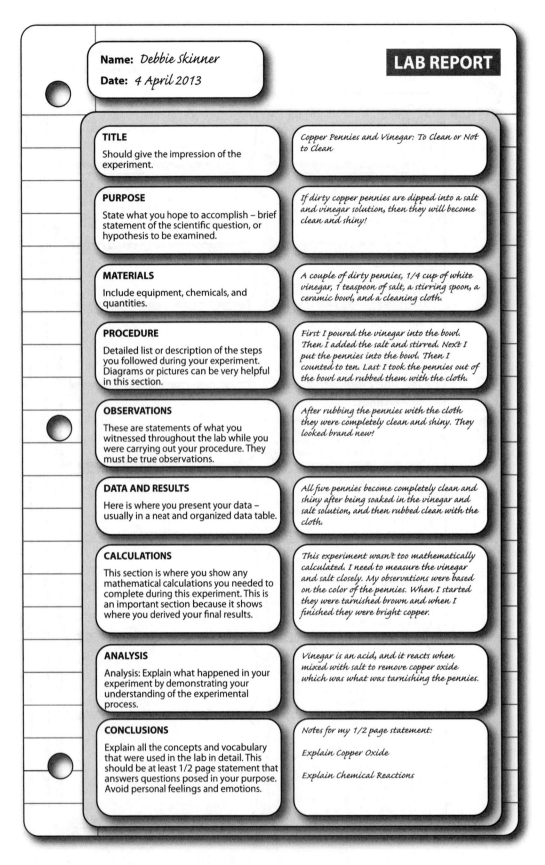

Name: *Debbie Skinner*

Date: *4 April 2013*

LAB REPORT

TITLE

Should give the impression of the experiment.

Copper Pennies and Vinegar: To Clean or Not to Clean

PURPOSE

State what you hope to accomplish – brief statement of the scientific question, or hypothesis to be examined.

If dirty copper pennies are dipped into a salt and vinegar solution, then they will become clean and shiny!

MATERIALS

Include equipment, chemicals, and quantities.

A couple of dirty pennies, 1/4 cup of white vinegar, 1 teaspoon of salt, a stirring spoon, a ceramic bowl, and a cleaning cloth.

PROCEDURE

Detailed list or description of the steps you followed during your experiment. Diagrams or pictures can be very helpful in this section.

First I poured the vinegar into the bowl. Then I added the salt and stirred. Next I put the pennies into the bowl. Then I counted to ten. Last I took the pennies out of the bowl and rubbed them with the cloth.

OBSERVATIONS

These are statements of what you witnessed throughout the lab while you were carrying out your procedure. They must be true observations.

After rubbing the pennies with the cloth they were completely clean and shiny. They looked brand new!

DATA AND RESULTS

Here is where you present your data – usually in a neat and organized data table.

All five pennies become completely clean and shiny after being soaked in the vinegar and salt solution, and then rubbed clean with the cloth.

CALCULATIONS

This section is where you show any mathematical calculations you needed to complete during this experiment. This is an important section because it shows where you derived your final results.

This experiment wasn't too mathematically calculated. I need to measure the vinegar and salt closely. My observations were based on the color of the pennies. When I started they were tarnished brown and when I finished they were bright copper.

ANALYSIS

Analysis: Explain what happened in your experiment by demonstrating your understanding of the experimental process.

Vinegar is an acid, and it reacts when mixed with salt to remove copper oxide which was what was tarnishing the pennies.

CONCLUSIONS

Explain all the concepts and vocabulary that were used in the lab in detail. This should be at least 1/2 page statement that answers questions posed in your purpose. Avoid personal feelings and emotions.

Notes for my 1/2 page statement:

Explain Copper Oxide

Explain Chemical Reactions

Figure 6.17b   Sixth-Grade Science Lab Preparation, Student Sample

SOME FINAL THOUGHTS

We can easily apply the instructional structure of literature circles to other content areas such as science, mathematics, and technical subjects. Instead of literary works like novels, students can read articles, newspapers, primary source documents, and other content-applicable texts. And by paying special attention to the underlying purpose of student-generated lab reports, we can help students address CCSS literacy goals while they learn content.

CHAPTER SEVEN

Technology Tools for Twenty-First-Century Learning

The Common Core State Standards call for the effective integration of technology for the understanding and representation of content knowledge. This chapter will explore how to use technology tools for twenty-first-century learning.

Earlier generations of standards placed technology in a separate category. Often technology was seen as an add-on or afterthought, and even considered to be a luxury. As we move further into the twenty-first century, our thinking about technology must evolve. The CCSS authors address the need for technology in the classroom to develop literacy skills and content knowledge. The Common Core documents the rigorous expectations for students' use of technology for career and college readiness:

> *They [students] use technology and digital media strategically and capably.*
>
> *Students employ technology thoughtfully to enhance their reading, writing, speaking, listening, and language use. They tailor their searches online to acquire useful information efficiently, and they integrate what they learn using technology with what they learn offline. They are familiar with the strengths and limitations of various technological tools and mediums and can select and use those best suited to their communication goals.*
>
> (CCSS 2010, p. 7)

Before we dig more deeply into the role of technology in the Comment Core era, I need to make it clear that many of us teach in schools where resources and equipment can be challenging. Since the Smarter Balanced and Partnership for Assessment of Readiness for College and Careers (PARCC) assessments will be web based, it becomes even more necessary to increase the use of technology in our classrooms. If students are going to be assessed in an online environment, they need to be able to navigate within it with some automaticity. I am not advocating the integration of technology solely so that students can perform well on assessments. The integration of technology is completely necessary in the twenty-first century for students to become college and career ready. This fact is what is most important in the discussion of technology to develop literacy skills and content knowledge.

My suggestions and advice in this chapter are meant to inspire and raise awareness of how we might be able to use technology to enhance teaching and learning.

HOW COMMON CORE STATE STANDARDS INCORPORATE TECHNOLOGY

Today's students are preparing for a world in which technology will be integral to the research, organization, and presentation of ideas—in both college and the workplace. Fortunately, technology is easily incorporated into the classroom. Giving students the opportunity to use technology to develop literacy skills and acquire content knowledge prepares them to accept their roles as fully engaged citizens in twenty-first-century society.

Reading

7. *Integrate and evaluate content presented in diverse formats and media, including visually and quantitatively, as well as in words.*

This standard is further explained in tables 7.1 and 7.2, which articulate the standards for the grade levels.

Anchor reading standard 7 calls for the inclusion of a wide variety of sources (other than the traditional textbook) that are in text and digital format. Using texts like blogs, websites, online reference materials, and other online resources are part of this expectation.

A research or inquiry project is an example of how this might look in the classroom.

Table 7.1 Anchor Reading Standard 7 as Articulated for Each Grade Level for English Language Arts

	Grade 6 Students	Grade 7 Students	Grade 8 Students
Literature	*Compare and contrast the experience of reading a story, drama, or poem to listening to or viewing an audio, video, or live version of the text, including contrasting what they "see" and "hear" when reading the text to what they perceive when they listen or watch.*	*Compare and contrast a written story, drama, or poem to its audio, filmed, staged, or multimedia version, analyzing the effects of techniques unique to each medium (e.g., lighting, sound, color, or camera focus and angles in a film).*	*Analyze the extent to which a filmed or live production of a story or drama stays faithful to or departs from the text or script, evaluating the choices made by the director or actors.*
Informational text	*Integrate information presented in different media or formats (e.g., visually, quantitatively) as well as in words to develop a coherent understanding of a topic or issue.*	*Compare and contrast a text to an audio, video, or multimedia version of the text, analyzing each medium's portrayal of the subject (e.g., how the delivery of a speech affects the impact of the words).*	*Evaluate the advantages and disadvantages of using different mediums (e.g., print or digital text, video, multimedia) to present a particular topic or idea.*

	Grades 9–10 Students	Grades 11–12 Students
Literature	*Analyze the representation of a subject or a key scene in two different artistic mediums, including what is emphasized or absent in each treatment (e.g., Auden's "Musée des Beaux Arts" and Breughel's "Landscape with the Fall of Icarus").*	*Analyze multiple interpretations of a story, drama, or poem (e.g., recorded or live production of a play or recorded novel or poetry), evaluating how each version interprets the source text. (Include at least one play by Shakespeare and one play by an American dramatist.)*

Table 7.1 Continued

	Grades 9–10 Students	Grades 11–12 Students
Informational text	*Analyze various accounts of a subject told in different mediums (e.g., a person's life story in both print and multimedia), determining which details are emphasized in each account.*	*Integrate and evaluate multiple sources of information presented in different media or formats (e.g., visually, quantitatively) as well as in words in order to address a question or solve a problem.*

Table 7.2 Anchor Reading Standard 7 as Articulated for Each Grade Level for Literacy in History/Social Studies, Science and Technical Subjects

Grades 6–8 Students	Grades 9–10 Students	Grades 11–12 Students
Integrate visual information (e.g., in charts, graphs, photographs, videos, or maps) with other information in print and digital texts.	*Integrate quantitative or technical analysis (e.g., charts, research data) with qualitative analysis in print or digital text.*	*Integrate and evaluate multiple sources of information presented in diverse formats and media (e.g., visually, quantitatively, as well as in words) in order to address a question or solve a problem.*

The standards emphasize the importance of students reading a wide variety of resources with increased complexity. Let's say that I am a biology teacher preparing a unit on alternative energy. I can propose an essential question like "Should fossil fuels be banned?" The students can take a position on this question, either pro or con (and I might add that this activity also addresses writing standard 1, which focuses on argumentation). I can offer them a variety of resources, which can include the following web-based sources:

▶ Procon.org has an excellent list of resources that address this question. (http://alternativeenergy.procon.org/view.answers.php?questionID= 001350)

- ▶ The Discover Channel website has many excellent articles and pages on the fossil fuel debate (http://news.discovery.com/earth/tags/fossil-fuels.htm)
- ▶ The US Department of Energy has the resources on fossil fuels at (http://energy.gov/science-innovation/energy-sources/fossil

These are just a few examples of the kinds of materials that I can find in digital libraries. The students would develop the reading anchor standard 7 skills through their reading and exploration of a variety of media, extending far beyond the more traditional approach of reading a chapter from a textbook. Students would be exposed to multiple points of view as they read, analyze, and synthesize the information.

Figure 7.1 (on evaluating websites) and figure 7.2 (on evaluating web-based resources for content information) are tools that can support a student's analysis of web-based texts and digital media.

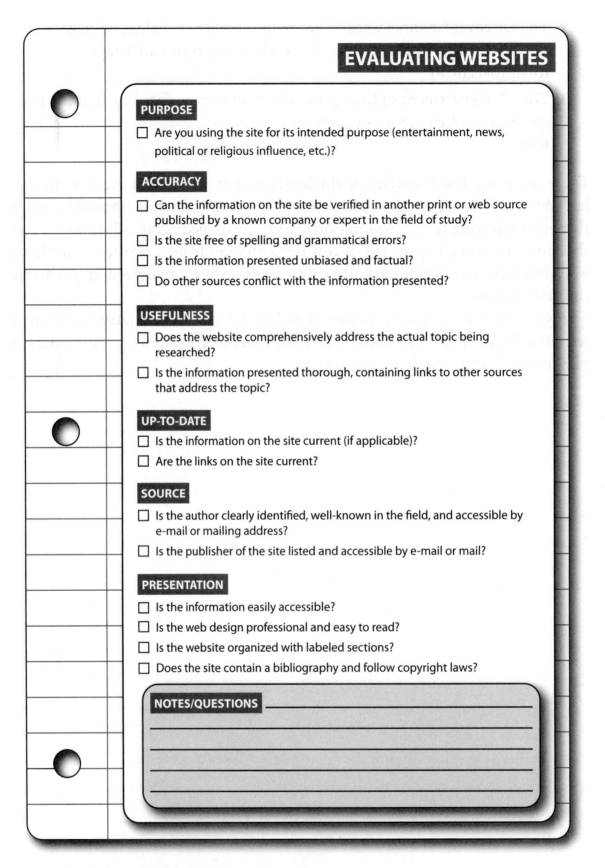

EVALUATING WEBSITES

PURPOSE

☐ Are you using the site for its intended purpose (entertainment, news, political or religious influence, etc.)?

ACCURACY

☐ Can the information on the site be verified in another print or web source published by a known company or expert in the field of study?

☐ Is the site free of spelling and grammatical errors?

☐ Is the information presented unbiased and factual?

☐ Do other sources conflict with the information presented?

USEFULNESS

☐ Does the website comprehensively address the actual topic being researched?

☐ Is the information presented thorough, containing links to other sources that address the topic?

UP-TO-DATE

☐ Is the information on the site current (if applicable)?

☐ Are the links on the site current?

SOURCE

☐ Is the author clearly identified, well-known in the field, and accessible by e-mail or mailing address?

☐ Is the publisher of the site listed and accessible by e-mail or mail?

PRESENTATION

☐ Is the information easily accessible?

☐ Is the web design professional and easy to read?

☐ Is the website organized with labeled sections?

☐ Does the site contain a bibliography and follow copyright laws?

NOTES/QUESTIONS _____

Figure 7.1a Evaluating Websites Template

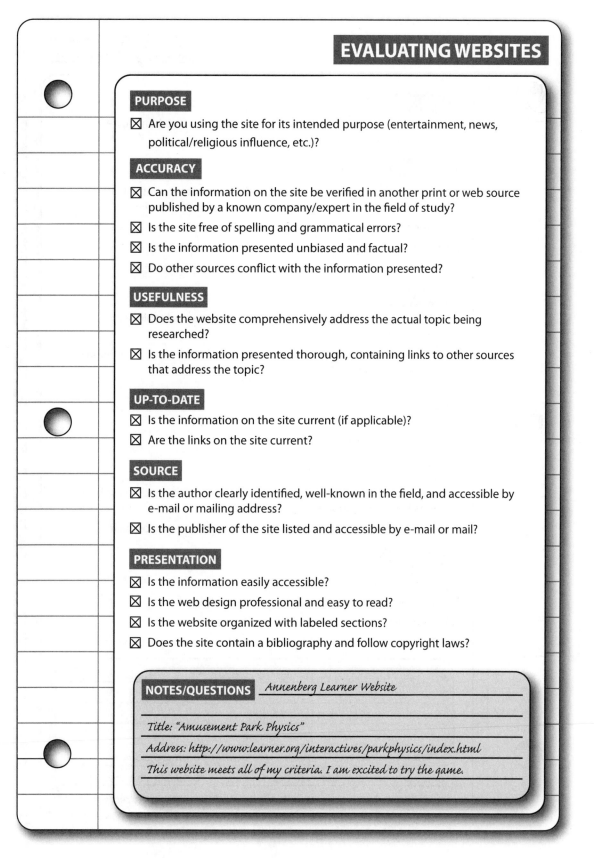

EVALUATING WEBSITES

PURPOSE

☒ Are you using the site for its intended purpose (entertainment, news, political/religious influence, etc.)?

ACCURACY

☒ Can the information on the site be verified in another print or web source published by a known company/expert in the field of study?

☒ Is the site free of spelling and grammatical errors?

☒ Is the information presented unbiased and factual?

☒ Do other sources conflict with the information presented?

USEFULNESS

☒ Does the website comprehensively address the actual topic being researched?

☒ Is the information presented thorough, containing links to other sources that address the topic?

UP-TO-DATE

☒ Is the information on the site current (if applicable)?

☒ Are the links on the site current?

SOURCE

☒ Is the author clearly identified, well-known in the field, and accessible by e-mail or mailing address?

☒ Is the publisher of the site listed and accessible by e-mail or mail?

PRESENTATION

☒ Is the information easily accessible?

☒ Is the web design professional and easy to read?

☒ Is the website organized with labeled sections?

☒ Does the site contain a bibliography and follow copyright laws?

NOTES/QUESTIONS _Annenberg Learner Website_

Title: "Amusement Park Physics"

Address: http://www.learner.org/interactives/parkphysics/index.html

This website meets all of my criteria. I am excited to try the game.

Figure 7.1b Evaluating Websites Student Sample

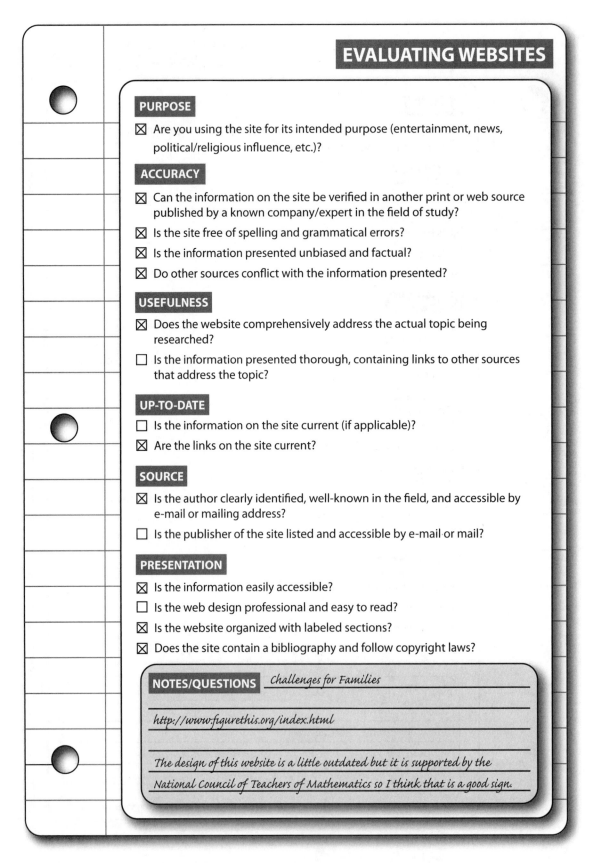

EVALUATING WEBSITES

PURPOSE

☒ Are you using the site for its intended purpose (entertainment, news, political/religious influence, etc.)?

ACCURACY

☒ Can the information on the site be verified in another print or web source published by a known company/expert in the field of study?

☒ Is the site free of spelling and grammatical errors?

☒ Is the information presented unbiased and factual?

☒ Do other sources conflict with the information presented?

USEFULNESS

☒ Does the website comprehensively address the actual topic being researched?

☐ Is the information presented thorough, containing links to other sources that address the topic?

UP-TO-DATE

☐ Is the information on the site current (if applicable)?

☒ Are the links on the site current?

SOURCE

☒ Is the author clearly identified, well-known in the field, and accessible by e-mail or mailing address?

☐ Is the publisher of the site listed and accessible by e-mail or mail?

PRESENTATION

☒ Is the information easily accessible?

☐ Is the web design professional and easy to read?

☒ Is the website organized with labeled sections?

☒ Does the site contain a bibliography and follow copyright laws?

NOTES/QUESTIONS *Challenges for Families*

http://www.figurethis.org/index.html

The design of this website is a little outdated but it is supported by the National Council of Teachers of Mathematics so I think that is a good sign.

Figure 7.1c Evaluating Websites Student Sample, Continued

EVALUATING WEB-BASED RESOURCES FOR CONTENT INFORMATION

ACCURACY OF INFORMATION

- ☐ Is the information presented biased or unbiased, fact or opinion?
- ☐ Are you using the site for its intended purpose (entertainment, news, political or religious influence, etc.)?
- ☐ Can the information on the site be verified in another print or web source published by a known company or expert in the field of study?
- ☐ Do the other sources conflict with the information presented?
- ☐ Is the site free of spelling and grammatical errors?
- ☐ Are the research methods explained?
- ☐ Does the information meet your needs?
- ☐ Does the website comprehensively address the topic being researched?
- ☐ Is the information presented thorough, containing links to other sources that address the topic?

SOURCE

- ☐ Is the author clearly identified, well-known in the field, and accessible by e-mail or mailing address?
- ☐ Is the publisher of the site listed and accessible by e-mail or mail?
- ☐ Is the information on the site current (if applicable)?
- ☐ Are the links on the site current?

PRESENTATION

- ☐ Is the information easily accessible?
- ☐ Is the web design professional and easy to read?
- ☐ Is the website organized with labeled sections?
- ☐ Does the site contain a bibliography and follow copyright laws?
- ☐ Are security and/or encryption systems employed when necessary?

NOTES/QUESTIONS

Figure 7.2a Evaluating Web-Based Resources for Content Information Template

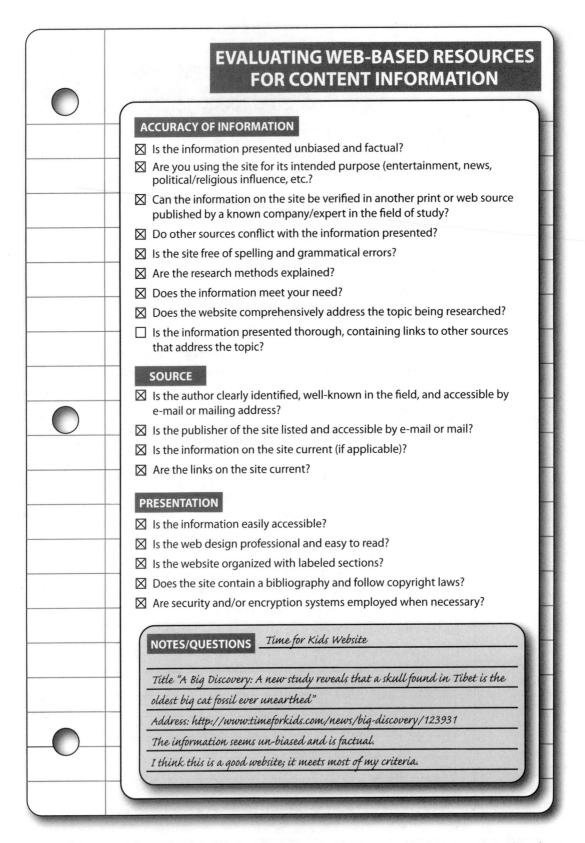

EVALUATING WEB-BASED RESOURCES FOR CONTENT INFORMATION

ACCURACY OF INFORMATION

☒ Is the information presented unbiased and factual?

☒ Are you using the site for its intended purpose (entertainment, news, political/religious influence, etc.?

☒ Can the information on the site be verified in another print or web source published by a known company/expert in the field of study?

☒ Do other sources conflict with the information presented?

☒ Is the site free of spelling and grammatical errors?

☒ Are the research methods explained?

☒ Does the information meet your need?

☒ Does the website comprehensively address the topic being researched?

☐ Is the information presented thorough, containing links to other sources that address the topic?

SOURCE

☒ Is the author clearly identified, well-known in the field, and accessible by e-mail or mailing address?

☒ Is the publisher of the site listed and accessible by e-mail or mail?

☒ Is the information on the site current (if applicable)?

☒ Are the links on the site current?

PRESENTATION

☒ Is the information easily accessible?

☒ Is the web design professional and easy to read?

☒ Is the website organized with labeled sections?

☒ Does the site contain a bibliography and follow copyright laws?

☒ Are security and/or encryption systems employed when necessary?

NOTES/QUESTIONS _Time for Kids Website_

Title "A Big Discovery: A new study reveals that a skull found in Tibet is the oldest big cat fossil ever unearthed"

Address: http://www.timeforkids.com/news/big-discovery/123931

The information seems un-biased and is factual.

I think this is a good website; it meets most of my criteria.

Figure 7.2b Evaluating Web-Based Resources for Content Information Student Sample

EVALUATING WEB-BASED RESOURCES FOR CONTENT INFORMATION

ACCURACY OF INFORMATION

☒ Is the information presented unbiased and factual?

☒ Are you using the site for its intended purpose (entertainment, news, political/religious influence, etc.?

☒ Can the information on the site be verified in another print or web source published by a known company/expert in the field of study?

☒ Do other sources conflict with the information presented?

☒ Is the site free of spelling and grammatical errors?

☐ Are the research methods explained?

☒ Does the information meet your needs?

☒ Does the website comprehensively address the topic being researched?

☒ Is the information presented thorough, containing links to other sources that address the topic?

SOURCE

☒ Is the author clearly identified, well-known in the field, and accessible by e-mail or mailing address?

☒ Is the publisher of the site listed and accessible by e-mail or mail?

☒ Is the information on the site current (if applicable)?

☒ Are the links on the site current?

PRESENTATION

☒ Is the information easily accessible?

☐ Is the web design professional and easy to read?

☒ Is the website organized with labeled sections?

☐ Does the site contain a bibliography and follow copyright laws?

☒ Are security and/or encryption systems employed when necessary?

NOTES/QUESTIONS   *AAA Math Resource Website*

Title: AAA Math

Address: http://www.aaamath.com/

The design of this website seems a little outdated and I don't know who the publisher is.

Figure 7.2c   Evaluating Web-Based Resources for Content Information Student Sample, Continued

Writing

Like reading, the writing standards also incorporate technology. Specifically, writing anchor standard 6 identifies how technology and writing skills are connected:

> *Use technology, including the Internet, to produce and publish writing and to interact and collaborate with others.*

Writing anchor standard 6 is further articulated at the different grade levels as outlined in tables 7.3 and 7.4.

Anchor writing standard 6 identifies the skills that students need to develop for twenty-first-century writing for college and career readiness. Here are some ideas for the development of these skills in the classroom.

Blogging: Short for "web log," the use of blogs for information sharing and discussion has exploded in the past few years. We read blogs for information, and students can write blogs to share what they know and understand with the entire world. Blogs certainly transform our notions about audience.

Digital Storytelling: In this electronic platform, students can create stories that integrate text, images, video, and narration. Students can use digital storytelling to present their analysis of a historical event or a narrative story.

Google Docs: There is tremendous power in Google Docs. Students can write and collaborate in the same document. In groups, the students document their analysis and discussion of a short story with three to five classmates. I particularly like the fact that students can view one another's discussions and thinking. Since the thinking is in written text, the students can use this document for future thinking and final draft writing. There are so many uses for Google Docs in the classroom; I urge you to learn about this resource.

Table 7.3 Anchor Writing Standard 6 as Articulated for Each Grade Level for English Language Arts

Grade 6 Students	Grade 7 Students	Grade 8 Students
Use technology, including the Internet, to produce and publish writing as well as to interact and collaborate with others; demonstrate sufficient command of keyboarding skills to type a minimum of three pages in a single sitting.	*Use technology, including the Internet, to produce and publish writing and link to and cite sources as well as to interact and collaborate with others, including linking to and citing sources.*	*Use technology, including the Internet, to produce and publish writing and present the relationships between information and ideas efficiently as well as to interact and collaborate with others.*

Grades 9–10 Students	Grades 11–12 Students	Grade 8 Students
Use technology, including the Internet, to produce, publish, and update individual or shared writing products, taking advantage of technology's capacity to link to other information and to display information flexibly and dynamically.	*Use technology, including the Internet, to produce, publish, and update individual or shared writing products in response to ongoing feedback, including new arguments or information.*	

Table 7.4 Anchor Writing Standard 6 as Articulated for Each Grade Level for Literacy in History/Social Studies, Science and Technical Subjects

Grades 6–8 Students	Grades 9–10 Students	Grades 11–12 Students
Use technology, including the Internet, to produce and publish writing and present the relationships between information and ideas clearly and efficiently.	*Use technology, including the Internet, to produce, publish, and update individual or shared writing products, taking advantage of technology's capacity to link to other information and to display information flexibly and dynamically.*	*Use technology, including the Internet, to produce, publish, and update individual or shared writing products in response to ongoing feedback, including new arguments or information.*

Speaking and Listening

Although the speaking and listening strand is not included in the interdisciplinary standards, it needs to be addressed. Let's look at the speaking and listening anchor standard that integrates technology. Table 7.5 sets out the standard as articulated for the different grades.

Table 7.5 Anchor Speaking and Listening Standard 5 as Articulated for Each Grade Level for English Language Arts

Make strategic use of digital media and visual displays of data to express information and enhance understanding of presentations.

Grade 6 Students	Grade 7 Students	Grade 8 Students
Include multimedia components (e.g., graphics, images, music, sound) and visual displays in presentations to clarify information.	*Include multimedia components and visual displays in presentations to clarify claims and findings and emphasize salient points.*	*Integrate multimedia and visual displays into presentations to clarify information, strengthen claims and evidence, and add interest.*

Grades 9–10 Students	Grades 11–12 Students
Make strategic use of digital media (e.g., textual, graphical, audio, visual, and interactive elements) in presentations to enhance understanding of findings, reasoning, and evidence and to add interest.	*Make strategic use of digital media (e.g., textual, graphical, audio, visual, and interactive elements) in presentations to enhance understanding of findings, reasoning, and evidence and to add interest.*

Author's note: Please remember that the speaking and listening strand is not included in the literacy in history/social studies standards. I include speaking and listening in this book because it is an important skill for students to develop while learning content.

What does this standard mean for ELA, mathematics, and science teachers? Like the writing standard 6, speaking and listening anchor standard 5 outlines the expectation that students should be proficient in using technology to express what they know and understand and to enhance a presentation. Here are some tools you can use in the classroom:

▶ **PresentMe** is a presentation tool that integrates slides (like those that you may have created with PowerPoint) and your video presentation of the material. I can think of several learning advantages when students use this web-based site. Think of your shy students. They can make a presentation without having to stand in front of their peers. Going through presentations eats up a lot of class time. Students can create their presentations and then e-mail you the link. Any learning opportunity for students to integrate speaking and listening with writing to demonstrate content comprehension is the highest level of critical thinking, the representational level.

- ▶ **Recording tools like Audioboo and Vocaroo** allow students to record narration to accompany a written piece or to demonstrate what they know and understand about a topic.

- ▶ **YouTube and other video sites** support listening skills. Students can learn about different topics through a variety of selected videos and media.

- ▶ **PowToon** is one of my favorite tools. Students can create an animated presentation with their original narration.

There are many more Web 2.0 tools that we can use in the classroom, and I have provided a list in this book as well as in the online resource center. The technology is constantly changing.

- ▶ **Prezi** (http://prezi.com/) is a site where students can use cloud-based presentation software tools to create three-dimensional visual presentations.

- ▶ **PresentMe** (https://present.me/content/) is a site where students can upload slides, and then record and edit their audio presentation—sharing the entire presentation with a link.

- ▶ **PearlTrees** (http://www.pearltrees.com/) is a user friendly collaborative visual bookmarking and curation site. Students can collect, drag, and organize website favorites and personal photos and notes into units called "pearls" that can be organized into "pearltrees."

- ▶ **Dropbox** (https://www.dropbox.com/) is a file storage site where students can upload, store, and share pictures, videos, and documents.

- ▶ **Pixton** (http://www.pixton.com/) is a site where students can use original content or school content to create comics and graphic novels.

- ▶ **BoomWriter** (http://boomwriter.com/) is a site where students can share writing to create books. BoomWriter provides a starter chapter of a story and students continue the story. Student's work is voted on anonymously, and then the winning chapters become part of a book that can be published by BoomWriter.

- ▶ **iAnnotate** (available on iTunes) is an app students can use for reading, marking, and sharing PDFs. The app includes highlighting, search, and organization tools.

- ▶ **Fotobabble** (http://www.fotobabble.com/) is a site students can use to create and share talking photos. Students upload a photo, create audio content, and share.

- ▶ **PhotoPeach** (http://photopeach.com/) is a site where students create and share slideshows. Students upload photographs and use tools to add sound and text to help tell the story.

> ▸ **Animoto** (http://animoto.com/) is a site where students create visual presentations. Students upload photos and videos, edit them with style, music and text tools, and then share through social media sites.
> ▸ **Livebinders** (http://www.livebinders.com/) is a site students can use to create an online binder to organize and curate content on a topic.

SOME FINAL THOUGHTS

I know that the integration of technology to develop literacy skills and content knowledge may seem overwhelming. My advice is this:

▸ **Give in to the chaos**. You will never ever know about every single tool that you could use for teaching your content. I always ask other teachers for their ideas, and sometimes students will give me some great tips, too. The International Society for Technology Educators (ISTE) is a great resource; the website is constantly updated.

▸ **Take it slow**. Learn a few tools, learn them well, and **then** use them in your classroom. Remember, good teachers tinker. Good teachers are always messing with their lesson plans and teaching tools in order to meet the learning needs of their students. I like to take a few websites or apps each month and tinker around with them. If I get stuck, I usually Google my question, and voilà! A fellow educator out in cyberspace is ready to help me. Google and YouTube are my best friends. I learn about new education web-based sites or apps from search engines like Google, and then there's usually a video somewhere on YouTube showing me how to use the technology, often throwing in some great tips.

▸ **Embrace the newness and the fact that you are a student too**. My students are always very helpful and patient with me when I try to implement a new technology in my teaching. Embracing your "learner" status can make you a great model for your students; they see how **you** learn something new and how your tenacious spirit leads you to find solutions when you're stuck. Even more exciting, students will also bear witness to your joy when you achieve mastery and success!

CHAPTER EIGHT

Helping Students Become College and Career Ready

Now that we are at the last chapter, I want to take us back to the beginning. My purpose in writing this book was to connect the Common Core State Standards skills to classroom practices that are also rooted in research and theory. The content literacy movement was relatively young when I entered the teaching profession more than twenty-five years ago. Since the movement to teach reading and writing in the content area began more than thirty years ago, many studies have been done that consistently support the positive learning connections between literacy skill development and content knowledge.

The twenty-first century is different. It's not a question of good or bad; it's just different, very different from what I experienced as a teenage student. As a teenager and college student, I used technologies like an electric typewriter, microfilm, and microfiche. The mark of a great student in my generation was the ability to get your hands on information. Today the mark of a great student is **knowing how to use information**. Literacy skills facilitate students' use of information.

As teachers in the midst of the information age, we need to recognize that the quantity of new information produced in a little more than four years is equal to the amount of information compiled over the entire history of the world (Darling-Hammond and Bransford, 2005). Today's job market requires more advanced literacy skills and the ability to analyze and synthesize large quantities of information. Linda Darling-Hammond (Darling-Hammond and Bransford, 2010) indicates that 95 percent of jobs fit this category in the twenty-first century. Workers today are required to digest, with ever-increasing speed, large amounts of information, largely in the form of text, which makes it imperative that our students achieve higher levels of literacy competency if they hope to compete.

Since so many of us are familiar with Bloom's taxonomy, let's use it as a tool for furthering discussion. Figure 8.1 shows Bloom's original taxonomy (which I prefer to the newer version).

I would argue that those of us who used electric typewriters, microfilm, and microfiche spent more time on the knowledge level of Bloom's taxonomy. It's not that this fact is good or bad; it's just what we needed to do back then. We also memorized content because memorization was a tremendous time saver. I still have Library of Congress catalogue numbers memorized from when I was a graduate student because not having to look them up when I needed them saved me so much time. The students we teach today have a different experience. They more frequently operate on the analysis, synthesis, and evaluation level of Bloom's taxonomy as a result of the abundance and constant availability of information. Today, information is recorded and shared through technology devices with amazing speed.

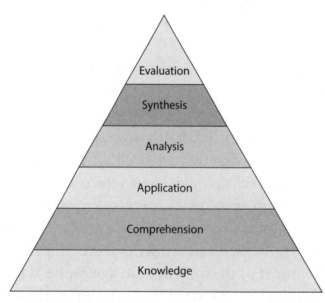

Figure 8.1 Bloom's Taxonomy

Here's an example of what students do now. I am sure that you teach students who play video games. My seventeen-year-old loves to play *The Sims*. What do teenagers do when they are stuck and can't advance to the next level of a video game? That's right—they look for a "cheat." They search the Internet to find different cheats and read about various strategies. Once teenagers have researched the cheats (and researching is an important skill for college and career readiness), they apply a cheat. Do you see that this is a higher-level skill according to Bloom's taxonomy? And this example doesn't stop there. Teenage gamers often go back and record comments and an evaluation of a particular cheat for their fellow gamers. Evaluation is the highest level on Bloom's taxonomy.

The CCSS authors identify the effect of the information age on education. We are still teaching the same literacy skills and content as we always have. The difference is that content is readily available, and students must learn how to use literacy skills to represent what they know and understand about content. As teachers, we want our students to be able to apply what they have learned. We've always wanted that for our students. I'm sure you've noticed, too, that the CCSS language contains verbs such as "analyze," "synthesize," and "evaluate," which are aligned with the highest levels on Bloom's taxonomy.

EXAMINING WHAT YOU CURRENTLY DO AS A CONTENT AREA TEACHER

Remember that in the introduction to the Common Core State Standards, the authors reminded us that it is teachers and curriculum specialists who know best how to develop the skills articulated in the standards? The standards do not require that the current curriculum should be discarded. In fact, what we should do is to analyze what we do as content area, discipline-based teachers and determine what is most effective and least effective. I'm sure you already do that as a reflective teacher. Examine the current curriculum and determine what is already Common Core friendly, develops literacy skills, and effectively teaches your content area. Once you've sorted that out, I'm sure you will soon realize that you're already teaching some lessons and units that are aligned with the Common Core and that integrate interdisciplinary literacy.

In taking a realistic inventory of what we do as teachers, we can "shore up" our curriculum and instruction to be more aligned with the Common Core. In my experience in working with teachers all over the country on aligning their curriculums with the Common Core, the following areas generally need the most "shoring up."

- ▶ **Argumentation**: Do your assignments contain opportunities for students to make a claim and provide evidence to support an assertion? Classroom activities like debates, document-based questions, and more formal writing assignments like essays and research papers develop students' skills and argumentation in writing, speaking, and listening.

- ▶ **Using research assignments to build and present knowledge**: Your unit and lesson plans should contain opportunities for students to engage in short and longer research projects that focus on questions. Homework assignments are often filled with low-level questions and rote memorization; worksheets generally don't meet this expectation. Instead, pose a challenging question for students to explore—a "how" or "why" question. For example, in a science class, students could discuss and write about questions like these: Why should there be public health agencies? How can people affect the environment?

- ▶ **Reading a wide variety of texts**: We have already discussed at length how important it is for teenage students to read a wide variety of texts. Create opportunities to develop content knowledge by exposing students to a variety of texts from different sources and at different reading levels. Students are going to be more engaged and interested in reading when they have some choices about the texts and are using information to respond to an interesting question. Variety promotes students' ability to analyze, synthesize, and represent large quantities of information.

SOME FINAL THOUGHTS

The strategies in this book are suggestions and ideas for developing literacy skills and content knowledge so that students can grow into even more advanced critical thinkers. These are not just literacy strategies; they are pedagogies. I believe in the power of teachers, and I know that powerful literacy strategies can not only deepen students' content knowledge but also better equip students for college and career readiness. I am optimistic about the Common Core State Standards, but I am also realistic in understanding that teachers need support and resources to make this vision a reality and to help our students match the portrait of a college- and career-ready student by regularly exhibiting the following characteristics of a literate individual.

They demonstrate independence.

Students can, without significant scaffolding, comprehend and evaluate complex texts across a range of types and disciplines, and they can construct effective arguments and convey intricate or multifaceted information. Likewise, students are able independently to discern a speaker's key points, request clarification, and ask relevant questions. They build on others' ideas, articulate their own ideas, and confirm they have been understood. Without prompting, they demonstrate command of Standard English and acquire and use a wide-ranging vocabulary. More broadly, they become self-directed learners, effectively seeking out and using resources to assist them, including teachers, peers, and print and digital reference materials.

They build strong content knowledge.

Students establish a base of knowledge across a wide range of subject matter by engaging with works of quality and substance. They become proficient in new areas through research and study. They read purposefully and listen attentively to gain both general knowledge and discipline-specific expertise. They refine and share their knowledge through writing and speaking.

They respond to the varying demands of audience, task, purpose, and discipline.

Students adapt their communication in relation to audience, task, purpose, and discipline. They set and adjust purpose for reading, writing, speaking, listening, and language use as warranted by the task. They appreciate nuances, such as how the composition of an audience should affect tone when speaking and how the connotations of words affect meaning. They also know that different disciplines call for different types of evidence (e.g., documentary evidence in history, experimental evidence in science).

They comprehend as well as critique.

Students are engaged and open minded—but discerning—readers and listeners. They work diligently to understand precisely what an author or speaker is saying, but they also question an author's or speaker's assumptions and premises and assess the veracity of claims and the soundness of reasoning.

They value evidence.

Students cite specific evidence when offering an oral or written interpretation of a text. They use relevant evidence when supporting their own points in writing and speaking, making their reasoning clear to the reader or listener, and they constructively evaluate others' use of evidence.

They use technology and digital media strategically and capably.

Students employ technology thoughtfully to enhance their reading, writing, speaking, listening, and language use. They tailor their searches online to acquire useful information efficiently, and they integrate what they learn using technology with what they learn offline. They are familiar with the strengths and limitations of various technological tools and mediums and can select and use those best suited to their communication goals.

They come to understand other perspectives and cultures.

Students appreciate that the twenty-first-century classroom and workplace are settings in which people from often widely divergent cultures and who represent diverse experiences and perspectives must learn and work together. Students actively seek to understand other perspectives and cultures through reading and listening, and they are able to communicate effectively with people of varied backgrounds. They evaluate other points of view critically and constructively. Through reading great classic and contemporary works of literature representative of a variety of periods, cultures, and worldviews, students can vicariously inhabit worlds and have experiences much different than their own.

(CCSS 2010, p. 7)

This may seem overwhelming at times, but remember: good teachers tinker! We are highly skilled professionals who know in our heads and hearts what good teaching and learning should be in our content classrooms. We are the ones who can make the Common Core vision—for our students to become college and career ready in the twenty-first century—a reality. And when it comes down to it, I don't think that the Common Core vision is all that different from what I have always believed as a lifelong educator—and probably not all that different from your own vision, my fellow educator.

APPENDIX A

List of Bonus Web Downloads

Many of the templates from the preceding chapters are available for free download from the publisher's website, along with a number of bonus materials. Individual classroom teachers may reproduce these for classroom use, but no other reproduction of these materials is permissible. (See the copyright page of this book.)

Templates may be downloaded at www.wiley.com/go/ccliteracy2. The password is the last five digits of this book's ISBN, which are **10203**.

APPENDIX B

Text Circles Resource Guide

This appendix covers the following topics:

▶ Background information about text circles
▶ Getting started with text circles in the classroom
▶ Creating and structuring mini-lessons

> Be sure to watch the videos on text circles on the publisher's website. The following pages are meant to complement those informational videos.

WHAT ARE TEXT CIRCLES?

Text circles are all these things:

▶ A translation of the adult reading group
▶ A way to offer students a genuine and authentic reading experience
▶ Also known as book clubs and reading groups

Consistent Elements

▶ Students choose their reading materials. It's important to offer a wide range of material on the specific content or topic. If an environmental science class is studying fracking for instance, students can read reports from traditional news sources like major newspapers, National Public Media, and the Associated Press. They can examine data and explore online reports from government agencies like the Department of Energy, Department of the Interior, US Geological Survey, and the Environmental Protection Agency. They can examine studies and graphs in specialty publications like *Discover* magazine, *National Geographic*, and *Scientific American*; and they can download support materials through reputable websites like PBS Learning Media and Smithsonian.gov. They can learn about the latest theories and proposals by evaluating papers that are published by professional scientific communities like the American Geophysical Union.

▶ Looking for reading material? Explore the websites that are mentioned elsewhere in this book, like www.mathelicious and The National Science Foundation. Scientific American has dedicated links for energy and sustainability, evolution, health, mind and brain, space, and technology. It also has a math link: www.scientificamerican.com/math/. Science Daily is a great source for the latest research news, and its website has dedicated links for computers and math, space and time, and matter and energy. And don't overlook the science and technology sections of traditional publications.

▶ Small groups are formed based on student choice. Grouping is by text choices, not by "ability" or other tracking.

▶ Groups meet on a regular schedule.

▶ Different groups choose and read different books. However, the first time through, all students use the same book, so you can teach students the structure of text circles.

▶ Members write notes that help guide both their reading and their discussion.

▶ Teacher-led mini-lessons should be scheduled before and after text circle meetings.

- The teacher does not lead any book but acts as a facilitator, fellow reader, and observer.
- Personal responses, connections, and questions are the starting point of discussion.
- The classroom has a spirit of playfulness, sharing, and collaboration.
- When texts are completed, the text circles share highlights of their reading through presentations, reviews, dramatizations, book chats, and other activities.
- New groups are formed around new reading choices, and the cycle begins again.
- How often you do a text circle will depend on your school's schedule; many teachers do at least ten per year.
- Assessment is by teacher observation and student self-evaluation. We'll discuss assessment at length in the pages that follow.

MINI-LESSONS

All mini-lessons can cover the following:

- Team building
- Reading strategies
- In-depth content instruction

Mini-Lessons in Team Building

Team-building mini-lessons teach social skills so that the students can collaborate in a text circle.

What Are Some Obstacles You May Encounter?

You may well run into some typical adolescent behaviors: one kid doesn't want to work with another kid, communication problems like one kid taking too much control, other kids reluctant to participate, and so on.

How Can You Overcome Those Obstacles?

You can devote the first few mini-lessons to learning social skills.

How Do You Build Classroom Community?

These are some helpful resources:

Mini-Lessons for Literature Circles, by Harvey Daniels and Nancy Steineke
The Second City Guide to Improv in the Classroom, by Katherine McKnight and Mary Scruggs

Note Group Brainstorming Ideas Here

No wrong ideas—write down anything that might help build a classroom environment where kids feel comfortable talking to each other.

_____

_____

_____

_____

_____

Mini-Lessons in Reading and Content

A reading strategy or literary strategy mini-lesson provides direct, explicit instruction for one specific teaching point. Remember, these are called "mini-lessons" for a reason—they need to be short. Aim for five minutes.

The structure of an effective mini-lesson is as follows:

1. Connect the lesson with the lesson from the day before, stating what will be learned and setting the purpose.
2. Teach the new strategy using a mentor text and modeling with a think-aloud. Be very explicit and model what proficient readers do to comprehend text.

Reading Strategies

▶ **Visualize**: Making pictures of mental images or sensory images as they read. The following student samples of Sequence Trails (figures B.1 and B.2) illustrate the use of visualization.

▶ **Connect**: The reader and experience connection. See the student samples in the "Stop and Write" section (figures B.3 and B.4). Note the personal point of view in "What I Think" section; it uses words *I*, *me*, *my*.

▶ **Question**: Interrogating the text.

▶ **Infer**: predict, interpret, synthesize.

▶ **Evaluate**: Critique and make judgments.

▶ **Analyze**: This is a good time to introduce or expand on discipline-specific information.

▶ **Recall**: Retell, summarize, and remember.

7ᵗʰ Grade Life Science with Ms. Yando
Photosynthesis

Name _Nancy Huerta_

Date _4/25/14_

1. Read the "Simplified Photosynthesis" handout. Take your time, read carefully. Look up words you don't understand.
2. Draw one picture for each step of photosynthesis as described in the handout. (How many pictures do you have to draw? Here's a hint: each paragraph describes one step.) Use the back of this sheet if necessary.
3. Label each picture with a complete sentence.
4. **EXTRA CREDIT OPTION**: THE HANDOUT IS CALLED "*SIMPLIFIED PHOTOSYNTHESIS*". WHAT STEP WOULD YOU LIKE TO KNOW MORE ABOUT? WRITE A QUESTION UNDER THAT PICTURE.

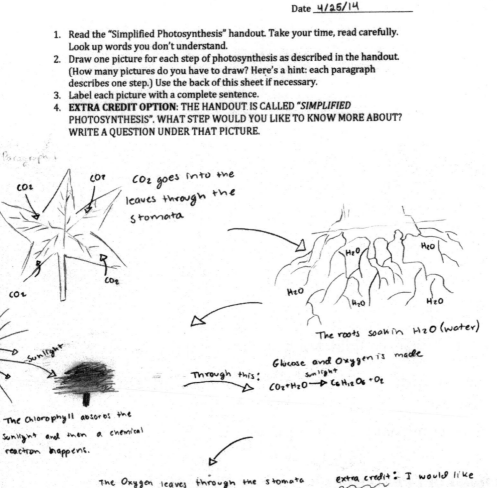

Figure B.1   Sequence Trails: Science Student Sample

Group #1 Activity
Faucets

1. Read the first two pages of the CONDUCTING A WATER AUDIT document from the Maryland Department of the Environment.
2. Go back and re-read the "Estimating Water Use Without A Meter " section on page 1.
3. Draw **four pictures** to illustrate the **four steps** you'll take to calculate the flow of faucets and showerheads. (You'll find these steps described under the first bullet point. The other bullet points tell you how to calculate the flow of toilets and appliances. YOUR GROUP IS JUST CONCERNED WITH FAUCETS!)

Figure B.2 Sequence Trails: Math Student Sample

▶ **Self-monitor**: Using individual skill set to understand and interpret the text.

▶ **Overcome obstacles independently**.

Examples of Mini-Lessons in Reading Content Strategies

Sticky Notes

We want students to listen to the voice in their heads. They should record these comments, questions, and connections on sticky notes. For guides, assessments, and student samples, go to http://www.ReadWriteThink.org.

Stop and Write

Students stop at various points and write summaries and reflections. There are a number of ways to do this activity. There are two variations in chapter 3. Figure 3.1 shows students writing "What I think" and "What I know." Figure 3.2 illustrates a student first summarizing "What I read" and then reflecting "What I think." Figures B.3 and B.4 show student sample Stop and Writes as adapted by individual teachers for classroom text circle or mini-lesson activities.

Science in the News

Choose a printed news article from this week's stack. Stop when you come to each of the marked stopping points. Fill out the chart below using complete sentences. You and other students who chose the same article will be grouped for discussion.

Name _Joe Levy_

Week of _Feb. 17, 2014_

Article _What Americans Don't Know About Science_ by Eleanor Barkham

Source/publication _The Atlantic Monthly_

	Summarize what you read.	What do you think about what you just read?
Stop #1	A biannual report has just been released. Two thousand Americans have just been asked simple science questions and a lot of them were wrong but so were respondents from	Respondants were all adults and 2,200 is a small sample size. other countries.
Stop #2	Read and interpret data in graphs: U.S. respondants sometimes give more wrong answers than right answers.	I had a hard time figuring out why other countries were in different order in these graphs. I think they're in descending order of correctness with U.S. alway on top. They are easy to read. I'm surprised were so bad.
Stop #3	This is not a comprehensive report. There is a gender gap. Results in last twenty years are stagnant. Questions could be reframed to filter out difference between religious belief and scientific knowledge.	I thought of some of these things and I am glad the author used them in her conclusion.

Figure B.3 Stop and Write: Science in the News Student Sample

What Are The Odds?

GENERAL MATH – TEXT CIRCLES
STOP & WRITE STATION

Name _Kashika Ombalawe_

Text _The Odds of Getting off the Elevator First by Carl Bialik_

Stop after every paragraph. Write at least one sentence in each box. Some texts are longer than others; continue on back if necessary.	
What I think:	**What I know:**
I can picture the elevator ride he is describing.	I found the definition of triskaidekaphobia on MirriamWebster. It means fear of the number 13.
I think I would have forgotten to not include the first floor if this was my problem.	I know how to write the math sentences for his assumptions.
I think the author's "simplifying assumptions" are bad. How does he know how many people walk?	I know he should base his assumptions on facts.
I think he's trying to be funny at the end.	I know he's good at math but he rounds a lot at the end.

Figure B.4 Stop and Write: What Are the Odds? Student Sample

READING LOGS

Reading logs aren't the same as mini-lessons—they're in addition to mini-lessons. A reading log should be a running record of a student's experience with the book. This could be a collection of a student's completed Stop and Writes as adapted by individual teachers for classroom text circle or mini-lesson activities.

- ▶ Students should write in the log every time they read.
- ▶ The emphasis should be on analysis and discussion; avoid excessive summarizing.
- ▶ The teacher or a student peer can respond to the reader's entries.

TEXT CIRCLE ROLES

The following are roles that a participant in a text circle can take. These ideas are adapted from http://www.ReadWriteThink.org.

Discussion Director

- ▶ Creates questions to increase comprehension (All group members suggest questions, and the discussion director fine-tunes them.)
- ▶ Asks who, what, why, when, where, how, and what if

Vocabulary Enricher

- ▶ Clarifies word meanings and pronunciations
- ▶ Uses research resources

Checker

- ▶ Checks for completion of assignments
- ▶ Evaluates participation
- ▶ Helps monitor discussion for equal participation

SCHEDULING

Table B.1 contains some general scheduling guidelines.

Table B.1 Scheduling Guidelines for Text Circles

Activity	Suggested Time Frame
Introductory mini-lesson	5–10 minutes
Small group activity	20–30 minutes
Sharing time and closing	5–15 minutes

TEXT CIRCLE LEARNING CENTERS

Keep in mind that learning centers can replace text circle roles. Set up all stations around your classroom and have students cycle through them in their groups. Students can move from station to station, doing a different task at each one. You should allow two to three days for this activity. The different stations can include the following:

- ▶ Listening Station
- ▶ Sequence Trails
- ▶ Vocabulary Detectives
- ▶ Discussion: "Whatcha think?"
- ▶ Content Analysis
- ▶ Illustration Station

ASSESSMENT AND EVALUATION FOR TEXT CIRCLES

This section includes a sample reading contract you can use with your students. A contract is not necessary in all cases, but because students may have an unusual amount of classroom autonomy during text circles, I've found contracts to be useful.

The template (figure B.5a) can be adapted to include an optional final project. The sample contract (figure B.5b) illustrates how a reading contract has been adapted for an Algebra II Text Circle activity.

Teacher: _____

Student: _____

Expectations and Guidelines

1. Be prepared (have text in class, any notes, questions, and thoughts about your reading).
2. Work with your group at each learning station in class.

I will read the following:

Text 1:

Text 2:

Text 3:

Due Date: _____

Signatures:

Student: _____

Teacher: _____

Figure B.5a   Reading Contract Template

Expectations and Guidelines

1. BE PREPARED! Read your text before class. You'll discuss your first text on Monday 12/8/14 and your second text on Monday 12/15/14. Bring your printed copies of texts to class, along with any notes, questions, and thoughts about your reading.
2. Work with your group at each learning station in class.
3. You and your group will make a presentation on one of your texts. Be prepared to explain how the author used the concepts *average*, *median*, and/or *mean* in his or her argument. Be able to restate the author's argument **in your own words.**

Figure B.5b   Reading Contract: Math Text Circle Sample

Expectations and Guidelines

I, _____, will read
TWO of the following texts.

Choose two texts from the list below by marking the boxes. You can view sample printouts of the texts on Mr. Jethmalani's projector table.

☐ *Are You Being Deceived by the Average?*
Author: Joe Manausa
Published by: *Tallahassee Real Estate* (3/24/14)

☐ Cost of a Wedding: Why Using The "Average" to Determine Cost May Be Misleading
Author: Erin Migdol
Published by: *The Huffington Post* (6/13/13)

☐ Five Myths about College Debt
Author: Vivek Wadhwa
Published by: *The Washington Post* (9/24/13)

☐ Report: NBA Median Salary Is $2.33 Million
Author: Ben Golliver
Published by: CBS Sports (8/20/11)

☐ The Importance of Being Median
Author: Josh Rosenau
Published by: *National Geographic*—Science Blogs (5/31/11)

☐ Mean vs. Median Income Growth
Author: Mark Thoma
Published by: *Economist's View* (9/2/11)

☐ Hall of Fame Musings: Figuring out the Median Positional Players in the Hall of Fame
Author: Nick Jaroszewicz
Published by: Harvard Sports Analysis (7/6/12)

Teacher sign here: _____

Student sign here: _____

Math is everywhere!!!

Figure B.5b   Reading Contract: Math Text Circle Sample, Continued

Table B.2   Sample Rubric for Project Assessment

Criteria	Exceeds Expectations	Meets Expectations	Does Not Meet Expectations
Project Appearance	Project is exceptionally neat, organized, and visually appealing.	Project is neat and organized.	Project is not neat or organized and could use some work on visual appeal.
Project Creativity	Creativity is noteworthy. Idea is innovative and/or artistically constructed.	Expresses knowledge in a creative and productive manner.	Project shows little or no evidence of creative expression.
Project Effort	Project is above and beyond the requirements. Excessive effort.	Student met criteria for final project.	Personal best is not evident.

Table B.2 is a sample rubric you can use in assessing student work on these projects.

SOME FINAL THOUGHTS

In your text circles, emphasize the value of student-centered classroom discussion instead of teacher-centered classroom discussion. Remember, students in charge of their own learning read because they enjoy it. Students who enjoy reading become lifelong learners—and that's the goal!

APPENDIX C

Resources and References

CHAPTER 1

National Governors Association Center for Best Practices, Council of Chief State School Officers (2010). *Common Core State Standards for English Language Arts & Literacy in History/Social Studies, Science, and Technical Subjects*. Washington, DC: National Governors Association Center for Best Practices, Council of Chief State School Officers.

Richardson, Motoko. (2013, August 15). "School Standards' Debut Is Rocky, and Critics Pounce." *New York Times*.

Sparks, Sarah. (2012, September 11). "Can NAEP Predict College Readiness?" *Education Week*.

CHAPTER 2

Beers, K. G. (2003). *When Kids Can't Read, What Teachers Can Do: A Guide for Teachers, 6–12*. Portsmouth, NH: Heinemann.

Daniels, H., & Steineke, N. (2004). *Mini-Lessons for Literature Circles*. Portsmouth, NH: Heinemann.

Manzo, Anthony V., & Casale, Ula p. (1985). "Listen-Read-Discuss: A Content Reading Heuristic." *Journal of Reading* 28, 372–374.

National Governors Association Center for Best Practices, Council of Chief State School Officers (2010). *Common Core State Standards for English Language Arts & Literacy in History/Social Studies, Science, and Technical Subjects*. Washington, DC: National Governors Association Center for Best Practices, Council of Chief State School Officers.

Rosenblatt, L. M. (1977). *The Reader, the Text, and the Poem*. Carbondale: Southern Illinois University Press.

Rosenblatt, L. M. (1995). *Literature as Exploration* (5th ed.). New York: Barnes & Noble. Originally published 1938.

Tovani, Cris. (2000). *I Read It, but I Don't Get It: Comprehension Strategies for Adolescent Readers*. Portland, ME: Stenhouse.

CHAPTER 3

Atwell, N. (1998). *In the Middle: New Understanding about Writing, Reading, and Learning.* Portsmouth, NH: Boynton/Cook.

Atwell, N. (2002). *Lessons That Change Writers.* Portsmouth, NH: Heinemann.

Britton, J. (1970). *Language and Learning.* London: Allen Lane. [2nd ed., 1992, Portsmouth NH: Boynton/Cook, Heinemann.]

Calkins, Lucy. (1986). *The Art of Teaching Writing.* Portsmouth, NH: Heinemann.

CERCA Education. (n.d.). CERCA. Retrieved October 15, 2013, from http://www.thinkcerca.com/.

Day, Alexandra. (1993). *Carl Goes to Daycare.* New York: Farrar Straus Giroux.

Day, Alexandra. (1998). *Follow Carl!* New York: Farrar Straus Giroux.

Day, Alexandra. (2009). *Carl's Snowy Afternoon.* New York: Farrar Straus Giroux.

Gere, A. R., Christenbury, L., & Sassi, K. (2005). *Writing on Demand: Best Practices and Strategies for Success.* Portsmouth, NH: Heinemann.

Graff, G. (2003). *Clueless in Academe: How Schooling Obscures the Life of the Mind.* New Haven, CT: Yale University Press.

Graff, G., & Birkenstein, C. (2010). *They Say I Say: The Moves that Matter in Academic Writing* (2nd ed.). New York: Norton.

Murray, D. M. (1985). *A Writer Teaches Writing.* Boston: Houghton Mifflin.

National Governors Association Center for Best Practices, Council of Chief State School Officers (2010). *Common Core State Standards for English Language Arts & Literacy in History/Social Studies, Science, and Technical Subjects.* Washington, DC: National Governors Association Center for Best Practices, Council of Chief State School Officers.

National Writing Project & Nagin, C. (2006). *Because Writing Matters: Improving Student Writing in Our Own Schools.* San Francisco: Jossey-Bass.

Romano, T. (1991). *Grammar and Teaching Writing.* Urbana, IL: National Council of Teachers of English.

Young, H. *Wordless Picture Book Lesson* (n.d.). Retrieved April 11, 2014, from http://www.makingmathematicians.com/Geometry.html.

CHAPTER 4

Audioboo—Empowerment and Transformation. (n.d.). Retrieved September 21, 2012, from http://www.audiboo.com/.

Ball, A., & Farr, M. (2003). "Language Varieties, Culture, and Teaching the English Language Arts." In J. Flood, D. Lapp, J. Squire, & J. Jensen (Eds.), *Handbook of Research on Teaching the English Language Arts* (2nd ed., pp. 435–445). Mahwah, NJ: Lawrence Erlbaum.

CERCA Education. (n.d.). CERCA. Retrieved September 21, 2012, from http://www.thinkcerca.com/.

National Governors Association Center for Best Practices, Council of Chief State School Officers (2010). *Common Core State Standards for English Language Arts & Literacy in History/Social Studies, Science, and Technical Subjects.* Washington, DC: National Governors Association Center for Best Practices, Council of Chief State School Officers.

Vocaroo Online Voice Recorder. (n.d.). Retrieved September 21, 2012, from http://vocaroo.com/.

Voki Home. (n.d.). Retrieved September 21, 2012, from http://www.voki.com/.

Voxopop—a Voice Based eLearning Tool. (n.d.). Retrieved September 21, 2012, from http://www.voxopop.com/.

CHAPTER 5

Blachowicz, C., & Fisher, P. (2005). *Teaching Vocabulary in All Classrooms* (3rd ed.). Englewood Cliffs, NJ: Prentice Hall.

Frayer, D., Frederick, W. C., & Klausmeier, H. J. (1969). *A Schema for Testing the Level of Cognitive Mastery.* Madison, WI: Wisconsin Center for Education Research.

Hillocks, G., & Smith, M. (2003). *Grammar and Literacy Learning*. In J. Flood, D. Lapp, J. Squire, & J. Jensen (Eds.), *Handbook of Research on Teaching the English Language Arts* (2nd ed., pp. 721–737). Mahwah, NJ: Lawrence Erlbaum.

Marzano, R. J., Pickering, D., & Pollock, J. E. (2001). *Classroom Instruction That Works: Research-Based Strategies for Increasing Student Achievement*. Alexandria, VA: Association for Supervision and Curriculum Development.

McCray, B. (n.d.). "Organelle Analogy Lesson." Unpublished.

National Governors Association Center for Best Practices, Council of Chief State School Officers (2010). *Common Core State Standards for English Language Arts & Literacy in History/Social Studies, Science, and Technical Subjects*. Washington, DC: National Governors Association Center for Best Practices, Council of Chief State School Officers.

National Institute for Literacy. (2007). *What Content-Area Teachers Should Know About Adolescent Literacy*. Retrieved from http://lincs.ed.gov/publications/pdf/adolescent_literacy07.pdf.

Noguchi, R. (1991). *Grammar and Teaching Writing*. Urbana, IL: National Council of Teachers of English.

Weaver, Constance. (1996). *Teaching Grammar in Context*. Portsmouth: Boynton/Cook.

Weaver, Constance (Ed.). (1998). *Lessons to Share: On Teaching Grammar in Context*. Portsmouth, NH: Boynton/Cook.

CHAPTER 6

Daniels, Harvey, & Steineke, Nancy. (2004). *Mini-Lessons for Literature Circles*. Portsmouth, NH: Heinemann.

Doyle, Terry. (2011). *Learner-Centered Teaching: Putting the Research on Learning into Practice*. Sterling, VA: Stylus Publishing.

McCombs, Barbara L., & Miller, Lynda. (2007). *Learner-Centered Classroom Practices and Assessments: Maximizing Student Motivation, Learning, and Achievement*. Thousand Oaks, CA: Corwin.

McKnight, Katherine S. (2010). *The Teacher's Big Book of Graphic Organizers: 100 Reproducible Organizers That Help Kids with Reading, Writing, and the Content Areas*. San Francisco, CA: Jossey-Bass.

Moeller, Victor J., & Moeller, Marc V. (2007). *Literature Circles That Engage Middle and High School Students*. Larchmont, NY: Eye On Education.

National Science Teachers Association. (2007, February). *The Integral Role of Laboratory Investigations in Science Instruction* [Scholarly project]. Retrieved from http://www.nsta.org/about/positions/laboratory.aspx.

Weimer, Maryellen. (2002). *Learner-Centered Teaching: Five Key Changes to Practice*. San Francisco: Jossey-Bass.

CHAPTER 7

Bergmann, Jonathan, & Sams, Aaron. (2012). *Flip Your Classroom: Reach Every Student in Every Class Every Day*. Eugene, OR: International Society for Technology in Education.

Carver, Ronald P. (2000). *The Causes of High and Low Reading Achievement*. Mahwah, NJ: Lawrence Erlbaum.

Chall, Jeanne S. (2000). *The Academic Achievement Challenge: What Really Works in the Classroom?* New York: Guilford.

Christel, Mary T., & Sullivan, Scott. (2007). *Lesson Plans for Creating Media-Rich Classrooms*. Urbana, IL: National Council of Teachers of English.

Christel, Mary T., & Sullivan, Scott. (2010). *Lesson Plans for Developing Digital Literacies*. Urbana, IL: National Council of Teachers of English.

Collins, Allan, & Halverson, Richard. (2009). *Rethinking Education in the Age of Technology: The Digital Revolution and Schooling in America*. New York: Teachers College.

Kist, William. (2005). *New Literacies in Action: Teaching and Learning in Multiple Media*. New York: Teachers College.

Kist, William. (2010). *The Socially Networked Classroom: Teaching in the New Media Age*. Thousand Oaks, CA: Corwin.

ProCon.org (2009, April 14). *Should the US Immediately Phase out Fossil Fuels?* Retrieved from http://alternativeenergy.procon.org/view.answers.php?questionID=001350.

Richardson, Will. (2006). *Blogs, Wikis, Podcasts, and Other Powerful Web Tools for Classrooms*. Thousand Oaks, CA: Corwin.

CHAPTER 8

Darling-Hammond, Linda, & Bransford, John. (2005). *Preparing Teachers for a Changing World: What Teachers Should Learn and Be Able to Do*. San Francisco, CA: Jossey-Bass.

Darling-Hammond, Linda. (2010). *The Flat World and Education: How America's Commitment to Equity Will Determine Our Future*. New York: Teachers College.

Jacobs, Heidi Hayes. (2010). *Curriculum 21: Essential Education for a Changing World*. Alexandria, VA: Association for Supervision and Curriculum Development.

Jensen, Eric. (1998). *Teaching with the Brain in Mind*. Alexandria, VA: Association for Supervision and Curriculum Development.

Jensen, Eric. (2006). *Enriching the Brain: How to Maximize Every Learner's Potential*. San Francisco: Jossey-Bass.

Jensen, Eric, & Nickelsen, LeAnn. (2008). *Deeper Learning: 7 Powerful Strategies for In-Depth and Longer-Lasting Learning*. Thousand Oaks, CA: Corwin.

Trilling, Bernie, & Fadel, Charles. (2009). *21st Century Skills: Learning for Life in Our Times*. San Francisco: Jossey-Bass.

INDEX

Page references followed by *fig* indicate an illustrated figure; followed by *t* indicate a table.

64–65, 112–114; language (including grammar and vocabulary) strand in the, 3, 13–16, 111–165, 190; the major shifts embedded in the, 7–10; overview of the, 2–3; reading strand in the, 3, 11–61, 189, 196–205*fig*; science labs aligned with goals of the, 188–190; speaking and listening strand in the, 3, 13–16, 101–110, 207–209*t*; standards focusing on English language arts classrooms, 4; Vocabulary Acquisition and Use, 115; writing strand in the, 3, 13–16, 63–100, 190, 206*t*–207*t*

Communication: CCSS on using technology to enhance, 103–104; technology impact on written, 69–70. *See also* Speaking and listening skills; Writing skills

Computerphile, 107

Connecting ideas, information, events skills: as anchor standard, 13; Sequence Trails strategy to develop, 47–51*fig*

Content area teachers: ELA Common Core State Standards (CCSS) implications for, 4–5; providing specific strategies to boost students' literacy and understanding to, 5; reading comprehension strategies deficiency by many, 11–12; self-examination of your current practices as a, 213–214; speaking and listening instructional ideas for English and social, 106–108; what the speaking and listening standards mean for science and mathematics, 105–106; what the vocabulary standards mean for, 115

Content areas: effective writing strategies in a, 63–100; focus on informational text in science and mathematics, 15; literature primarily taught in the English, 14–15; speaking and listening instructional ideas in the English and social studies, 106–108; strategies for building reading skills in a, 16–61

Content knowledge: building reading skills, 16–61; CCSS anchor standard on integrating ideas and, 14, 100; CCSS anchor standard on research to build and present, 9, 66, 98–100, 214; literate individual characteristics of building strong, 215; presentation of ideas and, 102; reading and comprehension required to develop, 12–13; research assignments used to build and present, 214; strategies for teaching effective content area writing, 63–100; strategies for teaching reading comprehension skills and, 16–61. *See also* Prior knowledge

Content literacy: CCSS identifying need for, 3–4; need for students to develop, 3–4

Content-specific text: cite textual evidence to support analysis of, 8*fig*; evaluating web-based resources for content information, 203*fig*–205*fig*;

giving students a voice for selecting increasingly challenging, 60; identifying craft and structure of, 14; identifying key ideas and details and, 13; integration of knowledge and ideas in, 14, 100; providing students with wide variety of, 214; student ability to read, 5; videos and audio versions to supplement, 61; visualizing, 47–51*fig*, 89–94, 159–165. *See also* Analyze and synthesize skills; Literary text; Text complexity

Cornell Notes strategy: additional tip for classroom implementation of, 30; connection to CCSS, 30; description of, 26; Proportions and Ratios Sample, 178*fig*; student sample of, 28*fig*–29*fig*, 177*fig*, 178*fig*; template for, 27*fig*; Vocational Agriculture/Horticultural Sample, 177*fig*

Cornell University, 26

Counterargument, 95

Craft and structure identification, description of, 14

Cultural sensitivity, 216

D

Daniels, H., 188

Darling-Hammond, L., 212

Day, A., 89

Defragging sentence fragments mini-lesson: description of, 128; materials needed for, 128; Part 1, 130*fig*; Part 2, 132*fig*; phrase slips for, 129*fig*; procedure to follow for, 131–132*fig*

Digital storytelling, 206

Discovery Channel website, 199

Dodge, B., 99

Doyle, T., 1686

Dropbox, 209

During-reading strategies: Cornell Notes, 26–30, 177*fig*, 178*fig*; description of, 16, 26; Questioning the Author, 30–34; SQ4R (survey, question, read, recite, review, reflect), 34–41*fig*

E

English Language Arts (ELA) standards. *See* Common Core State Standards for ELA in Science and Technical Subjects

English language learners, 110

Evaluating websites: for content information, 203*fig*–205*fig*; template for, 200*fig*–202*fig*

Evidence, 215

Expressive language, 101

F

Fix It Up Strategy Chart, 52*fig*

Follow Carl! (Day), 89

Fotobabble website, 103, 209

G

GIST strategy: description and connection to CCSS, 22; student sample of, 24*fig*–25*fig*; template for, 23*fig*

Monitoring comprehension skills, 34–41*fig*
Murphy, E., 94

N

Narrative writing: Cell/School Analogy example of combining visualization and, 163*fig*–164*fig*; PowToon to create animated presentation with, 208

Narrative writing skills: blogging used to develop, 206; CCSS anchor standard on, 66; digital storytelling used to develop, 206; literacy standards emphasis on developing, 6–7

National Assessment for Educational Progress, 7

National Assessment of Educational Progress (NAEP), 3

National Institute for Literacy, 111

National Reading Panel, 7

National Science Teachers Association position paper (2007), 189

Nevada's Northwest Regional Professional Development Program, 89

No Child Left Behind (NCLB) movement, 1

Numberphile, 107

O

Organelle Analogy: Centrioles, 162*fig*

Organelle Analogy: Endoplasmic Reticulum, 159*fig*

Organelle Analogy: Golgi Apparatus, 161*fig*

Organelle Analogy: Lysosomes, 160*fig*

P

Parabola Opens: vocabulary project: connection to CCSS, 108–109; description of, 108; directions and sample scene list,109–110

PARCC (Smarter Balanced and Partnership for Assessment of Readiness for College and Careers) assessments, 196

Passman, R., 121

PearlTrees website, 209

People/Content Poem strategy: connection to CCSS, 85; description of, 85; student sample on, 87*fig*–88*fig*; template for, 86*fig*

PhotoPeach website, 209

Pixton website, 209

Points of view: CCSS standard 1 from a student's, 8*fig*; CCSS standard 6 prompting evaluation of different, 15; interdisciplinary standards on understanding content, 14–15; literate individual's ability to understand other, 216; Questioning the Author strategy requiring inquiry into, 30–34

Postcards from the Past mini-lesson: description and materials needed for, 124; procedures to follow for the, 124–125

PowToon, 209

Predicting skills: Sequence Trails strategy to develop, 47–51*fig*; SQ4R strategy to develop, 34–41*fig*

PresentMe website, 103, 209

Preszi website, 103, 209

Prior knowledge: anticipation guide strategy to develop, 17–20*fig*; Questioning the Author strategy to develop, 30–34; SQR4 strategy to develop, 34–41. *See also* Content knowledge

ProCon website, 97, 99, 105, 198

Q

Question-Answer Relationship (QAR) strategy: connection to CCSS, 42–43; description and four types of questions used in, 42; student sample of, 45*fig*–46*fig*; template for, 44*fig*

Questioning the Author strategy: connection to CCSS, 34; description of, 30; student sample of, 32*fig*–33*fig*; template for, 31*fig*

R

RAFT strategy: Bloom's taxonomy and, 84*fig*; connection to CCSS, 84*fig*–85; description of, 78; student roles and suggestions for using, 78*t*; student sample on, 80*fig*–83*fig*; template for, 79*fig*

Read-alouds, 61

Readers: Lexile Framework on considerations of task and, 58*fig*, 59–60; motivation and engagement of, 60; providing a wide variety of texts to student, 214; visualizing text skills of, 47–51*fig*, 89–94, 159–165

Readers' Guide to Periodical Literature, 99

Reading between the Lines report (ACT, Inc.), 3

Reading comprehension skills: CCSS goal to develop college and career readiness of, 15–16, 195, 211–231*t*; CCSS interdisciplinary standards on, 3, 13–16; other tips for developing adolescent, 60–61; required to develop content knowledge, 12–13; science labs aligned with CCSS standards on, 189; to solve word problems, 12; strategies for building content area, 16–60, 196–205*fig*; visualization of words and their meanings, 47–51*fig*, 89–94, 159–165

Reading comprehension strategies: after-reading, 16, 42–52*fig*; before-reading, 16, 17–25*fig*; CCSS textual complexity model, 53, 58*fig*–60; close reading, 53–57*fig*; Common Core State Standards framework for learning, 12–13; during-reading, 16, 26–41*fig*; how CCSS incorporates technological tools into, 196–205*fig*; importance of teaching training on, 11–12; other tips for developing adolescent reading skills, 60–61

Receptive language, 101

Reif, L., 116

Research: to build and present knowledge, 66; greater emphasis of Common Core on, 9, 98–100; how Internet access has changed the process of,

ABOUT STAFF DEVELOPMENT FOR EDUCATORS

Providing educators with sustained professional development that is research-based, rigorous, and innovative, as well as practical, motivating, and fun, Staff Development for Educators' (SDE) mission is to create meaningful improvement in student attainment, teacher fulfillment, and school success.

Dedicated to helping build classrooms where all students can succeed, SDE's foundational work in the area of Differentiated Instruction and early advocacy of Singapore Math Strategies have helped it gain recognition as one of the nation's leading providers of professional development in education. SDE's Crystal Springs Books imprint exemplifies these same attributes to deliver important and timely resources right to the educator's desk.